Morning Glass

The Adventures of Legendary Waterman

Mike Doyle

with

Steve Sorensen

Front Cover painting by Mike Doyle
Back Cover photo by Craig Stecyk

Published by: Manzanita Press
               PO Box 720
               Three Rivers, CA 93271

Cataloging-in-Publication Data

Doyle, Michael
Morning Glass : The Adventures of Legendary Waterman Mike
Doyle / by Mike Doyle and Steve Sorensen
p.   cm.
1. Doyle, Michael, 1941-   —Biography.
2. Surfing.
I. Title
797.17

Library of Congress Catalog Card Number 93-78947
ISBN 0-9629418-2-4

Second Printing 1994
Printed in the United States of America

Contents

Maps

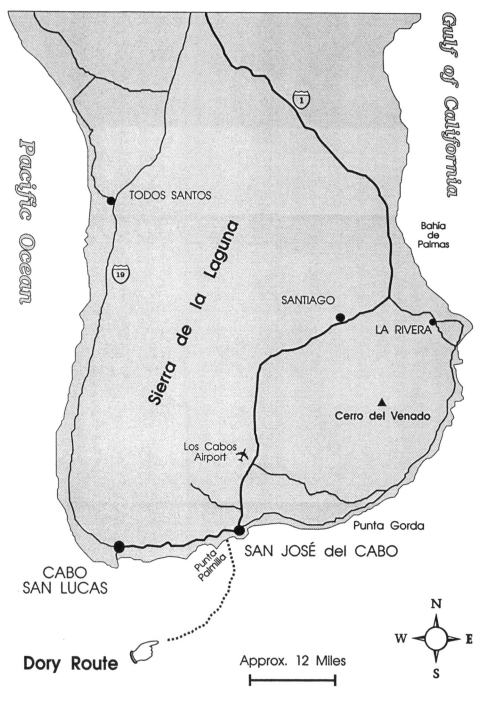

Gulf of California

Pacific Ocean

TODOS SANTOS

Sierra de la Laguna

Bahía de Palmas

SANTIAGO

LA RIVERA

Cerro del Venado

Los Cabos Airport

Punta Gorda

Punta Palmilla

SAN JOSÉ del CABO

CABO SAN LUCAS

Dory Route

Approx. 12 Miles

N
W   E
S

The Baja Peninsula

Ever since I discovered the ocean I've been an early riser. When I was just a boy I learned that morning is the time to be in the water, when the wind is calm and the surface glassy.

One winter morning not long ago, I got up at dawn, made myself a cup of coffee, and went out to have a look at the day. There's a hill behind my house, Gringo Hill, and from its summit I have a broad view of the Baja peninsula, from San José del Cabo to Cabo San Lucas. I climbed the hill in thirty minutes or so, then stopped to catch my breath and enjoy the sunrise over the ocean.

It was a beautiful day, calm and clear, and as soon as I felt the sun on my face I knew it would be warm. There was almost no swell, and the water was so clear I could see the dark reefs where the waves usually break at the cove in front of my house.

The weather patterns here on the Baja peninsula can be extremely complex, but over time I've learned to read them fairly well. If the wind is calm here, near the tip of the peninsula, then I know the wind is blowing on the Pacific side. If there's a north wind here in the morning, then I know it's blowing hard on the Gulf of California and glassy on the Pacific. But on this particular day the wind, like the swell, looked calm in all directions. I thought it would be a good day to go fishing.

The Baja peninsula is famous for being one of the best places in the world for sport fishing, but I'm not a sport fisherman. I don't like using a lot of fancy fishing gear, and I don't like putt-putting around in big fishing boats—the sound of the engines puts me to sleep, and the stink of the diesel exhaust makes me sick. Most of all, though, I don't like the way the crewmen on those boats do everything for you—bait your hook, tell you when to put your line in the water and when to reel it in. It reminds me of the fishing booth at the school carnival, where the little kids hang a line over the wall and somebody in back sticks a prize on the hook.

For me there's nothing more exciting than catching a big dorado out of a small boat, using garage-sale fishing gear. That style of fishing relies on the fisherman's knowledge and skill, minimizes the use of technology, and ensures a respect for the fish.

After jogging back to my house, I gathered up my fishing gear and, wearing only shorts and T-shirt, I hurried down the brushy hill in front of my house.

I keep a seventeen-foot dory on the beach. I've owned it for years, and I love it dearly. It's very sleek—about three feet wide and very narrow on the bottom. On a calm day I can row it six miles an hour.

I picked up one end of the dory, which only weighs about eighty pounds, and slid it across the sand. Most beaches are abrasive, like fine sandpaper, and are hard on the bottom of a boat; but here in Cabo the beaches are made of eroded shells, like shiny BBs, and the dory glided easily over them. I shoved the bow into the water, waded in to my ankles, grabbed the gunwales on either side, then leaped into the stern. Taking up the oars, I started rowing south, straight out to sea.

Just the day before, I'd heard that dorado had been biting off Punta Palmilla, maybe a mile from my house. It only took me a few minutes to reach that point; I had a sweat going by now, and the workout felt good. It also felt good to be on the open ocean, away from the sounds and smells of civilization. I decided to row out even farther.

After rowing hard for about an hour, Punta Palmilla was far behind me and just barely visible. Then, to my surprise, the wind started kicking up, creating a three-foot swell. The weather is so volatile here, it can change almost instantly. But I wasn't worried—I knew I was a strong rower, and I knew I was in good shape.

I put two fishing lines in the water, turned southwest, and started rowing downwind, with the swell. Settling into a familiar rhythm, I would row until I caught the swell, then ride it down into the trough, where I'd almost stall; then I'd give two or three quick strokes of the oars and take off again with the next swell. Each time I caught a swell, my lures would come almost completely out of the water, and I could see them spinning wildly. That kind of lure action really excites the fish, but you can't create it with a power boat. That's one reason why fishing in a dory can be so effective, and so much fun.

When I was about twelve miles offshore, both reels started screaming, and I knew I had a double hookup. I dropped my oars and started reeling in one of the lines. It felt like a big fish—maybe a dorado—and I had to work hard at bringing him in. But after just a few minutes, that fish slipped the hook and got away.

I started reeling in the second line, and right away I knew this fish was even bigger than the first. I reeled for ten or fifteen minutes before the fish jumped out of the water and I saw I had about a fifty-pound dorado—a speedy, bullet-shaped fish.

The dorado ran hard for about thirty minutes. I played him until the reel was hot, and the line felt like it was ready to melt. When I finally worked him close to the dory, his head came out of the water for a second, and he stared up at me with one big eye, totally calm, as if he knew something I didn't. As I reached down to gaff him, he flipped his head sideways, snapped the line, and was gone.

I laughed—two hookups and they'd both gotten away! That twist of fate was almost as fun as if I'd landed them both.

My shoulders and arms were aching now, more from working the dorado than from rowing. I leaned back in the dory for a minute to rest, looked up at the clear sky, and listened to the wind whistling over gunwales. What a feeling it was to be in an open boat, barely within sight of shore and only the strength in my arms to get me back.

As I sat up again, ready to row home, I realized that one of my oars was gone. When I'd dropped the oars to play the first fish, I must have forgotten to slip them back inside the boat. I knew better, but I'd developed a bad habit of dropping the oars from spending so much time fishing farther in, where small mistakes don't count for so much. Now I was fifteen miles from shore, in an open boat, in windy conditions that were growing worse by the minute . . . and with only one oar.

I stood up in the dory to see if I could spot the missing oar, wishing I'd been smart enough to paint them both fluorescent pink. But everywhere I looked there was nothing but a frothy mass of white water. I couldn't have seen the oar if it were only fifty feet away, and by this time it could easily have been a mile away.

The wind was really howling now, sideshore and offshore, creating about a four-foot chop, and the dory was rapidly being driven farther out, toward the southwest. I could still see the pink-and cream-colored mountains in the distance, but I couldn't see the shoreline at all.

My biggest worry by far was that I'd also drifted west along the coast about six miles toward Cabo San Lucas. If I couldn't somehow make my way to shore, I knew I would miss the cape completely and be swept out into the open ocean, where the wind and the surface chop would be even rougher. In those conditions, I would have no chance of surviving. It was like I was being sucked down a huge funnel, and the farther I got down the funnel, the faster I was going.

For just a moment, as I realized how serious the situation was, I felt my whole body go weak. As the sensation passed, I muttered out loud, "Well, Doyle, you really fucked up this time."

I knelt on one knee and nervously began canoe paddling, first on one side of the dory, then on the other. The dory was so narrow and light, I was able to make some progress in this way, but not enough. The paddling was very awkward, and I knew if I couldn't come up with a better plan, I would tire out long before I reached land.

This wasn't the first time in my life I'd been in a mess like this. I knew that these moments of ultimate reality, when you can see yourself and the world so clearly, can be the most valuable moments in your life. Also, I found some comfort and courage in knowing that if I had to die, this was the way I wanted to go—under a perfectly clear sky, the tropical sun blazing down, the ocean alive, and the wind blowing salt spray into my face. I would rather die sweating, relishing the joy of having flesh and blood, and fighting for my life; not lying in some hospital with tubes stuck in my throat, staring at the TV on the wall, already dead in every way except the final one.

In just a few minutes my left knee was bloody from chafing against the bottom of the dory, so I switched to my right knee and put my T-shirt underneath it for padding. In a few minutes more, though, that knee was bloody, too.

I figured I had four, maybe five hours before I drifted past the cape. As I tried to settle into the rhythm of paddling, I found my thoughts racing frantically in all directions. I'd learned a long time ago that fear can release enormous amounts of energy, but that kind of energy quickly fades to exhaustion. I felt weaker already. What I needed was the steady pace of the long-distance paddler, an old and familiar rhythm.

Once the initial rush had worn off, after thirty minutes or so, I was in control of my emotions again. The canoe paddling was still awkward, but the rhythm was comfortable and I knew I could maintain it for hours. Now came the long and monotonous struggle of trying to work my way back to land.

The mood that came over me then was strange—not fear or panic but a kind of calm, bittersweet nostalgia. When confronted with the real possibility of dying, I kept thinking over and over of people I knew and loved, of places I had been in my life, and of places I wanted to be again.

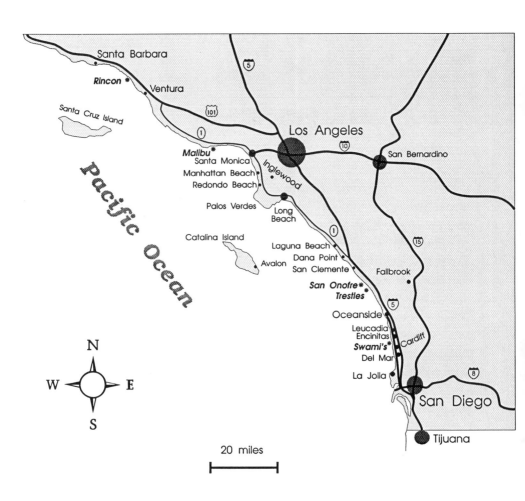

Santa Barbara

Rincon ✱

Ventura

5

Santa Cruz Island

101

1

Los Angeles

10

San Bernardino

Malibu✱

Santa Monica

Manhattan Beach

Redondo Beach

Inglewood

Palos Verdes

Long
Beach

Catalina Island

1

15

Laguna Beach

Avalon

Dana Point

San Clemente

Fallbrook

San Onofre✱

Trestles ✱

5

Oceanside

Leucadia

Encinitas

Cardiff

Swami's✱

Del Mar

La Jolla

8

San Diego

Tijuana

Pacific Ocean

N

W   E

S

20 miles

Southern California

TIKI MIKE

I was born landlocked, which in my case meant that I started out life disadvantaged. More than most people I've always needed the water, so in some ways those first ten years of my life were spent finding my way down to the ocean, where I knew I belonged.

I grew up in Inglewood, a suburb west of Los Angeles with blocks and blocks of small stucco houses. Most of the people who lived there were blue-collar workers who came in droves from all across the country to find jobs in the aircraft manufacturing plants during World War II. Every back yard, it seemed, had a makeshift machine shop.

My mother, Mary, married young and had me, her only child, in March of 1941, when she was just twenty-two. The marriage only lasted two years; then my mother and I moved in with my grand-mother in a small, one-bedroom house just a few blocks away. My grandmother, who spoke only Polish her entire life, had eight children of her own still living at home—some of them grown and with children of their own. Altogether there must have been twenty people living in that one tiny house. The kids would sleep half a dozen to a bed, all tangled up in each other.

Most of my mother's younger brothers were only a few years older than I, so in some ways my uncles were like my big brothers. They gave me my first taste of adventure. We liked to get up in the hills behind our house and run free. Los Angeles, before it grew so much, had lots of open fields where kids could play.

I was an awkward-looking kid with buck teeth and a large nose. All through grade school, the other kids called me "Beaver" or "Gopher," and I developed a lot of complexes about the way I looked. Later on, braces corrected my buck teeth, but it took me years to grow into my nose.

My fourth-grade teacher, Mrs. Schoenhair, was the first person to recognize that I had poor hearing. She moved me to the front of the class, where I was sure to understand what was going on; then she arranged for me to have some tests, which eventually showed that I had a congenital hearing problem. Several times a week I would get on a bus and go to lip-reading classes in Culver City. Most of the kids in the class were totally deaf, and a lot of them had other learning disabilities. I didn't think my hearing problem was really bad enough for me to be there, but I enjoyed learning how to read lips, which is a handy skill for anyone to have.

Mrs. Schoenhair showed a lot of interest in me. I wasn't one of her good students—in fact I didn't even like school—but she always made an effort to talk with me and helped me with art, which she knew was my favorite subject, and she generally helped to build my confidence. She was one of those exceptional teachers who really get involved with their students, and I credit her with easing me through what would have otherwise been a very painful time.

My mother worked at Northrop (an aircraft factory) during the days, and she was gone a lot in the evenings, too. I don't remember seeing much of her. Even so, I always knew she loved me very much, and over the years my relationship with her has always been very dear and strong.

When I was nine years old, my mother met a sailor, Walt Delaney. Walt had been in a lot of fistfights in his youth, and his nose was flat from being broken so many times. He was a good man, but he was the kind of person who didn't have a lot of patience with people. He had trouble expressing himself, and I think he tried hard to live up to the image of a tough sailor. After a few drinks, though, he would loosen up and become everybody's friend. Walt loved his dogs more than anything (he had several over the years), and he hated to see any animal hurt. He was very sensitive to animals, and I always liked that about him.

I don't think my mother was madly in love with Walt. I think she wanted to get me out of my grandmother's overcrowded house, and the only way she could manage that was to get married again, which she did.

The three of us moved into our own house in Westchester, next to Inglewood. Walt's notion of the perfect home was a trailer with a gravel yard—that way he could go play golf on his days off. My mother loved to grow things, and she wanted a house with a big yard and lots of plants and trees. The house in Westchester was sort of a compromise—not too big but with lots of plants.

Walt was often away at sea for six months or even a year at a time. My mother started working nights at Northrop and slept days. So I hardly ever saw either of them.

During those years we were living in Westchester, my mother had a lot of odd phobias. She had dizzy spells and used to worry that she was losing her mind. She didn't drive a car for forty years, which in Southern California is almost the same as being handicapped. She was terrified of being left alone, so Walt, when he wasn't at sea, took her with him everywhere. If he went to the corner store for a six-pack of beer, she went with him. If he went to play golf, she played too, even though she never really enjoyed the game.

My mother never had a lot of strict rules, but she did have a lot of simple, common-sense advice on how people should live their lives, and as I was growing up I heard those clichés over and over again: "Health is wealth. . . . Do what makes you happy. . . . Take time to smell the flowers. . . . Only boring people get bored." As a kid I never paid much attention to all my mom's little sayings, but looking back on it now, it amazes me how much they affected my outlook on life.

From my house in Westchester, the closest beach was Manhattan Beach, about fifteen miles away, in what is known as the South Bay. That whole area was densely populated, sometimes smoggy, and often overcast in the spring and early summer. When I was only seven or eight, I used to get on the bus and ride down to Manhattan Beach just to look at the ocean. From the first time I saw it, I was fascinated by how big and wild it looked. I knew I belonged in there, but I couldn't swim very well yet, so it took me a while to work my way into the water. I would take my skim board and ride it in the sand. Later I would take the skim board into the water and body board on it, just trying to get the feel and the rhythm of the waves.

Sometimes on the weekends, my mother would drive me and a friend down to the beach. We would swim and bodysurf together, mostly just goofing around, but in a competitive way. We used to play a game we called smelly moose. When there were two of us bodysurfing on the same wave, one would call out, "Smelly moose!" We'd kick and wriggle like seals, trying to see who could bodysurf the farthest up the sand. The guy who lost was the smelly moose. We played that game for hours, and it really taught us how to find the fastest part of a wave, how we could use our bodies to control our direction and speed, and most of all, how to feel comfortable in the water. By the time I was ten, I was a complete maniac for the ocean and never wanted to do anything except play at the beach.

In the seventh and eighth grades, I went to St. Eugene, a Catholic school. It was way too structured for my liking. I thought the nuns were stuffy, authoritarian, and mean. And the whole fairy tale about dying and going to heaven or hell never worked for me. My own experience, even at that age, was that heaven and hell were right here on earth, and over the years, nothing has really changed that opinion.

I was an altar boy for about a week. During the Sunday mass, it was my job to go up to the altar with a pitcher of wine and pour a little bit in the priest's chalice. I remember the priest had a big red nose, and I could smell alcohol on his breath. He reached down, grabbed my wrist, and twisted it until I was in pain. It took me a moment to realize he wanted more wine, so I just kept pouring until he finally let me go.

I didn't care much for confession, either. My parents never went, but they made me go. They said it would be good for me, that it would cleanse my soul, but I never felt I'd done anything bad enough to need any cleansing. I just didn't feel guilty. So at confession I would make up a few lies to keep the priest happy.

Out in the school yard one day, when I was in the eighth grade, a friend of mine said, "Do you know that Rita Babock is pregnant?"

Rita Babock was one of our classmates. She was always nice to me, but she was also years ahead of me in physical development.

She had very large breasts for a thirteen-year-old, and she went out with guys who were old enough to drive.

"Holy shit!" I said. "Rita Babock is pregnant?" The truth was, I didn't even know what being pregnant meant. I knew about men and women having sex, but I didn't understand that was how babies were made. Anyway, like a fool, I went and repeated the rumor to a couple of my friends.

It didn't take long for the story to get back to the sisters, and one afternoon a mean-looking nun came sailing into our class, marched directly over to my seat, and said, "Mother Superior wants to see you immediately."

That was the worst thing that could happen to a kid in Catholic school. As I walked down that long hall, I felt like I was going to see the witch in her castle.

Mother Superior was sitting behind her desk in her stiff black-and-white habit. Her skin was gray, her teeth yellow, and she had big blue bags under her eyes. She folded her hands, scrunched up her face, and said, "Young man, have you been telling untruths about Rita Babock?"

"Well . . . I don't. . . ."

"Don't lie to me!" she shrieked. "Did you or did you not tell people that Rita Babock is pregnant?"

"Somebody told me that . . . and I might have said it to somebody else. . . . I'm sorry if I. . . ."

"Enough!" Mother Superior waved her hands in front of me like I was supposed to disappear. Then her eyes narrowed, and she said, "What do you suppose your mother would say if she knew you were spreading lies?"

"Don't tell my mom," I begged. But I could see by the smile on Mother Superior's face that I'd made a big mistake by giving away my weakness.

"Why don't we just think about it for a few days," she said happily.

My life was hell for weeks after that, and I never did find out if Mother Superior said anything to my mother.

Then one day Rita Babock and I were working together on the set for a school play. We were in the rectory, behind the altar, all alone. It was kind of dark in there, and I was both nervous and excited about being alone with Rita. While we worked, Rita kept rubbing her breasts against my back and arms. I didn't know what that meant, or even if she was doing it on purpose. All I knew was that I got a tingly feeling every time she did it. Finally, I guess Rita grew impatient with me. She tapped me on the shoulder, and when I turned around in surprise she planted a big kiss right on my mouth.

The first time I ever saw somebody riding a surfboard was at the Manhattan Pier in 1953. As much time as I spent at the beach, you'd think I would have at least seen one surfer before then. But there were only a few dozen surfers in all of California at that time and, like surfers today, they were out at dawn surfing the morning glass. By the time the crowds arrived, they were gone.

But this one morning I took the first bus to the beach, walked out onto the Manhattan Pier, looked down, and saw these bronzed gods, all in incredibly good shape, happier and healthier than anybody I'd ever seen. They sat astride their boards, laughing with each other; at the first swell they swung their long boards around, dropped to their stomachs, and began paddling toward shore. From my viewpoint, it was almost as if I were on the board myself, paddling for the swell, sliding into the wave, coming to my feet, and angling the board down that long wall of green water. It was almost as if I already knew that feeling in my bones. From that day on, I knew that surfing was for me.

There were several surfers out that day: Dale Velzy, George Kapu, and Greg Noll. Greg was just a kid then, about sixteen years old, but he was hot. On one wave he turned around backward on his board, showing off a bit for the people watching from the pier. I was just dazzled, and said to myself, Oh, my god!

Another surfer out that day was Bob Hogan. He was blond and stocky, with very tightly defined muscles. He was probably about twenty-five at that time, a lifeguard, a great paddler, and an all-around waterman. As I left the pier, I happened to look in the back of Bob Hogan's car—a perfectly clean '46 Ford coupe—and saw lying there on the back seat a trophy he'd won in a paddling contest. I just knew he had to be some kind of superhero to own this piece of glitter, and I ran back onto the pier and watched him some more, trying to analyze what it was that made him so good.

Once I'd discovered there was such a thing as surfing, I began plotting my chance to try it. I used to stand out in the surf and wait until one of the surfers lost his board. The boards then were eleven feet long, twenty-four inches wide, and weighed fifty or sixty pounds. When they washed in broadside, they would hit me in the legs and knock me over. I would jump back up, scramble the board around, hop on, and paddle it ten feet before the owner snatched it back—"Thanks, kid"—and paddled it away.

One day in 1954, when I was thirteen, I was down at Manhattan Pier watching a guy ride a huge, old-fashioned paddle board—what we used to call a "kook box." It was hollow, square-railed, made of mahogany, about fourteen feet long, maybe sixty-five pounds, and had no skeg (or fin). It was the kind of paddle board lifeguards used for rescues; they worked fine for that purpose, but for surfing they were unbelievably awkward. When the guy came out of the water, dragging the board behind him, I asked if I could borrow it for a while. He looked at me like, "Get lost, kid." But when he sat down on the beach, I pestered him until he finally shrugged and nodded toward the board.

I'd watched enough surfing by then to have a pretty clear idea of the technique involved. I dragged the board into the water and flopped on top of it. After a while I managed to paddle the thing out beyond the shore break and get it turned around. To my surprise, after a few awkward tries, I managed to get that big clumsy thing going left on a three-foot wave. I came to my feet, right foot forward, just like riding a scooter. I had no way of turning the board—paddle boards are so awkward even expert surfers can barely turn them—but for a few brief seconds, I was gliding over the water.

As the wave started to break behind me, I looked back, then completely panicked. I hadn't thought that far ahead yet! My first impulse was to bail out, so I jumped out in front of the board, spread-eagled. That massive paddle board hit me right between the legs. I washed up on the beach, dragged myself onto dry sand, and lay there groaning. Within minutes my left testicle had swelled up to the size of a grapefruit.

My mother took me right to the doctor. He put me on his examining table and poked at my swollen testicle a couple of times until he was sure I was in pain. He muttered something to himself, then fumbled through one of his drawers. When I looked up, he had the biggest needle I'd ever seen in my life—it looked like a darning needle!

While I squirmed in agony, he inserted the needle into my testicle and drained out the blood. Then, without saying a word to me, he left.

As I lay there, sick with fear and pain, I could hear the doctor talking to my mother in the other room. "I think we might have to remove that testicle," he said. "But it's not really anything to be concerned about. You know he only needs one to have children."

Have children! What about just being in balance! I lay back on the table and groaned at my unbelievably bad luck. One wave, one nut. How much longer could my surfing career go on?

As soon as the doctor came back, I started begging him to let me keep my testicle. "Even when a kid gets polio in one leg, they don't cut it off," I pointed out. "Can't I wear some kind of brace on it?"

When the doctor saw how serious I was, he said, "Well, I suppose it wouldn't hurt to wait a while and see what happens. But if that testicle gets infected, we'll have to remove it. And I doubt very much that it will ever function properly again."

The doctor was right about that. To this day, I have one swollen testicle to remind me of my first wave.

After my accident, I had to stay out of the water for about a month. But I knew I wasn't going to quit surfing. In fact I used that first disaster to my advantage. I began pestering my mother for my own surfboard, arguing that if I'd had the right equipment in the first place, an accident like that never would have happened. I worked my mother every way that a kid knows how, trying to convince her how sorry she would be if I died and she never bought me the one thing I truly wanted. I can still hear her reply: "Michael, it'll be just like everything else you get. You'll use it for a week, and then you'll never use it again."

My mother and I still get a laugh every now and then over those words. But I usually got what I wanted from my mother, and this time was no exception. The only problem now was that I didn't know anything at all about surfboards and had no idea what kind of board I should buy. So one day down at the pier, I asked one of the older surfers what I should get. "Just go see Velzy and Jacobs," he said. "They'll fix you up."

Most surfers at that time were riding either hollow paddle boards (a wooden framework with a plywood shell), or solid redwood slabs, some of them twelve feet long and weighing more than a hundred and fifty pounds. The much lighter and much better balsa wood boards were just starting to appear. Dale Velzy and Hap Jacobs were making the only commercial balsa boards in California at that time. At first they had their sawhorses set up underneath the Manhattan Pier—they shaped their boards with draw knives and tossed the shavings right onto the sand. It was a bit crude, but it was the first facsimile of a surfboard shop in California. After a while, though, the city came down on Velzy and Jacobs, and they had to move their shop into a little building in Venice, right under an oil derrick.

The businessman in the partnership was Jacobs, a soft-spoken man who had grown up around Hermosa Beach and had been a star basketball player at Redondo High. Velzy was the salesman. He had style, charisma, and a silver tongue. He wore a diamond ring on his little finger, always had a pocketful of cash, and always drove a brand-new car.

Velzy was tending shop the day I walked in. Even though he had grown up on the beach—his dad had been a lifeguard at Hermosa Beach, and Dale had been a lifeguard himself—I thought he looked more like a cowboy than a surfer. He had a big cigar in his mouth, tattoos on his arms, and wore his hair slicked back. I could see right away why they called him "the Hawk"—he had a big hook nose.

I explained to Velzy that I wanted to buy a new surfboard. He looked down at me, then asked, "Where d'ya surf, kid?"

"I haven't really surfed anywhere yet," I said, leaving out that first disaster.

19

Velzy just nodded. "Don't worry about it. We'll make ya exactly whatcha need." He looked me over for a minute, mentally calculating my height and weight. Then he drew up an order, took my deposit, and said, "Be here first thing Friday morning."

Later I learned how Velzy did business: Every Friday morning there would be thirty or forty custom-made surfboards waiting on the racks. But anybody who walked through the door with cash in hand could buy any board on the rack—you just changed the name on the tag, handed Velzy the cash, and the board was yours. If you got there a little late, the board you ordered might already be sold.

I was late picking up my first surfboard, so I'm pretty sure it wasn't the board I'd ordered. But I didn't know that then, and it wouldn't have mattered anyway. I handed Velzy my mother's $75, and Velzy handed me a board off the rack. "Here, this one's perfect for ya, kid."

That first board was a 9′ 6″, and had sixty-four ants embedded into its surface coat of resin. It was what they called an "island-style" board, with a small fin and a pointed nose. Actually, it would still be considered a fairly contemporary shape today, except that none of the boards in those days had any rocker (or curve)—they were almost totally straight from nose to tail. You glued the balsa boards together, and they were only four inches thick to start with, so all the shaper could do was carve a small rocker.

That same day I took the sixty-four-ants board down to a place we called Rats Beach, between Torrance and Palos Verdes. I started out riding goofy foot, right foot forward, because I'm left-handed and that's the natural stance for lefties. Every time I took off that day, I pearled—the nose of my board plowed under the surface of the water, throwing me forward. I took off and pearled, took off and pearled—but at least I was catching some waves, and I was protecting my nuts.

A few days later, I dinged my new board on the Manhattan Pier. There was a big crack in the fiberglass on the nose, and I could see that water was leaking into the balsa wood. I had no idea how to fix it, so I called Velzy and asked him what to do. He said, "No problem, kid. Stop by the shop, we'll sell you some fiberglass and resin, and you can patch it yourself."

Walt, my stepdad, picked up the fiberglass, the gallon of resin, and a smaller can of catalyst. It didn't come with any directions, but somebody had told me you had to mix the catalyst with the resin for it to set up. So I dumped the whole can of catalyst into the gallon of resin, cut the fiberglass to cover the ding, then slapped on the resin with a paintbrush and waited for it to dry. After a while I went back to the garage to see if it had set up yet. The ding looked pretty good, at least for a first try, but the whole gallon of resin had set up, too, with Walt's paintbrush stuck in the middle of it.

Later that summer, when the surf wasn't good, I started hanging around the Velzy and Jacobs shop in Venice. I became fascinated with the whole process of making surfboards, and I wanted to learn as much about it as I could. After a while Velzy got tired of seeing me standing around, so he handed me a broom and said, "Here, you can see for yourself what a mess this place is. Why don'tcha clean it up!" So I started working there, sweeping the floor, running errands, and sanding boards. I didn't earn much, but I learned a lot. It was an apprenticeship that served me well over the years.

I had a good neighbor there in Westchester, Herb Duhe. He was married, about thirty, with his first kid. Herb had picked up surfing in the Marines, over in Hawaii, at Waikiki. He had a big paddle board, and he used to take it down to Corona Jetty on the weekends. I told Herb there were surfers at Manhattan Pier, which was news to him, and that it was my intention to learn how to surf. Herb got all stoked at the thought of having a surfing buddy, so when I bought my new surfboard, he bought a new board, too. Herb took me under his wing, and we went surfing together almost every weekend.

One day in the summer, Herb and I stopped at the Velzy and Jacobs shop in Venice. We had been up and down the South Bay looking for surf, but there just wasn't any to find. Velzy listened to us complain, then said, "These are all winter breaks along here, fellas. You gotta go up to Malibu. That's a great ride in the summer. I just heard it's breaking six feet right now."

We thought Velzy was putting us on, but Herb and I drove up to Malibu anyway, and sure enough, Velzy was right: Malibu was breaking set after set of long, ruler-perfect waves. That was when I first realized that it wasn't enough just to know how to surf. You also had to understand the seasons, the weather, the swell direction, and the wind pattern. Surfing was more than just kicks in the water. In order to be any good at this, you had to understand how your home planet works.

After that, Herb and I started surfing at Malibu every weekend. It was about a forty-five minute trip to Malibu, but the long drive was worth it. We would stop first in Culver City, at the old rail yard, and load up the back of Herb's '52 woody with railroad ties. As soon as we hit the beach, we'd start a big smoky bonfire that stank of creosote. There weren't many wetsuits in those days—sometimes when the wind was blowing hard, we'd wear a little wool sweater out in the water, but that was all we had. So as soon as we got out of the water, we'd run right over by the fire to get warm. When the fire burned down some, we'd wrap potatoes in tin foil and toss them in the coals. By the time we remembered to pull them out, they were usually charred black, but we'd crack them open anyway and eat them with salt. After surfing all day, those potatoes were a feast.

In the ninth grade, I went back to public school, at Inglewood High, where my mother had graduated. Every morning she would give me bus fare and lunch money, but I would pocket the bus money and hitchhike to school. At lunch I'd take the bus fare and gamble with it, lagging nickels and dimes with the Mexican guys at school.

I still wasn't comfortable with my looks. I was starting to grow some, but I was still thin and gangly, and my nose made me feel extremely self-conscious. When I'd look at girls, I'd look straight at them, so they couldn't see my profile.

And I never cared much for organized sports. Being picked to play on a team was more of a popularity contest than anything, and I wasn't popular. But I also thought organized sports were too restricting. To me baseball was a sport where one guy throws the ball, one guy tries to hit the ball, and sixteen other guys stand around and watch. I just couldn't imagine why anybody would think that was fun.

One of the P.E. teachers at Inglewood High was Jim Arnett, the guy who invented the adjustable starting block for track sprinters.

He was a very grumpy old guy. One day as I was walking to my gym class, he stopped me in the hall and told me I had slumped shoulders. I started to show him that I could stand up straight like a nerd if I really wanted to, but Arnett wasn't having any of that. He grabbed me right there and dragged me off to his corrective gym class.

Being in corrective gym was like having a big "D" for defective stamped on your forehead. Jim Arnett may have been a brilliant track man, but he didn't understand anything about teenagers, and his corrective gym class didn't do anything to help my slumped shoulders.

The South Bay surfers who were really ripping at that time— guys like Dewey Weber, Henry Ford, Freddie Pfahler, Mike Zuetell, and Peff Eick—had their own little clique, the 22nd Street Gang. They all lived in Manhattan or Hermosa Beach, and they all went to Mira Costa High. They hung out at the wall on 22nd Street, just north of the Hermosa Pier, which was the coolest place in Hermosa Beach, and where there were two or three great hamburger joints and the famous Green Store on the corner. They had their own style of talking and dressing. They wore faded jeans, blue T-shirts, bitchin' blue tennis shoes, and wore St. Christopher medals around their necks. Dewey Weber, who was a yo-yo champion, sometimes broke the gang's dress code by wearing his red Duncan Yo-Yo jacket; but other than that, they always looked like perfect clones of each other. And they did everything together. They surfed together every morning, and they drank together every night. All weekend long, they'd be standing there in front of the wall, talking about who got laid the night before, who got drunk, and who got put in jail. They'd be all hung over, with vomit stains on their pant cuffs and seaweed wrapped around their necks. They had their own little world, and I wanted so badly to be part of it.

But I was still landlocked out in Westchester, going to Inglewood High, where anybody who wore blue tennis shoes got the shit beat out of him. When I went down to the beach, the 22nd Street Gang called me a kook and a hodad. I couldn't surf like they could, and even though they were only two or three years older than I was, they were a lot more mature. I didn't know anything about drinking and carousing, other than what I'd heard.

Meanwhile, at my school there were only two social groups, the jocks and the *cholos*, and I didn't really fit into either one. I didn't play football or basketball, so I couldn't be a jock. For survival purposes, I dressed more like the *cholos* and had a blond jelly-roll hairdo. But I was a loner more than anything else, and being a loner meant I was easy prey.

The Mexican guys were into organized gangs, and the gang leader at Inglewood High was a guy named Art Carnero. His word was law. Art had black hair greased back with Finch's hair oil, long khaki pants, black shirts buttoned to the neck, and square-toed shoes—the *pachuco* look. Art had a real talent for sensing weakness. He and his buddies were like coyotes preying on stray dogs. They wouldn't mess with the jocks, who were bigger and stronger than they were and had their teammates to back them up. They picked on smaller and younger kids who were more vulnerable.

One day after school, Art Carnero and his buddies tried to talk me into going downtown with them to steal a bottle of vodka from the Sav-On drugstore. I was supposed to be their stooge, the guy who got caught if something went wrong. I wouldn't have anything to do with that plan, and I told them so. But Art and his buddies still sensed that I was afraid of them.

The next day at lunch, Art and his buddies got me down on the football field. They held me so I couldn't move and pulled up one of my pant legs. Then Art and another guy took out their knives and started playing tick-tack-toe on my leg, cutting into the skin just enough to draw blood. "Hey, Michael, what you so nervous about? We ain't gonna hurt choo."

I was scared to death, thinking if I even tried to move, I was gonna get stuck. I didn't know what to do. So I just lay there, wishing I were someplace else.

"Here's the deal, Michael. If I win this game, we gonna let you be our friend. But if my buddy here wins, then you gotta bring us a dollar a day. . . . Deal?"

I didn't answer. I just stared up at the sky, waiting for them to finish with me.

Finally, Art jumped to his feet, folded his knife, and stuck it back in his pocket. "Damn," he said. "You know, I never won nothin' my whole life. I always had to work for everything I got."

His buddies let me up, but before I could run away, Art said, "Now remember, Michael, you bring us a dollar every day, and we won't mess you up. But if you tell anybody about this, we gonna kill you."

I never gave Art Carnero any money—not because I was so brave, but because I didn't have any money. My lunch money and bus fare combined weren't a dollar a day. But every day I had to duck and hide from Art and his buddies, and every day I had to live with the fear that they would catch me and carve on me again.

All through those fearful high school years, I had a recurring dream of waking up in the morning and seeing the ocean out my window. I craved being near the water, and all I ever thought about was escaping to the one place where I thought I could be free and happy.

I tried to find as much literature as I could find about the ocean and surfing. There were no surf magazines in those days, but in the school library, in a copy of *National Geographic*, I found a photo of Waikiki, probably taken from an airplane or helicopter, showing a couple of surfers riding long, clean rollers. The water was so clear, you could see the coral bottom. The only beaches I had ever seen were the South Bay beaches, with sandy bottoms and murky water. But Waikiki looked so beautiful, it didn't seem to me like a place that could really exist. I kept trying to find the flaw in the photo, like it was some kind of trick. Every day for weeks, I went to the library to stare at that photo. I was in love with it, and I finally decided I just had to have it. So one day after school, I went to the library, found the copy of *National Geographic*, slipped it between two of my textbooks, and walked out with it. At home I hid it under my bed, and every day for two years, I would take it out and stare at that photo of Waikiki, planning for the day I would escape.

Later, another photo appeared in the newspaper that whetted my appetite even more for going to Hawaii. It was of three surfers— George Downing, Buzzy Trent, and Woody Brown—riding very straight, old-fashioned redwood boards at Makaha, on the west side of Oahu. The wave looked massive to me—at least twenty-five feet—a thick, boiling mountain of water. I'd heard about waves like that, but I'd never imagined they could look so beautiful and terrifying at the same time. And as far as I was concerned, the guys riding them were the most courageous men on earth.

Years later, after I got to know George Downing, I told him how much that photo had impressed me as a kid. George laughed and said, "That was really only about a twelve-foot wave. The photo was tilted to make it look twice as big as it really was."

One of the older surfers down at Manhattan Pier told me about a book called *California Surfriders* by Doc Ball. It focused on surfing in the 1930s and '40s, in San Onofre, La Jolla, and Santa Cruz—all places I'd never been before. I looked for the book at the school library and a couple of local libraries, without any luck. Then I told my mother about the book, and after a few phone calls, she learned that the Los Angeles County Library had a copy of it. She drove me to downtown Los Angeles so we could check it out.

I took Doc Ball's book home and studied each picture for an hour at a time, scrutinizing each grain in the black-and-white photos, the way the water flowed over the board, the way the wave was breaking—every detail—until I could feel what it was like trimming across a wall of water. I studied each of the surfers' styles, their hand movements, the way their feet were placed on the boards, and I came to understand that each surfer in that era—Hoppy Swartz, Leroy Grannis, Pete Peterson—had his own individual style.

I saw that the surfers in the book had a wonderful camaraderie that I didn't have in my own life. They were healthy and joyful, and they enjoyed being with each other. I could see a community spirit there that I wanted to be a part of.

But more than anything else, I saw from Doc Ball's book that surfing is as much an art as it is a sport. Before I had developed any elements of my own style, I came to appreciate that surfing at its highest level isn't supposed to be a macho struggle to defeat the wave, it's a form of dancing, with the wave as your partner, almost like ballet.

I was heartbroken when that book finally had to go back to the library, already days overdue. But my wonderful mother, seeing how enthralled I was with the book, somehow managed to find out that Doc Ball was running the Life's Highway Ranch for Boys, in Fort Seward, California. She wrote him a letter telling him how much her son loved his book, and a few weeks later, Doc Ball himself sent me a signed copy of *California Surfriders*. I received that book in 1956, and it's still one of the most precious things I own. Even today, every black-and-white photo in that book is as beautiful to me as the first time I saw it.

By the time I was fifteen, I'd already accepted the old tradition of the watermen as my own, and I set about the long process of mastering each of the waterman's skills. The tradition of the waterman comes from Polynesia and is different from the tradition of the sailor. The waterman's skills include surfing, paddling, rowing, and rough-water swimming. He might also be skilled at diving, fishing, spear fishing, tandem surfing, lifeguarding, and handling outrigger canoes. But he isn't necessarily skilled at sailing or navigation. The difference is that a waterman focuses on the coastal waters, while the sailor's realm is the deep water. By reading about the early days of surfing, I learned that the watermen who came before me didn't just go to the dive shop or the surf shop and buy the latest thing on the rack. They designed their own boards, their own dive gear, and their own outrigger canoes. They were constantly thinking and experimenting with other watermen about ways to perfect their gear. Nobody knew then how a surfboard should be designed. The only way to find out what worked and what didn't was to try it.

But the waterman tradition seems to be dying out with surfers today. A lot of younger guys are focused only on surfing, and they want to be masters of the sport before they've learned the fundamentals. There are some good surfers today who can barely swim. And I don't see much respect for the previous generations of surfers. When I was coming up, I didn't laugh at the older surfers on their redwood planks, because it thrilled me to think what they'd been able to accomplish on those old boards. They could paddle way outside and catch waves that surfers today wouldn't even try for.

And instead of being stuck in one place on a wave, they could drive through the flat parts and pick up a new section. What a thrill it must have been to stand up on a big plank like that—like riding a Cadillac downhill. I'm sure those huge redwood boards were as much fun as the little five-foot sticks that came into style in the 1980s and '90s. And to my way of thinking, the old style of surfing was more beautiful and creative than all the slashing and tearing that came along later. I realize that styles change, and that the slashing style fits the contemporary state of mind. But I think that surfers today are missing something really important when they don't try to learn from the watermen of the Thirties and Forties.

A lot of the California surfers from the Forties had served in the military in Hawaii, where they'd learned about surfing and Hawaiian culture. When they came back to California, they painted girls on their surfboards, just like Duke Kahanamoku, the great Hawaiian master; they had luaus on the beach, and carved Hawaiian tikis for their bamboo huts. Their whole beach scene was set up just like it had been in Hawaii.

Because I was landlocked, I had to work hard at creating my own surf scene out in Westchester. Though I'd never been to Hawaii, I'd seen pictures of the tikis, the Polynesian wood carvings that represented ancient gods, and I got caught up in the symbolism and magic of these tikis. Because I was lonely, vulnerable, and in many ways miserable, I figured I needed the magic of the tikis as much as the Hawaiians did. I took two periods of wood shop, the only class except art that I really enjoyed in high school, and spent most of my time carving wooden tikis. I started wearing them on leather thongs around my neck, like magic talismans, to ward off Art Carnero, Jim Arnett, and everybody else who was making my life difficult. I talked my mother into painting a beautiful full-length totem pole on my surfboard. And one day I dragged an old telephone pole back to my house and started carving it into a big totem; when it was finished, I mounted it in our front yard.

Deep down I suppose I hoped my tikis would win me some respect from the 22nd Street Gang, the group of guys I most wanted to be a part of. I thought the tikis would identify me as a true and devoted surfer who was spiritually in tune with the Hawaiian gods. But the first time I wore my tikis to Manhattan Beach, Dewey Weber, Mike Zuetell, and all the other bitchin' guys humiliated me. One of them grabbed the tiki around my neck, took a hard look at it, then flung it back at me. "Jesus, Mike, that's really hokey. Did your mother buy that for you?"

"No," I said. "I carved it myself."

From then on I was "Tiki Mike," the laughingstock of the South Bay.

When I turned fifteen and a half, my mother let me buy a Messerschmidt, a three-wheeled motorcycle with a bubble top. It was legally considered a motorcycle, but it could ride two people, one in back of the other. The whole bubble top would open up, like the cockpit of an airplane. I made a little rack for mounting my surfboard on top of the bubble, and I was set. I had my own wheels.

The first time I took my Messerschmidt down to Hermosa Beach, I parked it next to the sand, took my totem board off the bubble top, and went out surfing. While I was in the water, the 22nd Street Gang pushed my Messerschmidt onto the sand and turned it upside-down. When I came out and saw what they'd done, I just about broke down and cried. No matter where I was, at school or at the beach, I just didn't fit in. I was frustrated and unhappy, and I felt so alone.

The summer between my junior and senior years at Inglewood High, my stepfather, Walt, started working at the Point Mugu Naval Air Station, way up the coast, halfway to Santa Barbara. He'd leave every morning at six and drive up Highway 1, passing right by Malibu. So every morning, a few minutes before six, I rolled out of bed, grabbed my surfboard, and rode along with Walt.

I used to love passing through Venice in the morning. Not only was it interesting in an architectural sense, but there were so many strange characters coming out of the walls: winos waking up and blowing their snot on the sidewalk, women with tattoos, men with wigs and make-up, bikers, beatniks, artists, musicians—weirdos of all kinds. The place looked kind of rough compared to my own neighborhood, and very rough compared to the clean, quiet, high-rent area around Malibu, but I was fascinated by Venice because it was a place where it was okay to be a little bit different from everybody else. I could see that being different in Venice wasn't a liability, it was an asset.

Walt would drop me off at Malibu at seven or so. I'd collect enough Coke bottles to buy a quart of milk and a big package of Barbara Ann rolls. I'd eat the whole gooey dough ball, then I'd climb on my surfboard, paddle out, and stay out until almost dark. My feet would never touch dry sand for twelve hours. When Walt came to pick me up, I'd flop out in the back of the car and sleep all the way home. The next day I'd do it again.

Malibu was a magical place in those days. It was a beautiful beach, the wind blew side-offshore, the water had a crystal clarity, and it had the most ruler-perfect wave in California. It had the movie stars, and it had the surfing stars, and it was only a few minutes from downtown L.A., the center of wealth and power on the West Coast.

There were guys living on the beach at Malibu, building shacks and collecting Coke bottles to buy food. Nobody hassled them. Malibu wasn't that popular with beachgoers then, mostly just surfers, so the place was rarely crowded. When a good swell came up in the summer, there would be ten, twelve, maybe fifteen surfers out in the water.

But for me, Malibu meant the end of my misery. Not only did I get away from Art Carnero and his gang in Inglewood, and away from the 22nd Street Gang in Manhattan Beach, but I was able to make my own friends. Malibu didn't really have a local gang. The surfers there came from all over L.A., so none of us were outcasts. We were judged by our surfing ability—nothing else—and my surfing ability had improved to the point that I rated some respect.

One of my buddies at Malibu in those days was Lance Carson. We called him "Jet Pilot" because he had a perfectly pointed nose. Lance was from a wealthy family in Pacific Palisades, and every winter his parents sent him back East to some private military school. But in the summer he spent all his time at the beach. He was at a big disadvantage in some ways, because every year by the time he got out of school, the rest of us were already tanned and surfing really well, while Lance would still be all white and educated. But by the end of summer Lance would be surfing as well, or better, than any of us.

Besides having a very smooth, clean style of surfing, Lance became one of the greatest nose riders of all time. While most surfers could only run up to the nose and pose there for a few seconds, Lance could stand there almost indefinitely and in total control—he could actually maneuver the board from the nose.

Another good friend in those days was Kemp Aaberg. Kemp was a great surfer and was always in top shape. He also grew up in Pacific Palisades, and was the oldest of three boys. Kemp's little brother, Denny, later wrote a fine novel about surfing, *Big Wednesday*. I mostly remember Denny as a little beach rat hanging around his big brother, but later, after I read his book, I realized he'd been paying attention to everything we said and did.

All the little surf grommets like me, whose parents dropped them off at the beach, tried to make Malibu our own turf. We called ourselves "the judging panel," and we would lie there in the sand where we could see everybody who came down the stairs. To get by us, you had to pass our inspection, and it wasn't easy getting by the panel. We called you a "valley kook," a "hodad," and a "cowboy," but if you took the roasting with good humor, eventually you were accepted into our club. We challenged you in the beginning—out in the water we might even shove you off a few waves—but if you hung in there and took it, you got in.

When we weren't surfing, we used to sit there in the sand and work each other over, just to stay in practice: "You know something? You got a nose like an anteater."

"Yeah, well, the bigger the nose, the bigger the hose."

"Yeah, I've seen your hose. It looks like a little pink jellybean."

"That's not what your sister said."

"I don't even have a sister, you goofball."

Then we'd slobber all over our faces like idiots and roll in the sand like happy puppies.

Across the street from Malibu was a road that led up into the hills to a Catholic retreat. Along that road was a grove of orange trees with the best oranges any of us had ever tasted. Every now and then, one of the guys would say, "Let's go make an orange run." We'd wait until there were no cars going up the road to the retreat, then we'd charge across the highway, hop over the gate, and sneak up the road a ways. There was a little cabin there where the caretaker lived, and the grove was kept perfectly manicured all the time. Under the trees, every leaf was kept raked, yet we never saw a soul. The place had a mystical quality about it—we imagined that monks came down in the moonlight to care for the grove at night. We'd pull off our T-shirts, tie the sleeves in a knot, and fill them up with big ripe oranges. Then we'd run back to the beach to share the booty with our friends. After being out in the sun all day, and with salt water in our mouths, those juicy oranges tasted wonderful.

One of the wonderful Malibu characters from that era was Tubesteak, who was in his early twenties. He lived on the beach with another guy, Harry Stonelake. Everybody else came and went, but those two were always right there, taking life easy, surfing every day, and collecting Coke bottles to buy food. Tubesteak always wore cutoff pants with his big gut hanging over the waist, and he ate roasted hot dogs for every meal, which is how he got his name. The beach life suited Tubesteak perfectly, and he was always fat and happy.

Malibu was where I first started making a reputation for myself as a surfer. I was a goofy foot when I first started there. Malibu, like a lot of the great surf spots in California, breaks from left to right (as viewed by the surfer facing the beach). So a goofy footer at Malibu has his back to the wave—a disadvantage. In my case, the wave kept hitting me in the butt over and over, until one day I decided I'd better switch my stance to left foot forward. From that day on, my surfing ability began to improve dramatically.

Like all young surfers, I began by imitating the style of the older surfers, and one of the older surfers I admired most was Matt Kivlin. He was a very handsome man, and in the water he had a very casual style, very polished, with his board always in perfect trim with the wave. He surfed like a dancer, and out of the water he carried himself the same way. He was an outstanding waterman, an intelligent guy, and very well respected.

Another surfer I admired a lot was Mickey Muñoz, "the Mongoose." He was about three years older than I, short, dark, with a hatchet nose. Muñoz invented a lot of the stock poses we used in those days: El Teléfono, Quasimodo, El Spontáneo. They were sort of like compulsory exercises in gymnastics—every surfer had to master them in order to prove he'd reached a minimum level of skill.

Everybody was into nose riding in those days, and Muñoz had a board he called the duckbill. He'd extended the nose of the board with a piece of wood about a foot long; then he'd nailed a go-ahead (a rubber thong) onto it. Muñoz would walk all the way to the end of the board, then stick his foot out and slip it inside the go-ahead. That really impressed us.

But the unrivaled king of Malibu in those days was Mickey Dora, "Da Cat." He was about seven years older than I, or twenty-five at this time. His full name, which he had printed on his business cards, was Miklos Sandor Dora III. His father was a wine importer, and Mickey always had bottles of fine wine with his father's import label on them. Mickey's parents divorced when he was six, and he'd spent a lot of his youth in military schools.

It was Mickey's stepfather, Gard Chapin, who started taking him to the beach, at San Onofre. Gard Chapin had been one of the great California surfers of the 1930s and '40s, and a regular at Malibu. I think Mickey idolized Gard, and for a long time he went by the name of Mickey Chapin. Gard was a great waterman, but his personality put people off because he was arrogant and cocky. Gard Chapin later died under mysterious circumstances: The way I heard the story, he and some other people were on a yacht in the harbor at Cabo San Lucas. There had been an argument, Gard left angrily in a small dinghy, it flipped over, and he drowned. But I've also heard people who knew Gard say that version is ridiculous because Gard could swim extremely well. At any rate, Gard Chapin disappeared during the night and was later found dead.

Mickey used to say that his stepfather had been murdered, and when Mickey changed his last name back to Dora, he said it was for his own protection. I don't know if all that was true, or if it was just part of the mystery Mickey liked to wrap himself in.

One day I happened to notice that when Matt Kivlin was out

surfing, Dora watched him very carefully, studying every move Kivlin made. I realized then that Dora had imitated a lot of Kivlin's surfing style. Later I heard Dora refer to Kivlin as a genius of style. Because so many surfers, including me, imitated Dora, and Dora imitated Matt Kivlin, I think Kivlin had a much greater influence on the direction surfing took than many people realize today.

Dora had such charisma and style, and, like everyone else, I couldn't help but be very impressed with him. He wore full-length trench coats and drove around in classic old Duesenbergs and Bentleys, as if he were some European playboy enjoying his leisure at the beach. He had graceful little mannerisms and expressions— the way he would touch his sunglasses with just his thumb and forefinger, like a movie star, and smile at you. Every kid on the beach was going around doing Mickey Dora imitations. We drew iron crosses on the bottoms of our surfboards, and scrawled "Kaboom!" and "Kazam!" across the front of them. We didn't know what it meant, but we knew Mickey Dora did it, so it had to be cool.

Dora was always troubled by the world situation. I think he paid too much attention to the news. One day when I was going up and down the beach collecting Coke bottles to get gas money, Dora told me, "Buy gold, Doyle. The entire world economy is going to collapse. Buy gold."

I didn't have the vaguest idea what he was talking about. "Forget gold," I'd say. "Let's go surfing."

And Dora hated surf contests. He was always talking about how surfers were selling their souls for a few cheap trophies. One of his favorite tricks was to sign up to compete in a surf contest just to get everybody talking—"Is Dora really gonna show?"—then he would never appear. Or else he'd show up at the contest with an 11' 6" tandem board and just goof around on it while everybody else was competing, making a mockery of the whole thing.

Looking back on it now, I can see that Dora was manipulating the system to bring attention to himself. Dora was a promo man, and his favorite promotion was Mickey Dora. But everybody who knew him when he was in his prime had to admit that Dora was a genius. He stimulated everybody's imagination, and an awful lot of what became California surf culture was pure Dora.

One of the not-so-regular surfers at Malibu in the late Fifties was a guy named Tom Morey. I remember the first day I saw him at Malibu. He drove up to the beach in a new car and stepped out wearing a shirt and tie. He was very clean-cut but carried himself in a relaxed, slump-shouldered way. He pulled out a board he'd made himself, stripped off his suit and tie, and pulled on a pair of trunks. He was all white, like he didn't get out in the sun enough, and we expected him to be a real kook in the water. But Morey surprised us. He was a very smooth surfer, with a relaxed style and a light touch. He did beautiful cutbacks and had perfected a move called the standing island pullout, which some of us had never seen before.

We found out later that Morey worked for Douglas Aircraft as some kind of aeronautical engineer and he liked to play the drums in jazz bands on the side. He never really mixed with the crowd. He was kind of quiet and only showed up once in a while. But almost every time he came to the beach, Morey had a different surfboard—always something experimental, always something we had never seen before.

Another surfer I used to see at Malibu from time to time was Joey Cabell. He would pull up in a Volkswagen van with several surfboards on top. He was about six feet tall, thin in his upper body, and very wiry. He had penetrating blue eyes, clear skin, and a surprisingly quiet voice, but was high-strung and difficult to talk to.

Joey had been born in Hawaii and started surfing at Waikiki in 1946 when he was only seven. His first balsa board had been fashioned from an old army life raft. For spending money, he used to weave grass hats to sell to the tourists. Rabbit Kekai, a legendary surfer who had been the head beachboy at the Outrigger Canoe Club at Waikiki, recognized young Joey's talent and took him surfing all over Oahu. When I first saw Joey, he was on the mainland going to school at Orange Coast College in Costa Mesa. He was a couple of years older than I, which was a lot at that age, so we weren't close then. But I could see that he was a very talented athlete and a great waterman.

I remember the first time Gidget came down the stairs at Malibu. She was only about five feet tall, weighed less than a hundred pounds, and was carrying a borrowed surfboard that was so big, one end of it was dragging in the sand. She really caught our eye because there weren't a lot of girl surfers then. Tubesteak said, "Gee, here comes a girl."

Somebody else said, "God, she looks like a midget to me."

"Yeah, a girl midget—a gidget."

Somebody else started giving her a hard time, saying "Whatta ya think you're doing? Don't you know girls can't surf?"

Gidget (whose real name was Kathy Kohner) stopped halfway down the stairs, practically in tears. Tubesteak, who had a soft heart and needed a girlfriend, went over and said, "Hey, it's okay if you surf. Come on down."

Gidget never did become a very good surfer, but she learned to take our roasting in good humor, and eventually she was accepted into the crowd because all of us could appreciate somebody who tried as hard as she did. Like me and a few others in that Malibu crowd, Gidget was the kind of person who didn't really fit in back in her own neighborhood, but instead of feeling sorry for herself, she bought an old Buick convertible and a surfboard, and found her way to the beach. I really admired her for that.

I thought Gidget was cute: She had dark hair, fair skin, and nice legs. One day I told Gidget that the board she had was way too big for her, that she would have an easier time learning to surf if she used a smaller board. She asked me what kind of board she needed, and I said, "Why don't you let me find one for you." After looking around, I found a board that was just right for her. I got her a deal on it, too: fifteen dollars. Gidget and I became friends after that. I'd take her to the movies or just for a walk along the beach. But there were other guys taking her out during the same time, so we never had anything very serious going.

Gidget's father was a writer, and like all writers he was always searching for new material. One day he happened to listen in on one of his daughter's phone conversations and discovered that his daughter was right in the middle of a teenage subculture that the rest of the world knew nothing about. I'm sure he listened to me and Tubesteak and who knows who else talking about surfing, sex, all the nicknames and slang, and all the things that went on at the beach that parents weren't supposed to know anything about. He got a grip on the whole beach scene, and wrote a book on the subject before his daughter even knew what was going on.

We were kind of amused when the first Gidget book came out, because we knew it was about us. I don't think any of us really read it though, or the little bit we did read we thought was pretty hokey. You can't write about surfing if you aren't a surfer. A lot of writers have tried over the years, and I think they've done the sport a lot of damage by making it appear silly, frivolous, and self-indulgent.

We were more excited when the movie crews came down to Malibu to make the first Gidget movie. A lot of it was shot a few miles up the road from Malibu, at Leo Carillo State Beach. Some of us got paid to be the doubles in that movie. The money wasn't much, but they always had a big table of good food set up. We thought it was hilarious that somebody would pay us to surf, then feed us, too. We really didn't care if the movie turned out as hokey as the book.

Malibu is great in the summer, but the surf doesn't usually break there in the winter—at least not in the classic Malibu style. It took me a long time to figure that out. On the weekends after school started, I would lash my surfboard to the top of my Messerschmidt, drive up to Malibu and sit there on the windy beach all day long waiting for the waves to appear. They never did.

Again, it was Dale Velzy who educated me. He said I ought to go to Rincon, up by Santa Barbara. "On a north swell, the wave wraps around that point and you can get rides a half-mile long," he said. "In the winter, Rincon's the best wave in California."

Velzy was right, and before long Kemp Aaberg, Lance Carson, Johnny Fain, and I were driving up to Rincon almost every weekend. In those days it was nothing to drive 200 miles looking for good surf. Gas was twenty-five cents a gallon, and the highways weren't crowded. We used to drive from L.A. to Santa Barbara and back down to La Jolla, on the old highway, all in one day, just checking out the surf. There were only a few hundred really active surfers on the whole coast, and you knew most of them, so if you passed a car with a surfboard on top, that was a brother. You'd both pull over to the side of the road and exchange information: Where you been? How was the surf? Who'd you see? Who's hot this week? Even if you didn't know them, you'd still pull over and chat, exchange phone numbers, and end up being friends.

Another place we loved to surf in the winter was Swami's, down in San Diego County. The place got its name after an Indian spiritual leader, Paramahansa Yogananda, built one of his Self-Realization Fellowship retreats on the cliffs there overlooking the ocean. The place had a pair of big gold domes out in front that gave it a mystical quality.

Swami's was a thrill to surf because the swell came out of deep water, then jacked up on a reef 300 yards off the beach. It had a steep drop at the peak and a long, fast shoulder. On a good day, Swami's would get up to twelve feet. It was more of a Hawaiian-type wave than anything I'd surfed before.

The local star at Swami's was a freckle-faced kid named Rusty Miller, from Encinitas. I got to know him some then, and in later years he and I became close friends.

In those days we parked our cars on Highway 101, then walked through a big vegetable garden to a rickety old stairway that led down the bluff to the beach. The devotees at the retreat grew their own organic food, and they were always out there working quietly in the garden. To raise money for the retreat, they had a little stand on the highway where they sold mushroom burgers. We used to surf all day, then buy a bag of mushroom burgers for the drive home.

One of the classic surf spots in those days was San Onofre. The older guys who had learned to surf in Hawaii favored San Onofre because they thought it was a lot like Waikiki, with really long rides. Some of the younger surfers, though, didn't care for the wave at San Onofre because it came at you from all directions. I called it billiard surfing because there were so many angles, so many banks. I always thought it was an interesting wave.

What I loved most about San Onofre, though, was the creative energy there. The older surfers made tiki huts along the beach out of driftwood and bamboo so they could get out of the sun when they wanted. It was great to park there and lie in the shade of the tiki huts with rows of colorful surfboards lined up against their sides. There were guys living in old panel trucks they'd furnished in Polynesian style, with tapa cloth glued to the ceilings and sea shells glued to the dashboards; even their beer can openers were carved from wood, wrapped with string and varnished. They made their own canvas hats and reinforced them with big brass grommets, then decorated them with bottle caps. Some of the guys stitched big corks to the tops of their hats and wore them surfing; if they fell off their boards, the hats floated. Anything that washed up on the beach would find its way into some kind of sculpture: carved tikis hacked out with an ax, huge seagulls and little windmills made out of driftwood and mounted on long poles. When you were at San Onofre, you felt as if you were part of an ocean culture that had its roots in Polynesia.

The greatest surfer in the late Fifties and early Sixties was Phil Edwards. He lived down in Oceanside and had grown up surfing at Terramar, where the power plant in Carlsbad is today. His nickname was the "Guayule Kid." (Guayule was the name of a nearby rubber manufacturing plant.) Edwards had seen Mickey Dora surfing at San Onofre and was so impressed with Mickey's creativity and innovative style that he spent one whole summer surfing with Dora and copying every move Dora made. Later Edwards developed his own, totally original style.

For years I'd heard about Edwards doing things on surfboards that were phenomenal, but I'd never seen him surf myself. Everything I knew about him was by word of mouth. Other surfers told me he was a brilliant style master. They said he had one old board he'd been riding for about six years, and he loved it so much that when it would get all beat up, he'd carefully peel off the old fiberglass and reglass it. Everybody knew he was the best surfer in California, and probably the best surfer in the world, but his entire reputation in the surfing world was based on the respect of his peers, because Edwards usually wouldn't have anything to do with surf contests.

Every now and then we would hear rumors: "Edwards is coming up to Malibu. He's gonna show this weekend." I was always at Malibu, so I didn't have to worry about missing him if he did show. But I was always disappointed.

And then one day we got a huge summer swell at Malibu, and surfers from all up and down the coast showed up—from La Jolla, Oceanside, San Onofre, and Dana Point. That was one day I stayed out of the water, just so I could watch all these guys. There was Joey Cabell, with his perfect timing and gazelle-like moves; Mickey Dora, with one arm in the air, nose-tweaking and side-slipping up and down the wave; Dewey Weber, now known as the "Little Man on Wheels," running to the nose, then frantically backpedaling to the tail, slicing right, then cutting back again to the left; Lance Carson posing forever on the nose with his arms outstretched like a crucified Christ.

But the most impressive of all that day was Phil Edwards. What an inspiration it was to watch him at work! He'd do these totally original movements that weren't always functional but were expressive. He'd run up to the nose and stand there posing; then he'd snap out of it and run back. When the wave would start to break, he'd lean forward to let it hit him on the chest. He'd counter-rotate his lower body, as if he were winding up for a turn. He'd change his pace, like syncopated dancing. I thought his style was so beautiful.

One of Phil's moves that day absolutely astonished me: He took off on a big wave, but instead of turning right, he turned left, then backpedaled, planted his rear foot on the rail, swung the board all the way around to a full right, and immediately walked to the nose. I had never even imagined doing anything like that—but Edwards pulled it off so smoothly!

After watching Phil Edwards surf for the first time, I realized that all of us at Malibu had been imitating each other for so long, we'd become inbred and a bit stifled. From then on, my mind was open to new possibilities of what you could do with a wave.

The next day I stopped by the Velzy and Jacobs shop in Venice to order a new board. Watching Phil Edwards had changed my thinking about what kind of equipment I needed, and besides, I'd outgrown my old board. (I was only seventeen, but all of a sudden I was six feet tall and still growing.) I told Dale Velzy and Hap

Jacobs exactly what kind of board I wanted, and they listened patiently. Then I asked them how much a board like that would cost.

Hap Jacobs put his arm around me and said, "Well, Mike, I'll tell you what. We'll make you whatever kind of board you want, and it'll be from the best balsa we got. But we aren't gonna sell it to you. We're gonna own it. You can ride it all you want. When you decide it's time for a new board, you bring it back to us, and we'll make you another one."

I didn't get it at all. "Why would you do that?" I asked.

"Just trust us, Mike. This is something Dale and I want to do for you."

I still didn't get it. "That's great! But why?"

"Mike," Velzy said, "the way we hear it, you're getting to be one of the hottest young riders at Malibu these days. We just like to see the best surfers riding our boards."

I went home ecstatic that night and told my mother I'd won a free surfboard for being such a good surfer. I thought it was like winning a trophy in a contest.

You might say that was the end of my innocence. For the next fifteen years, I didn't pay for another piece of surfing equipment and rarely paid for a plane ticket.

The first surf movie I ever heard of was *The Big Surf*, by Bud Browne. We were all excited when it came to Culver City in 1957. I went with Herb Duhe in his '52 woody on opening night. I can remember driving around the corner and seeing the marquee that read, in giant red letters, *THE BIG SURF*.

The theater was one of those old-fashioned places with steep aisles, cheap baroque walls, and purple velvet curtains. By the time Herb and I got inside and found seats, the place was filled with a raucous crowd of surfers who had come all the way from Santa Barbara, to the north, and from Windansea, to the south. Every surfer (and wannabe surfer) in Southern California must have been there.

We all knew before the movie started that it was going to be about surfing in Hawaii—why else would it be called *The Big Surf?* Most of us had never seen film of Hawaiian surf before—just still photos. We expected the waves to be big, but when the film finally started and we got our first look at Sunset, Waimea, and other surf spots on the North Shore of Oahu, we were astonished at the speed and power of the waves. They were beautiful and fascinating, but also intimidating.

I can especially remember Conrad Kuna, a heavyset Hawaiian, riding Ala Moana; he had an old pig board he could turn with amazing speed. Another surfer who really stood out was our own Dewey Weber, from the old 22nd Street Gang, wearing bright red trunks at Makaha and running back and forth on his board like a little wound-up puppet. Dewey was really building a reputation for himself in the surfing world as the first ripper and slasher. He had grown up surfing the same waves I had, so I felt encouraged when I saw that he could handle the best surf Hawaii had to offer.

Mickey Dora was at the theater that night, pouting, it seemed, because everybody was paying more attention to the movie than to him. He was wearing a white sheet, like an Arab costume, but that wasn't good enough to compete with our first look at twenty-foot Sunset. Just as the movie was ending, we heard a series of loud concussions coming from the restrooms. Dora was throwing cherry bombs in the toilets.

They didn't show surf movies at that theater again for a long time.

The most famous surf spot in California during that era was Trestles, on the north end of the Camp Pendleton Marine Base. They called it Trestles because the train tracks crossed a lagoon there on a wooden trestle. It was a thick, heavy wave, a point break that was great for long boards. The marines, who used that area for amphibious training, tried hard to keep surfers out of Trestles. The penalty for being caught there was a $500 fine, six months in jail, or both; supposedly the FBI kept a list of violators. But no self-respecting surfer let the marines keep him out of Trestles. Great surf spots were gifts of nature, like the Grand Canyon and Yosemite, and as far as we were concerned, the military had no claim to them.

The trick to getting into Trestles was to drive to the bottom of a nearby arroyo, leave your car in the jungle of willows, then sneak down to the beach. If the marines came while you were in the water, you could paddle so far out they couldn't get you, then turn north and paddle to San Clemente State Park, where they didn't have the authority to arrest you. That really infuriated the marines. Several times after I worked that trick on them, they fired their automatic weapons in the water all around me. Sometimes the bullets would hit as close as ten feet away. Other times I would come back to my car and find that they had slashed my tires. It was a real war between surfers and marines, and it went on for years.

For a while I became obsessed with surfing at Trestles. I loved the wave, but I came to love the thrill of battling the marines even more. I bought an old 1946 Ford woody. The transmission only had two working gears, but I only paid twenty-five dollars for the thing, so I wasn't worried if the marines impounded it. I spray-painted the whole body in pre-hippie flower style and wrote on the side "Trestle Special."

One day I was surfing at Trestles with Mike McLellan, who was the fullback on the Orange Coast College football team. He probably weighed 220 pounds, and most of it was muscle. Mike was legendary for fighting the marines. As he and I were walking down the trail to the beach, carrying our surfboards under our arms, two marines dressed in jungle fatigues jumped out of the willows beside the trail. They pointed their guns at us, so of course we surrendered. They turned us around and started walking us back up the trail. There was a marine in front, then me, then Mike, and the other marine was bringing up the rear. All of a sudden, Mike jammed the tail of his board into the marine's chest, caved him in, then ran up and clobbered the other marine in the back of the neck with the nose of his surfboard. I was so surprised, I just stood there in shock. But Mike grabbed me, and we started running as fast as we could. I thought for sure the marines were going to fire on us. We knew about some side trails that we hoped the marines didn't know about, so we followed them back to our car, hopped in, and got out of there in a hurry.

One time, though, I did get caught at Trestles. We were sitting on the beach when the marines came out of the willow jungle. I picked up my board and started running for the water, but one marine ran after me and grabbed the back of my board. They caught me and five other guys and marched us back to their van.

They drove us to the base headquarters, which is about ten miles inland from the beach, then lined us up against the wall and asked us our names.

I said, "Mike Doyle."

The marine gave me a sarcastic look. "Right, fella. The last twenty surfers we had in here were either Mickey Doyle or Mike Dora."

I laughed. In a way, I was flattered.

None of us had any I.D., so the marines made us sit there for three or four hours worrying about what was going to happen to us; then they took our pictures and let us go. "Next time we see you at Trestles, you're going to jail," they said.

I didn't surf at Manhattan or Hermosa Beach much anymore. There were so many better places to surf, and besides, I had bad memories of the place. And except for Dewey Weber, the 22nd Street Gang didn't make it up to Malibu much. We never saw them at Swami's, Rincon, or San Onofre, either. They were all talented surfers, but they were afraid to leave their home turf, where they were unchallenged.

But then one day, maybe as an effort to break out of their rut, the whole 22nd Street Gang showed up at Malibu. I could see how nervous they were. Maybe they were afraid they would be treated as badly as they had treated outsiders on their home turf. They just sat on the beach for a while and watched the Malibu regulars surf.

I knew they were watching, so I showed off a bit. When I came out of the water, Henry Ford, who had always been their ringleader and mouthpiece, walked over to me and said, "Are you Tiki Mike, the guy we used to see down at Hermosa Beach?"

I laughed—nobody had called me Tiki Mike in years. I'd grown at least a foot and gained fifty pounds since the days when they had made my life so miserable. I didn't look so gangly anymore (some girls were even starting to give the impression they thought I was attractive), and I had the self-confidence of somebody who had found his own place in the world. I said, "Yeah, I'm Tiki Mike."

Henry got a pained look on his face, then said, "Jesus, how'd you get to be so good?"

I could see now how their tight little clique had retarded their growth. By being so cruel to me, they'd forced me to go out on my own—they'd shoved me into evolution. "I don't know, Henry," I said. "I've been working on it, I guess."

In 1959, my senior year in high school, my buddy Mike Majek and I started a business shaping balsa wood surfboards in my garage. Our major investment was a power planer. Foam surfboards had just started to come on the market, but their advantages hadn't been fully recognized yet. In fact, some surfers called foam boards "speedo sponges" or "flexi-fliers." So Majek and I stuck with shaping balsa boards. Beginning with a balsa blank, we would plane and sand each board into the shape we wanted, then coat it with fiberglass and resin. We shaped about 150 boards that year and sold them all, which put a little spending money in our pockets and gave us some independence.

One weekend, after Majek and I had each saved up a few hundred dollars, we flew up to San Francisco, then took a cab down to Burlingame, just south of the airport. There was a huge storage yard there filled with used ambulances and hearses: big beautiful Cadillacs with powerful V-8 engines and heavyweight suspensions. The mortuaries would buy new cars every year or so, no matter what condition the old ones were in; the cars had been well serviced, and hardly any of them had more than 15,000 miles, since they only went from the mortuary to the graveyard and back. There was almost no market for these cars—who wanted to own a used death-mobile?—but they made perfect surf wagons. So for $400 I bought a beautiful 1958 Cadillac with braided curtains and a burgundy velvet interior—a beautiful piece of metal and chrome. I remember the interior smelled liked dried flower petals.

Majek bought himself a Cadillac ambulance, and together we cruised down the Coast Highway, through Santa Cruz and Big Sur, in our plush wagons with their big engines purring. We were only eighteen and had our own Cadillacs.

As soon as we got home, I had my hearse painted canary yellow, and Mike had his ambulance painted fire-engine red. We liked to cruise side by side down Manchester Boulevard, in Inglewood, Majek in his ambulance and me in my hearse, while all the other cruisers in their lowered La Bamba '54 Oldsmobiles gave us angry stares. What thrilled us most of all, I think, was that we were thumbing our noses at the stifling Fifties mentality and getting away with it. We didn't have to act like square football jocks, and we didn't have to dress like tough *cholos* anymore. We had our own style now. The creative freedom and exhilaration we'd found in surfing was affecting our whole lives.

I loved taking my hearse to the beach. I carried my surfboards and wetsuits on the chrome coffin rack, so when I pushed a button, the whole rack would come sliding out. In midday I could climb in the back of the hearse to get out of the sun, and I slept in it when we went overnight to Rincon or Swami's. The only bad thing about that car was going to pick up a girl for a date. One look at my bed on wheels, and no girl's father would ever let his daughter see me again. So I learned after a while to park around the corner.

There was a whole flush of Nazi paraphernalia on the beach during this era: German helmets, swastikas, iron crosses. I don't know how all that got started—from Mickey Dora, I suppose. A lot of surfers had fathers who fought in World War II, so naturally the most rebellious thing they could do was pretend they were Nazis. One surfer I knew had a life-size painting of Hitler on the bottom of his surfboard. He also drove a white milk truck with swastikas painted on the sides. He used to drive around in that milk truck standing up, with the doors slid back, wearing a chrome German army helmet and a long trench coat covered with Nazi medals. One night he swerved to miss a dog in the road, the milk truck rolled over, and he was thrown out the door. He looked up to see the milk truck falling toward him, but the door casement landed right where he was. The truck was destroyed, but this guy wasn't touched.

Beginning about that time, 1959, Lance Carson started going through one of the wildest periods I've ever seen anybody go through. He refused to go back East to the military academy for his senior year, and <u>he started</u> acting up anywhere <u>he could find an audience.</u> He would go through a whole series of wild antics, rolling around on the ground and making bizarre sounds and faces, trying to see how silly he could get. His favorite trick was waving his bare ass at the world. After a surf movie at the Redondo High School Auditorium, while thousands of people were pouring out the doors, Lance stood at the bottom of the steps with his pants around his ankles, spreading his cheeks. After that his nickname became "No Pants Lance."

At first we thought Lance was just trying to get us all to laugh, but sooner or later he would push himself to the point that we wondered if he was going to lose control. He would punch his fist through a window or run out on the highway and see how close he could come to getting hit by a car. Another time Lance parked in front of Winchells Donuts and stood on the hood of his car with no pants on and a doughnut around his weenie, like a hood ornament. I thought it was beautiful—a kind of performance art that made a mockery of people's fear of nudity.

Years later I think it embarrassed Lance to be remembered for the wild antics of his youth. But in some ways Lance was years ahead of his time. He appreciated bizarre and outrageous situations, and if he couldn't find them, he would create them. I think Lance might have been the first punker.

I was at a surf contest down in La Jolla when I met a very beautiful girl, Marsha Bainer. She was just fifteen then, tall, part Mexican, with long black hair that fell to the back of her knees. She was from Torrance and had come to the contest with another guy, but we were immediately attracted to each other. Besides being one of the most beautiful women I'd ever seen, Marsha was intelligent (she was a straight-A student in high school), healthy, and fun. I wasn't the only guy in love with her. She had a number of admirers, including an entire generation of surfers who saw her as a bikini-clad model in the Jacobs Surfboard ads that appeared in surf magazines.

I asked Marsha out and, to my surprise, she accepted. From then on we started seeing a lot of each other. One night after Marsha and I had been out on a date, we went back to my parents' house in

Westchester. Walt was away at the time, and my mother had made a point of not being home. But she'd left a nice bottle of wine on ice for us and had turned the stereo to a quiet jazz station. Most surprising of all, she'd put fresh sheets on my bed and had turned the covers down. My mother had set everything up for me, and I couldn't figure out why. My mother has never been able to talk about sex—she has the typical Catholic sense of guilt—and to this day, seeing sex in the movies embarrasses her. The only thing I could figure out was that she was worried her son might be gay, and she wanted to steer me onto the right track, even if it meant making a sinner out of me.

One evening my stepfather, Walt, and I were talking. I was telling him how much I wanted to go to Hawaii and, maybe someday, see all of the South Pacific. Walt had been in the Pacific during World War II. He listened to me for a while, then said, "I hated the Pacific. I wouldn't go back there for anything."

"Why?" I asked.

It took some prodding, but I finally got Walt to explain. "I hated the Pacific because I lost so many friends there," he said.

Walt and I had never been very close. But once he was able to start talking about the war, it poured out in a flood. "I had a lot of buddies who flew planes in the Pacific," he said. "They'd take off, and they'd never come back. . . . Then a few days later, the Japanese would fly over our camp and toss out the arms and legs of our dead friends."

Walt paused, trying to get hold of his emotions, then went on. "One day we just couldn't take it any more. We went crazy with anger, climbed in our planes, and started flying up the rivers, shooting anybody with slant eyes. We didn't even know which side they were on, or care. If they moved, we shot them."

Walt broke down and started crying. This was something he'd kept buried deep inside for years. Once he'd finished telling me about his war experiences, he seemed embarrassed. And he never mentioned it to me again.

I hope it was good for Walt to get that story out in the open. I believe it was—both for him and me, because I learned something about the reality of war. It wasn't like the John Wayne movies that were so popular at the time. Sometimes it was just senseless killing that could haunt a person for the rest of his life.

As my senior year in high school drew to a close, I had no thought of going to college. My mother didn't encourage me to go—nobody in her family had ever gone. I was just waiting for high school to end so I could go to Hawaii.

On the last day of high school, in June 1959, everybody in my English class had to stand up and talk about what he or she planned to do with the rest of his or her life. One guy described how his dad was going to get him a job selling life insurance. One girl said she was going to marry her boyfriend, the same guy she'd been going with since the ninth grade. Another guy was going to join the army and learn about radio repair.

The teacher, Mrs. Tregeagle, was probably congratulating herself on how she'd helped these fine young people achieve adulthood. Meanwhile, all the other kids were listening nervously, trying to come up with stories good enough to outdo their classmates.

I was sitting in the back of the class, trying to keep a low profile. But Mrs. Tregeagle eventually called on me. I walked to the front of the class, looked at my classmates, then at the teacher, and said, "I'm gonna live on the beach at Malibu, and I'm gonna surf every day."

Mrs. Tregeagle was not pleased. "Now, Michael, you know you can't make a living surfing."

"Well, I've thought about that," I said. "I'll collect Coke bottles."

The whole class started giggling, not sure if I was serious. Mrs. Tregeagle gave me her most severe look.

"There's two guys down there doing it right now!" I said. "Tubesteak and Harry Stonelake. They work at it every day, and they get just enough money to eat. It's perfect!"

The other kids were really having fun now, watching me make a fool out of myself.

Mrs. Tregeagle got up from her desk, walked over to my side, grabbed me by the arm, and dragged me out of the classroom and into the hall. She was furious. "What do you think you're doing, trying to disrupt my class like that?"

I said, "I didn't do that to disrupt your class. That's really what I'm going to do."

Mrs. Tregeagle looked me directly in the eye and slowly began to realize that I really was serious. She let go of my arm, stepped back, and shook her head with disgust. "You poor, poor boy," she said.

A Garage Full of Trophies

*T*here was a swim coach at Inglewood High, Rudy Kroon, who surfed a little and worked as a lifeguard in the summer. Rudy knew I wasn't material for his swim team, but he also knew I spent a lot of time in the ocean. So he said to me one day just before school let out, "Mike, you know, I think you'd make a good lifeguard. They need guys who know the ocean, not just pool swimmers. Why don't you take the test?"

I liked that idea. It sounded more profitable than collecting Coke bottles at Malibu, so I started training for the lifeguard test.

I would get up every morning at five, eat a bowl of wheat germ and middlings, and hit the water by six. I'd take off from the Santa Monica Pier on my big paddle board, and I'd paddle to Topanga and back, about ten miles. Or, once in a while, I'd have somebody drive me up to the Malibu Pier, and I'd paddle back to Santa Monica, about eighteen miles. Other times I'd paddle straight out to sea, put a foam pad under my forehead as a rest, put my head down, get into the rhythm of the workout, and before I knew it I'd have ten miles between me and the shore. After I finished paddling, I'd swim a mile and then run for a couple of miles.

When it came time to take the City of Santa Monica lifeguard test, I was in great shape. I came in nineteenth, and they hired twenty-five, so I went to work as a lifeguard for the rest of that summer.

Lifeguarding was a great job for me. I wasn't landlocked anymore, I spent all day at the beach, and I was saving money to go to Hawaii in the winter.

Santa Monica wasn't a very active area for rescues. There weren't a lot of rip tides or other hazards. Sometimes there wouldn't be anybody at all in the water, so I would play volleyball with the locals.

One day I met a girl at my lifeguard tower. She was about sixteen and very attractive. She seemed to like me a lot—she hung around my tower all day—so after work I went over to her house. We kissed a while, and I was really surprised how sensitive she was to my touch. I had never known a girl that hot before.

Later I mentioned her name to another lifeguard, and he said, "You know she's a nympho, don't you?"

I said, "No kidding?" Then I thought about it for a moment. "What's a nympho, anyway?"

"Well, that's when a girl starts having sex and she can't quit."

"God," I said, "That's a really serious disease." Like most teenagers of my era, I was fairly naive about sex. I'd heard about Spanish flies: In those days it was common knowledge that if you slipped a Spanish fly into a girl's drink, she had to have sex with you. We always wanted to know where we could buy a Spanish fly, but we never found out. Anyway, the way I understood it, this nympho had whatever it was that a Spanish fly did to a girl, but she had it naturally.

Later that summer, when there was a lifeguard competition in Carpenteria, near Santa Barbara, I drove some of the guys on our team up there in my yellow hearse. A few of the guys took their girlfriends, and I took this nympho with me. On the way back I was kind of tired, so I let one of the other guys drive the hearse while I crawled into a sleeping bag in back. The girl joined me, and pretty soon we started fooling around. As soon as I touched this girl, she was just electric with sexual energy—she started quivering and making noises, even with other people there in the car. I thought, God, she does have it!

I stopped seeing her after that because she frightened me so much. I liked her a lot, but I just couldn't deal with a serious disease like nymphomania.

Every summer there was a paddling race from Catalina Island to Manhattan Pier, about twenty-eight miles. It sounded like the most grueling competitive event I could imagine, but a lot of my heroes—Ricky Grigg, Greg Noll, Bob Hogan—had competed in that race. It was one way you proved you were a serious, all-around waterman, and I decided to give it a try.

I knew my biggest rival in the race would be Kemp Aaberg. Kemp was a great paddler, and he was always in top shape. Kemp was working as a lifeguard, too, and sometimes he and I worked out together. He couldn't beat me in the short races, but he was really good in the longer distances, and I knew I would need an edge to beat him in the Catalina race.

I worked out every morning that summer, gradually increasing my daily paddling distance from eight, to ten, to twelve miles. I also became extremely conscious of my diet. I read everything I could get my hands on about how diet affected an endurance athlete's performance. I met a guy who was a nutritionist at UCLA, and he put me on a breakfast diet of horse meat, liver, kelp tablets, and seven-grain cereal with honey. For lunch I had fruit, a quart of yogurt, and sandwiches made from wheat bread, non-hydrogenated peanut butter, and honey.

About two weeks before the race, I increased my daily paddling distance to twenty miles. I was working out five hours a day, and every night when I went to bed I was totally exhausted. I was in fantastic shape; the only problem was that Kemp was doing the same workouts I was doing, and I still felt I needed an edge to beat him.

Then, a few days before the race, I happened to see Kemp on the beach eating a hot dog. I figured that was it—he'd broken training! Kemp didn't have a chance, now, and I was confident I would win.

The day before the race, the contest organizers took all the competitors, about a dozen of us, over to Catalina Island on a 200-foot yacht. To everyone's surprise, Mickey Dora had signed up to compete. Anybody could sign up if he wanted to, but we all knew Dora hadn't been working out. Kemp took one look at Dora's paddle board—an ancient, hollow kook box from the 1930s—and said to me, "That board will never make it across the channel." All the way over on the yacht, Dora was drinking champagne with the contest sponsors and having a ball.

That night we stayed at a campground just outside Catalina.

The contest organizers were in a party mood, and they put on a big feast of filet mignon and even more champagne. The competitors, of course, were still on strict training diets. We stuffed ourselves on wheat germ and peanut-butter sandwiches, and went to bed early. Dora stayed up late, drinking cocktails and partying around the campfire.

The next morning we left the harbor at first light, when the channel was still glassy. Each paddler was led by a motorized guide boat. It was the guides' job to calculate the current and wind conditions, and to plot the most direct route across the channel. So each of us, following our own guide boat, went our separate way.

Kemp had a hollow, veneer board—very light and very fast—but I'd made my own foam paddle board, which was almost unheard of at that time. It was about twelve feet long and twenty inches wide. It was faster than Kemp's board, and before long I was pulling away from him. Every time I looked back to find him, he was falling farther and farther behind, and after a while I couldn't even see him anymore. I just put my head down and stroked hard for the mainland.

After a couple of hours, I started noticing that my guide boat wasn't following a straight course. On the open ocean I couldn't even see the mainland, so I had no choice but to follow my guide. But I didn't like what I was seeing. As I watched more carefully, I saw the guys in the boat chucking empty beer cans overboard. I knew then my guides were drunk.

After about four hours of paddling, I was close enough to the mainland to get my bearings: I was south of Paddle Board Cove—way off course. So I ignored my guide boat now and turned north, stroking even harder to make up for lost time. Just off the Redondo Pier, I met Kemp, who had been led on a much truer course than I had. I'd lost all my lead trying to get back on course.

As Kemp and I paddled side by side, he started complaining that his hollow board was taking on water. He needed to stop long enough to tape up the leaky spots, but it was against the rules for him to touch his guide boat. I probably should have let him sink—having your equipment in order is part of winning a paddling race—but I was still confident I would win anyway, so I stopped and held his board while he swam over to his guide boat, got the tape, and mended his board. Without my help, his board would have drifted away or he would have touched his guide boat, which would have automatically disqualified him.

Kemp and I started talking back and forth, which both of us knew was a bad idea. The tendency in a long-distance paddling race is to get paired up to ease the loneliness. But then you become psychologically dependent on one another. To prevent that from happening, I started pulling away from him again.

About three miles from the finish, Kemp called over to me, "I've had it!" and he started paddling directly for shore. If he touched shore anyplace before the finish, he would have been disqualified.

I figured it was over now. Kemp was finally paying the price for having eaten that hot dog.

I stayed on course for Manhattan Pier, but by now I was totally drained, almost delirious—literally falling asleep on my board. I'd been drinking grape juice to keep from dehydrating, but the sugar kept giving me a jolt, like getting shot in the arm with adrenaline. The trouble with that was, ten minutes later, when the sugar rush had worn off, I was more drained than before.

It so happened there was an eight-foot south swell running that day, which was very unusual there. Once Kemp got close to shore, paddling just outside the surf line, he discovered there was about a four-knot drift sucking him toward the finish. Meanwhile, I was still way outside, getting tossed around by the swell. When Kemp saw he still had a chance to beat me, he started paddling hard again.

I tried my best, but as we approached the pier I saw Kemp turn the corner just a couple hundred yards ahead of me. He caught a wave and rode it to shore. After six hours of paddling on the open ocean, we finished less than a minute apart.

Mickey Dora was waiting for us on the beach with a big smile on his face and a beer in his hand. About a mile out of the Catalina harbor, his paddle board had sunk. He'd climbed into his guide boat and drunk beer all the way back to the mainland.

That summer I got a notice in the mail ordering me to appear at the induction center in Los Angeles for a draft physical. This was after the Korean War, but during the military buildup before the

Vietnam War. Cold War tensions were high all over the world, and young men my age were being drafted by the thousands. Along with other information in the induction letter, it said, "Bring your toothbrush." From talking with other guys who'd already had their physicals, I knew what that meant: If you passed, they put you on the bus and took you straight to Fort Ord.

All I knew about the military was what Walt had told me and from battling the marines at Trestles. As far as I was concerned, the military was the enemy. Now they wanted to force me into becoming one of them. But I wasn't going to fight in their war. No way. I knew I wouldn't go, no matter what I had to do. In fact, I was so sure I wouldn't go, the day of the physical, I loaded my hearse with surfboards and wetsuits. And I didn't take my toothbrush.

When I walked through the door at the induction center, there were already about 200 guys ahead of me. Some hairy ape in a uniform and smoking a cigar stood up in front of us and said, "A lotta you assholes here today think you're gonna get out of military duty. Well, I'm here to tell you that none of you are gonna get out. You're all going, because your country needs you!"

He ordered us to strip down to our shorts, then lined us up single file and told us to follow the painted lines on the floor.

The guy in front of me had shit stains in his underwear. A couple of guys passed out, they were so scared. One of them bounced against a window and broke it. I remember thinking I'd never seen such poor physical specimens in my life as the guys around me. They were almost all skinny, white, and sickly, with pimply backs and bowed legs, chicken-breasted, swaybacked, knock-kneed, and gimpy. But I'd been working out and surfing every day. I was tanned and in great shape—the prime of my life. I remember thinking, nervously, I'm the healthiest guy in this room.

Somebody told us to pull down our shorts, bend over, and spread our cheeks. A doctor walked by sticking his finger in every guy's ass. What a demoralizing thing. Then they herded us down the line like cattle.

At one point they handed us paper cups and told us to pee in them. I saw one guy take a pin from his underwear, prick his finger, and squeeze a drop of blood into his cup.

Later on, some guy in a uniform saw that I was holding some papers in my hand, and he asked me what they were.

I said, "They're from my doctor." (The papers documented my hearing problem all the way back to my lip-reading classes in grammar school.)

The guy growled at me and said, "Lemme have 'em!"

I had a pretty good idea how the system worked: If I gave my papers to this jerk, they'd get lost in the shuffle and I'd be on the bus to Fort Ord. So I told him, "No way. I'm keeping these." He tried to grab the papers from me, but I held on to them until I got to talk to a doctor. I knew those papers were my only hope.

Eventually, they put me in a hearing booth. I'd taken so many hearing tests over the years, I knew how to make my hearing seem even worse than it was.

Finally, after several hours, we all came to the end of the painted lines, back in the big room where we'd started. I looked out the front window and saw my yellow hearse with the boards inside. Just then, two big orange buses pulled up to the curb, waiting to carry fresh meat for the war machine.

The ape with the cigar reappeared, this time with a long list in his hand. He started walking down the line, reading names from the list, grabbing guys by the shoulders, and shoving them toward the bus. "Accepted . . . accepted . . . accepted. . . ."

Then he came to me. He looked at the list, looked at me, looked at the list again. "Rejected?" He gave me a dirty scowl, but I knew he couldn't touch me. I turned away from him, broke into a big grin, and ran outside.

What a glorious sense of freedom. I felt like somebody had given me my life.

One of the best things about being a lifeguard was that a lot of the older guys I'd idolized for years—Buzzy Trent, Ricky Grigg, and Dave Rochlen—also worked as lifeguards, and I got to see them almost every day.

Buzzy Trent, who was about nine years older than I, had a tight muscular body, with short arms and legs, a tiny waist and a big chest. He'd grown up in Santa Monica back in the Forties; he and Matt

Kivlin used to ride their bikes to Malibu. But Buzzy had a real craving for adventure and at some point decided he had to have bigger thrills than California surfing could offer. He started spending his winters in Hawaii and became one of the great pioneers of surfing on the North Shore of Oahu.

The Hawaiians who developed the modern style of surfing in the early part of this century, Duke Kahanamoku's generation, had spent most of their time at Waikiki. Some of them worked at the hotels as professional beachboys, taking rich tourists out on tandem boards and outrigger canoes. They were fantastic watermen, but they had kind of a cushy life there, living off their tips and hustling the tourist women. They didn't want to go over to the North Shore of Oahu, where the waves were so big and thunderous you couldn't even sleep at night.

The next generation of surfers, which included Hawaiians, as well as *haoles* (whites), had been terrific watermen too, and they rode some big waves at Makaha, on the west side of the island, but they didn't have the equipment and the madman mentality to go after the biggest waves they could find.

It was the California crazies in the Fifties who really pioneered big-wave surfing. They were the ones who discovered that a relatively short stretch (less than ten miles) of the North Shore was blessed with the biggest and best surf in the world: Sunset, Pipeline, Pupukea, Waimea, and Haleiwa. If the California crazies had anything in common it was a wild, restless, sometimes almost self-destructive energy. They had a bohemian lifestyle, some were hard drinkers—always looking for that quick rush—and they might have been considered misfits at any vocation other than riding big waves.

But to me, Buzzy Trent was a super-hero. I was thrilled just to know him, and every time I saw him I pumped him for information about the North Shore. "What's Sunset like? When that big wave hits you, how long do you have to hold your breath?"

Buzzy would say something like, "Listen, you've surfed at Swami's when the surf was twelve-foot, right? Well, wait'll you surf Sunset. It's ten times as powerful as that. It would kill most California surfers."

It scared the hell out of me to hear Buzzy's stories, but at the same time I couldn't get enough of them.

The other lifeguard I admired a lot was Ricky Grigg. Buzzy had taught Ricky how to surf at Malibu when he was just a kid. Ricky wasn't a big guy, about 160 pounds, but well built. He had blond hair that was already thinning and a great big smile. He always looked comfortable in the water, and was absolutely fearless. Ricky had already spent one winter surfing in Hawaii, and everytime I asked him about it he encouraged me to go to the North Shore and see it for myself.

One afternoon I was sitting in my lifeguard tower with absolutely nothing going on, when I looked down the beach and happened to notice a girl crawling along the sand on her stomach. She got closer and closer, and when she got to the bottom of the tower I looked down and saw she had the most gorgeous, crystal-clear eyes I'd ever seen. I said, "What in the world are you doing?"

"My girlfriend bet me ten dollars I couldn't crawl on my elbows from one tower to another," she replied.

"Well, it looks like you win," I said. "Tell you girlfriend I'll pay the ten dollars."

We started talking, and Sparkle Eyes (that became her nickname) told me she was from Laguna Beach. "I go down that way to surf at San Onofre and Trestles all the time," I said.

"Come and see me next time you're in town," she said.

Sparkle Eyes and I started seeing each other after that. She had a great-looking sister, too, so I set her up with Mike Majek. I'd pick up Sparkle Eyes in my yellow hearse, Majek would pick up her sister in the red ambulance, and we'd all go up in the Laguna Hills to park.

Sparkle Eyes' father was in the marines, and Mike and I were terrified of him because of all the trouble we'd had with the jarheads at Trestles. We tried to avoid the sisters' house when we knew the old man was around, and we were always careful not to park my hearse or Majek's ambulance out front where he could see them.

But one evening Majek, the two sisters, and I were at their house. In fact, Sparkle Eyes and I were in her parents' bed, and we had the front door locked just in case the parents came home.

All of a sudden we heard a banging on the front door. "Who's in there?" their father called. When he didn't get an answer, he started trying to break down the door with his shoulder.

Mike and I ran out the back door with Sparkle Eyes, and her sister stayed behind to stall the old man while we made our getaway. We ran around front (the father was inside the house by now), Mike jumped in the red ambulance, Sparkle Eyes and I jumped in the yellow hearse, and we all took off.

I never went back to Sparkle Eyes' house again. We only met secretly, away from her father.

Although I was beginning to feel my oats when it came to sex, I mostly stayed away from drinking and partying at that age. I spent most of my time working out, lifeguarding, or sleeping. But one night I did go to a party put on by some of the lifeguards. I borrowed my aunt's car, a clean '57 Chevy, and took a date.

The party was a big blowout. In those days lifeguards were expected to be wild and out of control, so naturally they all tried hard to live up to that reputation. They had a dory filled with ice and beer, and everybody got smashed. For some reason, maybe because I was nervous about being with this girl, I started drinking beer, too. It was the first time I ever drank, and I only had two bottles of Rainier Ale. I remember we all got down on the ground and wrestled, but I don't remember anything after that.

I woke up the next morning in the front seat of my aunt's car, with the door open. Somebody's automatic sprinklers had turned on, and there was water running down my hands and arms. I didn't know how I got there. I didn't know how my date got home. I didn't remember leaving the party.

I went home and called the girl. She said I'd behaved like a perfect gentleman and she had no idea what had happened to me after I took her home.

I was in a daze for a week after that. Out surfing, I'd just sit there on my board watching while a wave broke on top of me. I thought I was losing my mind.

Looking back on it, I think I'd been so serious about training and so conscientious about everything I put in my body, I somehow convinced myself that even one beer would destroy me. When I had those two beers, I was so disappointed with myself, I blocked out the entire experience.

Even in those days, Santa Monica was kind of a perverted place. There were always guys whacking off under the pier, and we busted a lot of sand pumpers. In fact that was a code with the other lifeguards: "Got a sand pumper behind tower three!" I guess there was some kind of cult of sand pumpers, I don't know. But what they'd do was crawl up behind these girls sleeping on the beach, until they were about fifteen feet away; then they'd poke holes in the sand, pull their weenies out, and hump away in the sand. Some of those guys liked people to see them—they actually got a thrill out of getting caught.

Little by little, I discovered that this perversion involved the lifeguard force, as well. The ocean at Santa Monica was never very demanding, and the job just wasn't active enough to keep the lifeguards on their toes. None of the older guys ever worked out, and they'd booze it up every night. They were bored, and the boredom turned into sexual degeneracy. In fact, it was said to be the most degenerate lifeguard force on the whole coast.

The Santa Monica beaches used to get a lot of Europeans, particularly Scandinavians: big, blonde Swedish girls who were a lot less inhibited about sex than American girls. They just loved lifeguards, which the lifeguards learned very quickly. When the girls came up to the tower to talk, all wet from being in the ocean, the lifeguards would offer them nice warm showers. Then the lifeguards would start playing with them, getting all giggly, and before long they'd be screwing them right there in the tower. Some of the girls would come back several times a week.

There were two lieutenants on the force who worked at an area called North Beach. We'll call them Al and Ron (not their real names). One of the locals at North Beach was a gay Chinese fellow we'll call Jong Chiu (not his real name, either). He liked lifeguards as much as the Scandinavian girls did. He'd run down the beach on his tiptoes and wave at the lifeguards until they'd pay attention to him. The guys would laugh and make fun of him, and the more they did that, the more excited he got.

One day all the lifeguards were at the main tower working on our outrigger canoes, sanding the paddles and checking the rigging, getting ready for a lifeguard competition. Jong Chiu happened to walk by, and Al and Ron invited him up into the tower. It was a big tower, the substation, with a shower and restroom upstairs.

As I sanded my paddle, I kept hearing the toilet flush. Some of the other guys had climbed up the back of the tower and were peeking into the shower stall, watching and giggling. One by one, most of the guys took a turn upstairs. I didn't know what was going on, but I knew enough to ignore it.

After a while, more lifeguard trucks pulled up, with lifeguards and a lieutenant from South Beach. They all went up there, too.

Finally, one of the lieutenants said to me, "Okay, Doyle, it's your turn next."

I kept sanding on my paddle, like I didn't know what he was talking about. When he insisted I go upstairs, I looked at him and said, "If you think I'm going up there, you're out of your mind."

After that, the lieutenant left me alone, but I could see it made him nervous that I wouldn't participate.

Nothing more came of the incident at that time, and I did my best to forget about it. But later on, it came back to haunt us all.

In 1959 Dale Velzy and Hap Jacobs dissolved their partnership. They still kept the name Velzy & Jacobs on their surfboards, but Jacobs took over the shop in Venice, while Velzy moved his wife and family to San Clemente, about fifty miles south of L.A., and opened a new shop there.

I bought a 1957 Ranchero that summer, and to help pay for it I started running balsa wood blanks down to Velzy's shop twice a week.

San Clemente was a sleepy little beach town then, but I liked it so much I started staying down there and shaping boards for Velzy when I wasn't lifeguarding. There were three other guys working for him, Kimo Hollinger, Duke Brown and my old friend Kemp Aaberg. We all slept in a big loft above the shop; we were like Velzy's guard dogs, keeping burglars away at night. The loft was about three feet deep in balsa shavings left over from shaping boards. Balsa comes off the planer clean and smooth, and it smells wonderful—not like Styrofoam and fiberglass, which are itchy and smelly. So we just threw our sleeping bags down in those balsa chips and slept like we were in surf rat heaven.

Every morning at first light, we'd jump out of our bags, hop in a van, head to the doughnut shop for a quick breakfast, then hit Trestles at the crack of dawn. We'd surf the morning glass, then come back and work on surfboards during the middle part of the day. Later, we'd head back to Trestles for the evening glass. We didn't do anything except make surfboards and surf.

Velzy didn't shape that many surfboards himself anymore; he just concentrated on keeping the materials coming in the shop on Monday and the finished boards going out on Friday. If there was an order for a racing board or a big tandem board—something that caught his fancy—he would shape it himself. But Velzy's real passion was cars. He always had a fast hot rod with a surfboard sticking out the back, or a sleek little Mercedes.

Velzy paid us by the piece. If you shaped a board you got $5, if you sanded a board you got $3, and so on. We had a clipboard hanging on the wall, and every time we finished a job, we'd put a check by our name. Every Friday Velzy would add up the check marks, pull a big roll of cash from his pocket, and peel off whatever he owed us. For Velzy every transaction was always in cash—no checks, no bookkeeping, no bother.

We all thought Velzy was rich because he drove a Mercedes SL 300 gull wing and wore a big diamond ring. Anybody as slick as the Hawk had to be rich. But one day, late that summer, some guys in three-piece suits showed up at Velzy's shop. I didn't know who they were, but one of the other guys said they were from the IRS. I didn't even know what that meant. Whoever they were, they shut the place down and put a big lock on the door.

After that, Velzy's shop was finished. He took off for Montana, saying he was going to try his hand at gold mining. The Hawk always had an eye for striking it rich.

One night I was staying with friends at Laguna Beach. I had to be to work lifeguarding at eight in the morning, and I needed a couple of hours for my morning workout, so I rolled out of bed at four o'clock.

I was still kind of groggy as I headed up the Coast Highway. Between Newport and Huntington Beach a light fog was rolling in off the ocean. There was almost nothing there in those days, just the ocean on one side of the road and open fields on the other. About a mile away, I spotted a pair of headlights coming toward me. They looked like they were in my lane, and I wondered if maybe this was a drunk trying to find his way home.

I kept watching the lights as they got closer and closer. Then I glanced in my rearview mirror and saw a car a couple hundred yards behind me. I couldn't tell if the car behind me saw the car coming toward us, so I tapped my brakes a couple of times, hoping to warn the driver.

I could see now that the car coming toward me was going really fast—maybe eighty miles an hour. I wasn't sure what to do, but I realized that if I stayed in my lane, I'd be dead. I tapped my brakes a couple more times; then, at the very last moment, I swerved into the left lane.

The car in front went roaring by me, and a few moments later I heard an enormous crash. The two cars had smashed head on.

I pulled over and ran back to the cars. I'd had some paramedic training as a lifeguard, and I thought maybe I could do something to save a life. In the car that had been behind me there had been four people, but they were all lying on the highway now. One by one I went around checking them. No life there . . . no life there . . . no life there. . . . The car that had caused the accident was crushed so badly, it was impossible to get inside of it. And there were no other cars anywhere in sight. You would expect somebody to be out driving at that hour, but there wasn't a soul. It was so eerie, I felt like maybe I was dead, too.

So, everybody here is dead, I thought. The only thing I can do is go for help. I got back in my car and drove on to Huntington Beach. I stopped at the first phone booth, parked my car, and ran over to call the police—and there on the floor of the phone booth was another body, all crumpled up and twisted so the door to the booth wouldn't open.

I ran back to my car, hopped in, and rammed the phone booth a couple of times with the bumper to see if I could wake the guy up. But he didn't move.

I started to pull back onto the highway, and just then a police car cruised by. I whipped my car around and pulled in front of him. I jumped out, ran over, and told him what had happened.

As the cop took off down the highway, I got back in my car and headed north again, trying to make some sense out of this vision of death. I'd only driven a short way up the highway when a huge moth with a five-inch wing span landed on my windshield. I watched the moth for a moment, then realized it was dead, too—only the force of the wind was holding it in place.

All this had to mean something; it had to be some kind of omen. But if it was, I couldn't figure it out. After two or three miles, I turned on the windshield wipers and knocked the moth off.

When that summer came to an end, I'd saved enough money to make my trip to Hawaii. Buzzy Trent, Ricky Grigg, and a few other California surfers had a place on the North Shore they rented every winter. They told me that if I flew to Honolulu, they would pick me up at the airport and let me stay at their place until I could get a place of my own. My plan was to spend all winter, and I was starting to get really excited about it. But at the same time, there was something scary about knowing my greatest dream was about to come true. If you put all your hopes into one thing and that one thing turns out not to be as wonderful as you'd thought, what do you do next?

Also, the thought occurred to me that until now surfing had mostly been just for fun. But in Hawaii, there would be a very real element of risk. Every now and then we would hear reports through the grapevine of big-wave riders on the North Shore drowning, and for the first time I began to understand why so many of the great California surfers never gave the North Shore a try, or if they did, they came back home and never tried it again.

In September I bought my ticket on USOA—United States Overseas Airlines. The price was only $80 round trip but, as the saying goes, you get what you pay for. The rumor was that USOA stood for "Use Some Other Airline." Their only plane was a rickety

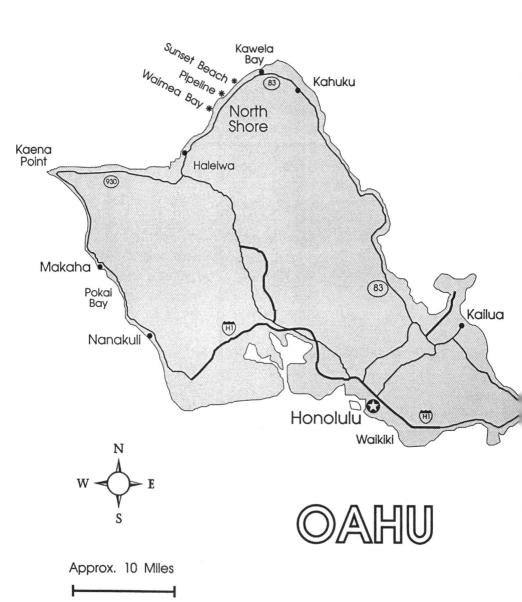

Pacific Ocean

Sunset Beach ✳
Kawela Bay
Pipeline ✳
Waimea Bay ✳
83
Kahuku

North Shore

Kaena Point

930

Haleiwa

Makaha

Pokai Bay

83

Nanakuli

H1

Kailua

Honolulu
☆

H1

Waikiki

N
W ← → E
S

OAHU

Approx. 10 Miles

old DC-6, and they treated the passengers worse than they treated the freight.

It was my first time on an airplane, and I was so nervous about flying, I took along as carry-on luggage my swim fins, wetsuit, and a blowup surf mat, thinking that if we crashed, I'd have a better chance of survival.

The plane was supposed to leave from the Lockheed terminal at the Burbank airport, but right before departure, one of the engines broke down. We had to wait at the YMCA in Burbank for two days while they pulled the engine out, repaired it, and got it back into the plane again.

When the plane was finally ready to fly, they canceled the tickets for about three-fourths of the passengers because they needed the space for a load of Avon cosmetics bound for Honolulu. I was lucky to get a seat—all but about fifteen of them had been removed to make room for the Avon boxes. As we took off, the plane was so overloaded I was worried we'd fall into the ocean, but after a couple of hours I decided there was nothing I could do about it. I climbed on top of the boxes of cosmetics, with my surf mat by my side, and went to sleep.

We landed at the Honolulu airport late that night. I knew we were coming in over Waikiki, and I was looking out the window trying to get my first glimpse of Hawaiian waves, but it was too dark.

Buzzy Trent and Ricky Grigg were waiting for me at the airport. With them was Peter Cole, another Californian who now lived in Honolulu, where he taught at the Punahou prep school. He was thin, with a receding hairline, had a studious look, and was quieter than the others; but I knew he was a legendary big-wave rider. The winter before, 1958, he'd become the first *haole* to win the Makaha International, the most important surf contest in the world.

We grabbed my luggage and surfboard, and climbed in Peter's car. The war stories started immediately: "You shoulda seen the wipeout Peter took at Sunset yesterday," Buzzy said. "God, it was horrible! We didn't think he was ever coming up again."

It only took us an hour to drive across Oahu to the North Shore, but it was dark out and I couldn't see any of the scenery or get my bearings. I felt disoriented and uncomfortable. As we got out of the car, I could hear the waves pounding on the beach. Just by the sound I could tell they were unlike any waves I'd seen before.

Buzzy and Ricky lived in an old army barracks Quonset hut just a few feet back from the high-tide line. The place had one big room in front, a kitchen and bath, and some small bedrooms in back. There was no furniture except a few old smelly mattresses thrown down on the floor. The kitchen was piled high with dirty dishes and trash. They had a big sack of beans, a big sack of rice, and several cases of beer. It was the only house of surfers on the whole North Shore, and the guys rented it for something like $75 a month.

Buzzy welcomed me to their house by saying, "Doyle, you want my wife for the night?" Buzzy's wife, Violet, was a Filipino who grew up in Hawaii. She looked soft and dark and, I thought, beautiful.

Buzzy didn't mean any harm—it was just his idea of a joke. But I was so embarrassed, I just looked at the floor and pretended I didn't know what he was talking about.

"Ah, come on, Buzzy, lay off him," Ricky said. "He just got here."

"Well, then here, have a shooter," Buzzy laughed, and handed me a glass of whiskey. "Tomorrow we ride the big surf!"

Buzzy and the others stayed up late that night drinking whiskey, but I unrolled my sleeping bag on the floor and tried to sleep. I couldn't, though. The impact from the waves made the floor of the hut shake, and I kept thinking, What am I doing here with these madmen?

I was relieved when dawn finally arrived. As soon as I heard the others stirring, I got up and went outside. Right in front of the Quonset hut was the most incredible shore break I'd ever seen— eight-foot barrels crashing on a reef. It was the fastest, tightest wave I could imagine, and I just stood there staring at it.

When the others came out, they looked hung over. Buzzy scratched his belly, pointed at the shore break, and said, "Well, this is it, Doyle. This is where we surf when Sunset's not breaking."

I looked at the shore break again, then back at Buzzy. "Are you serious?" I asked. The place looked like death to me.

"Yeah, some good lefts out there. Here, lemme show ya." And he started pointing out the line-up. "Now, you wanna paddle out right over there. It's a bit tight, sure, but get up on the nose right after takeoff, and you'll make it. We'll come out as soon as you get a coupla rides."

I took my board and paddled out, thinking to myself, This is way out of my league.

I sat outside and watched the waves breaking for a minute or two. I figured the only way I could make a wave like that was to get my board angled left on the takeoff and then just go for it. If I had to drop in, then turn, I'd be eaten alive.

So I gave it a try and found, to my surprise, that I could actually pull it off. My board didn't really fit inside that tight barrel, so there was just one quick, screaming slide to the shoulder. I rode three or four waves before I noticed that none of the others were coming out to join me. They were standing on the beach watching me. So I paddled back in, thinking maybe I was doing something wrong.

Buzzy said, "Way to go, kid."

Nobody else said a word.

I didn't find out until later I'd been surfing what they called the Banzai Pipeline. The bottom was shallow rock, with hollow caves where you could be trapped and drowned. It was considered too dangerous to surf.

In later years a lot of surfers claimed to be the first to have ridden the Pipeline. I don't know who rode it first, and I don't really care. I do know, though, that I did ride it then, in September 1959. And it was only utter ignorance that made me do it.

We ate breakfast out on the porch, and I asked the others what their plan was for the day. Buzzy said, "We're gonna go down to Sunset."

"Yeah?" I said. "Where is it?"

He pointed down the beach, about two miles away, where we could see a wave breaking way out. Buzzy said, "That's Sunset. It should be good today. Probably about fifteen feet."

In Hawaii, a fifteen-foot wave is no big deal. But in California that's about as big as waves get. I thought to myself, Ohhhhh, noooo. . . .

When we got to Sunset, nobody else was out. We got our boards off the car and waxed up. This time I waited until the others put their boards in the water before I followed them, and we all paddled out together.

There were no more practical jokes. Buzzy and the others all wanted somebody new to surf with. I'd already proved I had the ability to play with them; all I needed now was the experience. They really took me under their wing that day.

"The line-up at Sunset is critical," Ricky said, sitting astride his board and pointing toward the beach. "But everybody has his own reference points to find it. I like to use that house with the palm tree in front and that radar tower on the hill." He was shouting above the roar of the waves, and I could see the excitement in his eyes. "The wind often blows ten to fifteen knots here, so you have to watch your line-up all the time or you'll get blown into no man's land, where you'll miss the wave. On a big day, it'll start to feather on an outer reef, maybe a half-mile out, and then you know there's a big set coming. When you see that, you have to paddle like hell, straight out, or you'll get caught inside."

He looked at me to see if I understood. I nodded that I did, so he turned and paddled away.

I sat on the shoulder for a long time. I'd never seen waves that big and that fast before, and I forgot all about surfing. I was hypnotized by just watching them build up to mountainous peaks and then crash.

The others tried a few waves. Buzzy was the most aggressive of the bunch. He didn't surf with great style and grace, but he was indestructible and totally fearless. He had a wide, hunched-over stance, and no part of his upper body moved. Just making the wave was his goal.

Peter, who was very nearsighted without his glasses, would pick and choose his waves more cautiously, and his style was more fluid than Buzzy's. But Ricky combined the best of each: He was fearless—he would take off on anything—and he surfed with a looser, more relaxed style that showed he was really in control. This was only Ricky's second winter in Hawaii, but by watching and learning everything he could from the older guys, he had been able to avoid going through the long, painful, learning process they had gone through. He was already one of the best big-wave riders in the world.

I started out with a smaller wave, took the steep drop, but barely kept the nose of my board from pearling. I pulled off a cautious turn, survived to the shoulder and, as carefully as I could, eased my board out the back. As the wave passed under me, my board and I flew ten feet into the air. I was so stoked, I screamed.

After riding a few more waves, I started to gain confidence. To feel the speed trimming down the face of those big waves way out in the ocean, and to feel that strong offshore wind, and to sense the camaraderie of the older surfers I respected and admired—it was the thrill of my life.

There were some problems: My board wasn't performing the way I'd hoped it would. It tended to pearl much too easily. But I was usually able to compensate for that.

After only a couple of hours in the water, though, I made a big mistake. I caught a big wave and made the drop-in; a nice shoulder built up, I ran it out, and continued on to the inside section. But instead of building up again, the inside section sucked out over a shallower reef and wrapped around me on both sides like a horseshoe. I could see I was going to get caught in the impact zone, and I decided it was time to bail. In California I was used to bailing off the nose, but that doesn't work in the much faster Hawaiian waves. As I bailed off the nose, the board kept coming and smashed me in the back. The wave pounded me down, and I hit bottom with a crushing impact. I was stunned for a few moments. Finally I got oriented, found the bottom with my feet, and pushed off with all my strength. But before I could reach the surface for a breath of air, I got caught in the turbulence, spun around again, and the next thing I knew I hit bottom a second time. This time I was held down even longer, but I fought and fought for the surface until I finally got air.

As I swam for the shore, the joy and elation were gone, and all the old doubts came back. This is too much, I thought. I'm not good enough for this.

When I finally got to shore, nobody made a big thing out of it. Peter Cole said, in an offhand way, "It probably would have been better if you'd dived off the back of the board." Nobody else said a word, but I could feel their support. They were watching out for me like big brothers.

Over the years that inside section at Sunset has nailed a lot of surfers. It was just one of the many things you had to learn if you wanted to surf there. I went back out and worked my way through most of my fear. I made sure I never bailed off the nose again, and I avoided the inside. But because of that one terrible wipeout, Sunset has always scared the hell out of me.

During the next few weeks I became more and more comfortable riding the big waves at Sunset, Waimea and Makaha. Comfortable isn't quite the word. I was dancing with forces of nature that were so powerful, they could destroy you if you made one wrong move. But if you learned to dance with skill and grace, you were rewarded with an incomparable feeling of euphoria.

The only real problem I had now was my equipment. My board was too straight, too wide in the nose, too narrow in the tail, and too heavy. I'd made that board myself—it had been my idea of what a big gun should be, but at the time I'd made it, I hadn't surfed any really big waves. I was able to ride it, but I had to stand way back on the tail, and I was still pearling. I went over the falls a lot, too—instead of riding the slope in front of the wave, I was entering too late, getting sucked over the top of the wave, and pounded into the impact zone at the bottom of the wave. You can't do that very many times on twenty-foot waves without getting hurt.

I asked Buzzy, Peter, and some of the older guys what they thought of my board. They just shrugged, but I could see by their expressions that they weren't too excited about it. They said, "Wait'll Curren gets here."

I didn't know who they were talking about, so I asked Buzzy who Curren was.

"When you go hunting rhinos, you take a big gun," he said. "Well, Curren's the guy who makes the rhino guns."

Little by little, I learned more about Pat Curren: He made his living as a professional diver working on the offshore oil platforms back in California. He was from La Jolla and close to thirty years old. He was a bit of a loner.

Peter Cole called Pat Curren the King of Waimea. "He's so damned patient," Cole said. "Curren will sit out there and wait while everybody else rides wave after wave. Then, when everybody else has gone in, Curren will be in perfect position for the wave of the day. He does it over and over, while the rest of us are just sitting there on the beach, thinking, 'Why didn't I wait?' "

From the way people talked about Pat Curren, I imagined him to be the greatest surfer in the world, a magnificent physical specimen, with an electrifying personality. But when Curren finally arrived and we met him at the airport, I was disappointed. He was gaunt and pale, with a pointed chin, sunken cheeks and worried eyes. He had a military haircut, was real quiet and moody. On the drive back to the North Shore, he didn't say one word.

I soon found out that Curren wasn't the dazzling surfer I had imagined. He had guts and he rode the hell out of the biggest waves, but what really set Curren apart, and won him the admiration of the others, was that he made the most beautiful, streamlined surfboards any of us had ever seen. Each one of his boards was a cross between a work of art and a weapon, like some beautifully crafted spear. Curren had learned how to attach slabs of wood to the nose and tail of a board to get more rocker, or curve. And his boards went like rockets. In those days, speed was everything. Riding big waves wasn't about style or looking pretty or making graceful cutbacks or any of that. It was about going for the biggest wave and hoping you didn't get killed. Curren's boards were designed to go straight down the line, hard and fast. They gave you a chance at survival.

After one look at Curren's big guns, I knew that my board was a primitive piece of junk.

Meanwhile, back at the Quonset hut, Buzzy and Violet fought constantly. They loved each other a lot, but they expressed their affection in a way that I wasn't able to understand. Sometimes after they'd been fighting for days, Buzzy would take Violet to her mother's house on the other side of the island and leave her there.

When he got back to the North Shore, he'd say to the rest of us, "Now, let's surf!"

The whole situation at the Quonset hut made me nervous. But after a couple of weeks, I was joined by another group of friends from the mainland who were closer to my age: L.J. "Little John" Richards, Mark Portrif, Adrien Esnard, and a few others. I put down a deposit, and we rented a house from the Kahuku Sugar Plantation, which owned six houses at Kawela Bay, just northeast of Sunset. The house we rented cost $300 a month. That was a lot of money in those days, but we split the rent among eight guys and became only the second house of surfers on the North Shore.

At first we all decided we would share the household expenses. We would go shopping together, cook our meals together, take turns washing dishes, clean house together, and so on. That plan lasted about three days. There were constant arguments: Who took my bowl? Who got in my peanut butter? Who's turn was it to wash dishes last night? The house was a filthy mess, and nobody ever washed a dish. So we changed the rules: Everybody bought his own food, everybody put a lock on his own cupboard to keep the other guys out, and everybody washed his own dishes.

There were no girls on the North Shore at that time, except for a couple of local Hawaiian girls, and they were off limits. If you messed with a Hawaiian girl, her big brother stomped your face. We didn't care about girls, though. We were dedicated surfers, there to ride the waves. If it had been girls we wanted, we'd have stayed in California. Too many times back home we'd seen one of our friends meet a girl, then the next morning he wouldn't answer the wake-up call. He couldn't go surfing because he had a new girl-friend. We felt sorry for him. None of that here—our time on the North Shore was too precious to waste on girls.

To get around the island, we pooled our money together, bought a big four-door '48 Chrysler, and bolted our surfboard racks right to the roof. At five every morning, all eight guys would pile into the Chrysler and go check the surf. We'd drive from Kawela Bay to Haleiwa, about twenty miles, and pick out the place where we thought the waves were the best.

Sometimes the surf got so big the whole North Shore closed

out. Rather than peeling off cleanly from the peak of the wave out to the shoulder, the waves were breaking in one long thunderous crash. On days like that we'd drive around the point of the island to Makaha, about an hour and a half away, where the surf usually wasn't quite as big. But no matter where we surfed, we were almost always the only guys out, and we'd stay out all day long.

One day that winter, when the whole North Shore was closed out and Sunset was breaking over twenty-five feet, a bunch of us piled into our old cars and drove around to Kaena Point. The older guys told us that Kaena Point had the biggest surf in the world, and we wanted to see it for ourselves. The road wasn't paved between Haleiwa and Makaha—in fact there wasn't a road, just a muddy rut. Pat Curren knew the way better than anybody else, so he led the caravan. We had several flat tires, and one car lost a muffler. But it was worth it. The waves were at least fifty feet that day, and a stiff offshore wind was blowing the tops off them. We sat there silently, watching that amazing wonder of nature. Nobody even considered going out.

In December I entered the Makaha International—my first world-class surfing competition—but I didn't really have enough experience with Hawaiian waves to compete on that level yet. I lost my board in the preliminaries and didn't even qualify.

There was a filmmaker living at Kawela Bay, Bud Browne, who'd made the first surf movie I'd ever seen, *The Big Surf.* They called Bud "the Barracuda" because he was so thin and because he was a great swimmer. Bud was eccentric in some ways. Back in California he lived in a one-room apartment above a garage in Costa Mesa. He'd been a schoolteacher before he started making films. He only ate one meal a day, dinner, and most of that was sugar; canned pears and fudge were his favorites. Because he was so fond of sweets, he had a lot of bad teeth that had been repaired with gold bridgework.

Every winter Bud would go to Hawaii to work on his surf films. He was very innovative, and they say he developed one of the first underwater cameras. He was also a very kind man. He appreciated my surfing ability and took me under his wing. I lived right next door to him at Kawela Bay, so when he took off every morning to go filming, I jumped right in his car. Bud and I spent a lot of time together, driving around the island looking for surf.

When Bud Browne made a movie, instead of just showing a whole bunch of guys out surfing, he would pick a couple of surfers he thought were hot, and he'd build the whole movie around them. It made a nice story, with real characters that people could relate to. And instead of just showing all surf shots, Bud liked to record the day-to-day lives of surfers living on the North Shore—the house, the cars, going to town for groceries, and so on. One time he took a group of us up to Waimea Falls, where he filmed us jumping from the cliffs to the water eighty feet below. Once we went up to Na Pali, where the high winds blow; we'd lean off the cliff and let the wind blow us back. And another time he filmed us sacrificing old cars and old surfboards to the surf gods, a ritual surfers still practice.

During that winter I met another photographer and filmmaker, John Severson. He'd been a high school art teacher in San Juan Capistrano but had just recently started making surf films. He was a very creative person, and kind of nervous. I remember he had large hands and feet, was kind of stooped in the shoulders, and he always had a great tan.

Like Bud Browne, Severson followed our little band of surfers around the North Shore, taking photos of us all. He told us late that winter that he was going to start a glossy surf magazine, and we were all pretty excited about that because there had never been a magazine about surfing before.

After about five months on the North Shore, I felt I was doing as well on big waves as any surfer there. But I knew I couldn't get any better using the equipment I had. I knew I needed one of Pat Curren's boards. The trouble was, I was terrified of Pat Curren, and during that entire winter I never worked up the courage to say one word to him.

It was really more complicated than that. I didn't just want one of Curren's boards, I wanted his template, his design, so I could make my own board. I knew the path to excellence in this sport lay in making your own equipment, customizing it for your own needs, adding your own touches. That way you were never dependent upon somebody else and your equipment always matched your physical abilities. Curren was certainly a much better craftsman than I was and could have made a better board than I could, but his real genius was in that one strip of Masonite that recorded the rail curve of his rhino guns. Curren developed that template through years of big-wave riding, countless wipeouts, who knows how many scars and bruises, endless hours at a drafting table, plus an enormous amount of natural talent. I knew that if I had Curren's template, I could avoid years of trial and error with my own designs.

But asking Curren if I could borrow his template wasn't like asking an ordinary favor. It was kind of like asking him if I could borrow his wife—but his template probably meant more to him than his wife. His life's work, his entire reputation, his whole identity was based on that template, that one simple curve.

I hoped that as a fellow waterman, Curren would understand how important it was for me to make my own equipment. But then again, I could imagine him saying to me, Why don't you just buy one of my boards, Doyle? Whatsa matter, they not good enough for ya?

So I was stuck. I had the physical ability and the youth to surpass what the previous generation of surfers had accomplished on the North Shore, but I lacked their knowledge of board design, and the only one who could really help me was a tweaked-out deep-sea diver who scared the living hell out of me.

I left Hawaii that spring to go back to California, where my lifeguard job was waiting for me. After Hawaii, California looked gray and bleak to me. Driving on the freeway through L.A., I felt like one tiny blood cell flowing through a vein. And I'd forgotten how square everything was: square buildings on square lots on square blocks.

One day, not long after I'd been back, I drove down to Encinitas to see Rusty Miller and to surf at Swami's.

I'd surfed with Rusty at Swami's several times, but the first time I ever saw him out of the water was at a party in Palos Verdes. He'd been wearing a tweed coat and slacks, and was smoking a pipe with his arms crossed, looking very much like a professor of history, which was what he wanted to become at the time. He had a freckly complexion, kind of a bent nose, and reddish-brown hair. I remember thinking, This guy's really got his act together, going to college, dressing like a professor. He made me feel like a goofball.

Rusty lived with his parents on the bluff in Encinitas, just a half mile or so from Swami's. It was kind of strange going to Rusty's house. His father was extremely overweight, and every time I saw him he was sitting in a chair in the living room smoking cigarettes. Rusty's mother had a deep, raspy voice, and she chain-smoked, too. The ceiling in their house was stained brown from all the cigarette smoke, so it was easy to imagine what the insides of their lungs looked like.

Anyway, Rusty and I surfed at Cardiff Reef that morning, and I explained to him the problems I'd had with my surfboards in Hawaii that winter and how badly I needed one of Pat Curren's designs.

Rusty said, "You know, Curren just opened a surf shop here in Encinitas. You oughta stop by and see him."

I tried to explain how terrified I was of Curren.

"I know what you mean," Rusty said. "He scares me, too. But I still think you oughta go see him."

That afternoon I stopped by Curren's shop on D Street. I parked around the corner and sat in my car for a few minutes, working up my courage. When I finally got out and walked around the corner, I saw a sign on the shop window: Be back sometime.

I peeked in the window, and in the dim light I could see a row of Curren's big guns standing against the back wall, like dark tiki gods. I stood there trying to memorize their shapes, trying to capture that one magical line. But I knew it couldn't be done.

I started walking away—then stopped. Right there on the sidewalk, drawn in grease pencil, was a full-scale drawing of Curren's template. It was about 9' 6"—just my size—a masterpiece of art and design, right there where people could walk on it, spit on

78

it, or make off with it. I stepped inside those magical lines, then looked down at my feet to see how the water flowed over and around me. It was a miracle!

But how could I get it off the sidewalk and into my hands? I knew right away what I had to do. I ran up D Street, across the Coast Highway, then up the hill to the Mayfair market, where I bought ten feet of butcher paper and a felt pen. I ran back down the hill to Curren's shop, unrolled the butcher paper over the template, placed rocks at all four corners to keep the paper from blowing away, then got down on my hands and knees, and began tracing the lines.

I had most of the template on paper when I realized somebody was watching me. I looked up and saw Curren standing on the street corner. His forehead was all twisted up in anger, and his eyes were scrunched down into mean little slits. I wasn't sure if he even recognized me. Should I try to explain myself? Or should I just run for it now, while I still had a chance?

Curren stared at me for a long time, putting it all together: the North Shore, the Quonset hut, the kid with the lousy surfboards. Finally, as he fumbled for the keys to his shop, Curren said, "You didn't have to steal it, Doyle. Though I have to admit that's kind of flattering. Just don't forget to tell people where it came from, all right?"

As he disappeared through the doorway, I saw a smile on Curren's face.

That summer, 1960, I took the L.A. County lifeguard test, scored well, and was assigned to Manhattan Beach. Working for the county was a welcome relief from the Santa Monica lifeguard force. The county had a well-organized, well-disciplined lifeguard force, a lot of the lifeguards there were good surfers, and they had a very competitive Taplin team.

The Taplin was an annual competition for lifeguards from all over California. Named after George Taplin, a lifeguard who started the event, it included competitions in three events: rough-water swimming, rowing, and paddling. The lifeguard forces liked their guys to train for the Taplin because it kept them in top shape; plus it was a lot of fun and helped build morale.

Early that summer, it was announced that at the National Lifeguard Championships, there would be an extra-grueling Taplin competition in which the competitors would swim half a mile, paddle half a mile, and row half a mile. It would be called the Ironman—the first time that name was used for an athletic competition. When the L.A. County lifeguards heard about the new event, we were excited and we started training very hard.

I also had the Catalina-to-Manhattan Pier Paddling Race to prepare for. After my bitter loss the summer before to Kemp Aaberg, I wasn't taking any chances. I built myself a new paddle board that was long, slim, and very fast. In our daily workouts, none of the other paddlers was coming even close to me.

Once again, though, luck wasn't with me. The day of the race was very stormy. The organizers started the race anyway, but as soon as we were on the open ocean we had to fight ten-foot ground swells. Every now and then the swells would break, and we'd have to push through the soup. I realized the current was carrying us to Point Fermin, way off course, but I wasn't that worried about it. I was in such great shape, I knew that if I had to, I'd paddle all the way to Long Beach, then follow the coast north to Manhattan Pier.

But with the heavy seas, the guide boats were taking even more of a beating than the paddlers. The boats needed more speed to head into the swells, and some of them started taking on water. So when we were about mid-channel, the Coast Guard asked the organizers to call off the race. The paddlers came out of the water and rode the guide boats back. If we'd been allowed to paddle just a bit farther, we'd have rounded the point at Palos Verdes and been in glassy conditions again.

After that disappointment, I was even more eager to prove what I could do in the Ironman competition.

The Ironman was held at Redondo Beach, at night. Huge searchlights were mounted to light up the water, the newspapers and TV stations sent crews to cover the event, and a large crowd came to watch. I'd never competed in anything quite like that, and I was very nervous.

Right before the contest started, the order of the events was drawn from a hat. Each lifeguard wanted his strongest event to be held first. I was the strongest paddler on the coast at that time, so naturally I wanted paddling to be held first. I was a fairly strong rower, too. If I had a weakness, it was in swimming. Not that I was a bad swimmer, but in Southern California some of the lifeguards were world-class, Olympic-caliber swimmers.

When they drew the order of events, it came out swimming first, rowing second, paddling third. For my abilities, it was the worst possible order.

It had been a very windy day, and it was still blowing maybe fifteen knots, with a three-foot chop on the water. For the swimming event, they had fifteen lanes marked on a quarter-mile course, straight out into the ocean. At a quarter-mile, they had several big white buoys with searchlights aimed right at them. As we gathered at the starting line, standing right next to me was Tom Landis, UCLA's top swimmer.

At the sound of the horn, we ran and dived into the surf. I quickly lost track of where the other swimmers were in the choppy water, and concentrated on swimming as hard as I could. I knew that a lot of the competitors were used to swimming in pools, following straight lines, and making flip turns. I'd spent a lot more time in the open ocean than they had, but I still didn't think I had a chance against guys like Landis. I figured my only hope was to keep from looking like a complete fool.

As I finished the first leg and rounded the buoy, I lifted my head to see if I could find the other swimmers, but the surf was just too big and I couldn't see anybody around me. I put my head down and stroked hard for the beach.

Now my knowledge of the ocean started to help me. I took advantage of what we called "railroading." When you feel the wave picking you up, you power hard with the rhythm; if you time it just right, you can move forward about four extra feet for every wave. Then on the inside section, I caught about a four-foot wave and bodysurfed it part way in.

When my feet first touched sand, I still didn't know where I was in the crowd. I sprang out of the water and ran up on the beach, disappointed to see there was no one else around me. Just as I feared, I'd finished dead last.

Then I heard people in the crowd screaming at me and pointing behind me. I looked back and saw some of the other swimmers just coming out of the water. I wasn't in last place, I was in first!

After winning the swimming event, I had no real challengers. I dominated the paddling and rowing events, and ended up winning the first Ironman.

One day I was sitting in my lifeguard tower at Manhattan Beach, when a lifeguard truck pulled up. Two plainclothes policemen got out, climbed the tower, and handed me a subpoena to appear in court.

I didn't know what the hell was going on, but after talking to my lieutenant, I got this story: The Santa Monica Police Department had been trying for some time to take over the Santa Monica lifeguard force, the outfit I'd been with the summer before. Somehow the chief of police had heard the story about Jong Chiu up in the tower that day; he figured if he could turn that into a public scandal, that would be the perfect excuse to move in and take over the lifeguard force once and for all.

Before the court date, I had to go see the Santa Monica chief of police. As I passed through the front office, I saw Jong Chiu waiting outside. He smiled at me.

The chief of police told me, "We know you were there that day. If you tell us the truth, you won't be implicated."

I told the police what I'd seen, which wasn't much, really, and they seemed satisfied.

Two weeks later I had to go to court and listen to the whole ugly story being told in public. It was in open court, with all the lifeguards, their families, and anybody else who wanted to be there. They put Jong Chiu on the witness stand, and one by one the prosecutors asked him about each of the lifeguards who had been there that day. "Oh, yes," Jong Chiu would say, pointing to one of the lifeguards. "He was there that day, and I enjoyed him very much."

Meanwhile, the lifeguard, with his wife next to him, squirmed in agony.

A lot of the guys broke down and cried, and told the police

everything. It was a total disaster—they were all fired. The only exception was one shrewd lieutenant. He was as guilty as any of them, but he refused to admit anything, even though the others said he had been there. After the trial, he was reinstated and collected back pay for the whole time the investigation and trial had taken place. Then he quit.

In those days every little beach town up and down the coast had its own summer beach festival. It was a chamber of commerce-type thing to attract tourists. They held swimming, rowing, and paddling contests, volleyball tournaments, sand castle contests—whatever they wanted. When surfing started to become popular, they added that event, too. Since I was training every day to stay in shape as a lifeguard, I used to enter all those contests as a fun way to check my level of conditioning. If there was a paddle board contest anywhere in Southern California, I was in it. If there was a rowing contest, I'd enter that. And, of course, I was in the surf contest, too. In no time at all, I'd collected a whole garage full of trophies.

Looking back on it now, I'd have to say I went to the extreme. I became a contest junky. But at that age, nineteen, I craved the recognition. I think because I'd had so many complexes about my appearance and my hearing difficulty, I needed the trophies to help build my self confidence. I see that kids today are the same—they love to win a trophy—and I think that's good for them.

Competing in paddling contests taught me that I had certain natural talents—broad shoulders, long arms, and fairly large hands—which made me ideally suited to paddling. I designed and built my own paddle boards, which meant my equipment was always matched to my abilities. And I was in great shape. I knew that if I practiced and trained, I would be almost unbeatable. And for several years I was.

Paddling races also taught me a lot about the psychology of competition. There were a few great big guys who were just animals at paddling, but they didn't know how to compete. I would plan each race ahead of time, then stick to the plan. If it was an eight-mile race, I'd stay with the pack the first couple of miles, then make my

83

move on the third mile and power out until I'd buried them. I'd be almost exhausted, ready to die, but the guys behind thought I could still keep going, so they'd quit, at least in their minds. And when they gave up, I could slow down and conserve my energy for the rest of the race.

I really loved competing in paddling races—much more than I ever loved competing in surf contests. Paddling had a finish line, which made it real.

But some of those first surf contests were so bad, it was kind of funny. Usually the judges didn't even surf. The local president of the chamber of commerce would get his mother-in-law, who was a gym teacher, and his brother, who was a fan of big-time wrestling; he'd get the owner of the local pharmacy, who'd donated money for the trophies; and maybe his neighbor, who'd been on the swim team in high school. And they were considered qualified to judge a surf contest, even though none of them had ever been on a surfboard before. The judges had no concept of wave selection, wave positioning, or style. So if some guy in the contest did something really silly, like stand on his head, the judges thought that was just fantastic and the guy would win the contest. It was ridiculous, and the surfers knew it.

Even the surfing trophies were ridiculous. In those days it was hard for the contest organizers to find surfing trophies, so they used to take a basketball trophy with the basketball player jumping up to make a one-arm dunk. They'd cut the basketball off his hand, cut under his feet at the base, then lay him down on a small, hand-carved paddling board. It looked like a basketball player being carried out on a stretcher.

The truth is, I never felt that surfing as a competitive sport made much sense. Surfing is very difficult to judge because there's an act of god that influences how each wave will behave. It's so subjective. If you have eight great surfers out in the water, any one of them could be considered the best. And oddly enough, if you leave them out in the water for an hour, you can usually see who's surfing the best. But if you try to break it down into a point system, the whole thing falls apart.

But probably the worst thing about surf contests is that they're contrary to the very essence of the sport, which is freedom. If you make up a bunch of arbitrary rules that are supposed to define good surfing, the creative freedom of surfing gets destroyed.

I wasn't the only surfer of my era who felt this way. There were a lot of great surfers—Kemp Aaberg, Lance Carson, Phil Edwards, and Mickey Dora—who rarely entered contests. If a big contest was being held at Malibu, they'd much rather go down the road someplace and surf by themselves all day.

As a young man I was caught in the middle of all that. I wasn't against competition—I loved competition. If you put me in a paddling contest, I'd grind it out till I coughed blood, because in a paddling contest, the first guy to cross the finish line wins. That made sense to me. But in a surf contest, I never felt there was a fair way to decide who won.

After I got a little older and began competing every winter in world-class surfing contests, the judging became somewhat better. But I still never felt the contests had any real validity. I competed because surf contests were my free ride. How I placed in contests one year would determine whether or not a sponsor would pay my way to Hawaii the next year. If I hadn't competed in the big surf contests and done well, I would never have been able to spend half the year traveling and surfing. So in a way, competing in surf contests became a job.

I was working at Zuma Beach, north of Malibu, one day, when I got a call from my captain saying that lifeguards all the way down the coast had spotted three killer whales swimming north. Since there were a lot of people in the water at the time, he wanted me to go out in our rescue boat, a small powered boat, find the killer whales, follow them up the coast, and notify the towers along the way if they got too close to shore.

So I got in the boat and headed south until I saw the big, black fins of three killer whales cutting slowly across the surface of the water. The fins looked huge to me. One was a little bigger than the others, but they were all sticking three or four feet out of the water. I started following about 200 feet behind them.

When they rounded Point Dume, the killer whales veered in

closer to the shore. There's a large buoy there, about thirty feet in diameter, marking the point. As usual, there was a bunch of seals resting on top of the buoy. When the killer whales reached the buoy, they threw their bodies up against it, knocking the seals into the water, and then went around chomping and snapping the seals in two. After they'd killed all the seals, the whales swam on again, without even stopping to eat their kills.

Seeing that made me think about all the swimming and paddling I did far from shore. The ocean is still a wild place, and there are big things out there that can kill you.

I followed the killer whales until they were beyond the heavily populated beaches, then I turned around and headed back to Zuma.

The next morning, when I went out for my paddling workout, it was foggy along the coast. But I didn't mind working out in the fog, because the ocean is usually calm on foggy days. I got on my fourteen-foot paddle board and started toward Point Dume, cutting across the glassy surface of the water with long, smooth strokes. In the distance I could hear the bell on the buoy, so I headed toward that.

Then I heard something else, very faint—or maybe I felt it in the water, I don't really know. I looked over to my side and saw the silhouettes of two big fins about a hundred feet away, which was about as far as I could see in the fog. The fins weren't moving, or just barely wavering, like two big cardboard cutouts.

I stopped paddling, pulled my hands up out of the water, and just lay there. I could sense that the killer whales knew I was there. They had to have felt the vibration of my board or heard my arms moving through the water. My first impulse was to turn and sprint out of there as fast as I could. But I knew I couldn't outrun them, and I was afraid the thrashing in the water would only excite them. So I did my best to be still.

I lay there for a long time, not moving. Then all of a sudden, both fins rotated in the water and came straight at me. When they got five feet in front of me, they dove. I looked over my shoulder and watched them pass under me. The water was extremely clear, and I could see their dark shapes moving swiftly. One of them was about thirty feet long, and the other was a bit shorter.

I waited a few moments more, until both killer whales were completely out of sight. Then I turned and paddled for the beach as fast as I could go.

I was driving home from work one day, when I pulled up to a corner stoplight and noticed a poster stapled to a telephone pole. The poster was advertising a new surf movie that was going to play at the Pier Avenue School in Hermosa Beach. There was a photo on the poster of a powerful, Hawaiian-looking wave. The surfer in the photo was leaning hard into the wave, crouched down with one hand on the rail and one hand raised in the air. There was something vaguely familiar about it. Then I realized the movie was Bud Browne's latest, *Surf Happy*, and the surfer on the poster was me.

Some people have forgotten how surf movies were distributed in those days. The regular film distribution channels weren't open to surf movies—there just weren't enough surfers to make it worthwhile for the big film distributors. So filmmakers like Bud Browne, John Severson, and Bruce Brown had to create their own channels. Every little beach town up and down the coast had a civic auditorium, a high school gym, or YMCA that could be rented for one or two nights. The filmmaker would send out a crew a few days in advance of the showing to nail posters on telephone poles and bulletin boards. Then the news would spread by word of mouth. The filmmaker would roll into town with the film the day of the showing and help set up chairs in the auditorium. He would even sell the tickets at the door himself. Because a lot of the early films didn't have sound, he would do his own live narration. If a good crowd turned out, he might have enough money to get a motel room for the night. If not, he would sleep in his car.

I went to the first showing of *Surf Happy* at the Pier Avenue School and took a seat in the back with some of my surf buddies. When the movie started and I watched myself on film for the first time, I became very uneasy—almost sick to my stomach. Even though other surfers in the room were hooting and cheering, I thought my style of surfing had a lot of room for improvement. I knew I'd done well my first winter in Hawaii, but I also knew there were a lot of surfers in the room who might have done as well if they'd been there too. More importantly, though, being the center of attention wasn't what I'd imagined it to be. I enjoyed the recognition, all right, but I began to realize I was now the object of jealousy.

After the lights came on and we were all on our way out, I could see guys I didn't know pointing at me and saying, "That's the guy in the movie." I tried to pretend I didn't see them, but I did. One of my friends came up to me and said, "Hey, Mike, you really did good." But I could feel a new distance between me and my old surf buddies, and that made me feel sad.

One evening that summer, John Severson, who I'd met in Hawaii the winter before, called me at home and said, "Hey, Mike, we're going down to Tamarack, in Carlsbad, tomorrow to do a photo session for my new surf magazine. Phil Edwards will be there. Why don't you come along, too?"

I'd almost forgotten that Severson had said he was going to start a surf magazine. And now he wanted me to do a photo shoot with my idol, Phil Edwards? "I think I can make it," I said.

I wore a pair of red, size-52 baggies, which I thought looked really cool—my first fashion statement. John set up his tripod on the cliffs at Tamarack and got some good shots of Edwards and me that appeared in the first issue of *Surfer* magazine. That first issue, which came out in January 1960, also featured José Angel at Sunset, Lance Carson and Kemp Aaberg at Rincon, and Mickey Dora at Makaha. It was all in black and white, with very grainy, poor-quality photos. But surfers, hungry for any news about their sport, snatched it off the store shelves, and it immediately became a collector's item.

That fall John Severson told me he wanted to make his first surf film, in Hawaii, and wanted to use me as the featured surfer. He said he would pay for my trip to Hawaii that winter and cover all my expenses while we were working on the film. I couldn't believe it—I could pocket all the money I'd saved working as a lifeguard that summer!

In December, John and I already had our tickets to Hawaii when, at the last minute, he told me he wanted to take along an airline stewardess he'd met just a few days before. I've already explained how, to hard-core surfers, having a girlfriend in Hawaii was considered a big drawback because it cut into your surf time. But John was paying for my trip, so how could I object? Still, something about the glassy look in John's eyes when he talked about this girl made me uneasy.

When I met John's girlfriend, Louise, at the airport, I could see why he was all hot over her: she was a tall, pretty blonde, with a curvaceous figure.

In Hawaii we rented the Quonset hut right on the beach at the Pipeline, where Buzzy and his bunch had stayed the year before. I retreated to one of the smaller back bedrooms and let the two lovebirds take over the front of the house. But that back bedroom became my prison cell. From the first night, and every night after, I lay in there listening to John and Louise making passionate love. I couldn't sleep. At dawn every morning I would peek out my window and see huge waves breaking on the beach. I was dying to get out there and surf, but I couldn't because John and Louise wouldn't stop long enough for me to slip through the front room and out the door. And of course we weren't getting any work done on our film.

After a few days of that, I knew I had to get out of there. When John and Louise cooled down enough to go buy some groceries, I slipped out with my surfboards and went over to Kawela Bay, where the guys I'd lived with the year before had rented a house again.

What a joy it was to be with my surf buddies again! I forgot about Severson and the movie we were supposed to be working on. I just went surfing every day and enjoyed the life of a beach rat.

Later that winter, Severson cooled down just a bit, and we finally got some work done on his film. He and Louise got married not long after that, and they're together still.

The first time I paddled out at Waimea that winter, the waves looked impossibly big and fast. I watched another surfer dropping in on a fifteen-foot wave, and I thought, God, that's impossible! It was so intimidating. The North Shore really is a whole different level of surfing.

But after a week or two, I was back in the groove again. I was thinking fast, and after a while a fifteen-foot wave just didn't look that big anymore. Besides, I was riding the boards I'd made from Pat Curren's template. This year, not only did I have the experience, but my equipment was as good as anybody's.

I surfed Waimea one day that winter when it was at least twenty-five feet, maybe thirty. It was the biggest I'd ever seen it, and there were only about a dozen guys out. Every surfer has his bad days, when he just can't do anything right, and every time he takes off, he gets creamed. But I'll always remember this one day, because I could do no wrong. Other guys were going over the falls, and boards were crunching all around me. But I'd take off and angle right, hang high at the top of the wave, then drop down twenty feet and swing around into the curl. I felt so calm, I kept wondering if I was doing it right. It seemed so simple, like surfing a three-foot shore break back in California. But when I looked up at the waves, they were huge.

I had one bad day at Waimea that winter I'll never forget, though. It was late morning, on a fifteen- to eighteen-foot day—big, but not monstrous—with choppy surface conditions. There were also four-foot wedges coming in at an angle from the north and breaking. The surf was decomposing, and it was about time to go in, but I wanted to catch one more good ride. I was sitting right off the point, which can be a bit tricky. If you lose your board there, the waves will carry it right into the rocks. I paddled for what looked like an average wave, but as I dropped in, it reared up to about eighteen feet. As the wave passed over the boil, it churned violently and, in classic Waimea fashion, the top of the wave pitched way out. Before I was completely in the wave I could see it was going to get nasty, so I sat back on my board, trying to stall out. But I was too late. The wave hit me in the back and threw me over the falls while I was still sitting on the rear of my board. I had no idea how to bail out of something like that, but as I was free-falling down the face of this eighteen-foot wave, I swung my right leg over the board and rolled off to the side. To my surprise, when I hit the water, instead of being pounded to the bottom, as on most bad wipeouts, I was pitched out like a beach ball. I bounced along in front of the white water, thrashing and spinning, unable to dive under or break away. Luckily, I was able to suck a little air through the foam. The white water drove me in about 150 yards, in a course parallel to the rocks, but only about ten feet away from them. I could very easily have been dragged along the top of the rocks, in which case I would have been ground to hamburger. When I was finally able to stop myself, I saw that I was right in front of the rocks. As I watched in horror, the waves crashing on the rocks tore my board into a hundred pieces. Slowly and carefully, I eased myself away from the rocks, and swam all the way to shore.

It's odd how, out of thousands of waves and hundreds of wipeouts, one wipeout like that has stayed with me for years. Not because it turned out so badly, but because if things had gone just a little bit differently it might have been the end of my life.

Some surfers seem to love the wipeouts even more than the great rides. It's almost as if they try to wipe out, just for the bizarre thrill of it. I can understand that in a way, because during those few awful seconds, when it's all out of your control, you arrive at a state of consciousness that is completely out of the ordinary. I think having your life in danger causes you to appreciate life all the more.

It's funny, too, but the seriousness of a wipeout isn't always proportional to the size of a wave. Sometimes a huge wave will pass right over you and leave you untouched. And then other times, an eight-foot wave will hold you down until you think you're going to drown. If you open your eyes underwater while a twenty-five-foot wave breaks over you, you can see that there are turbulent columns of white water, like cyclones, that are being pushed violently to the bottom. But in between the white columns are areas of blue water that are relatively undisturbed. If you are captured in one of the white columns, you get battered down, but if you get bounced into the blue calm, you just float to the surface, unharmed.

Mickey Dora showed up in Hawaii that winter. His reputation in the world of surfing was growing, but more as a personality than as a big-wave rider. He was great back in Malibu, where he was the king, but when he came to Hawaii he showed up with all the wrong equipment, like it didn't really matter to him, or like he was trying to make a mockery of big-wave riding. I don't think Dora ever got the thrill from big waves the way others of us did. I think it was the surfing lifestyle that intrigued him more than anything else. He didn't fit into mainstream society, with a steady job and a little house out in the suburbs; but at the beach, Dora always felt at home.

Dora had been surviving by doing stunt work in Hollywood—awful movies like *Bikini Beach Blanket,* with Frankie Avalon and Annette Funicello. But the movies didn't pay enough to live the kind of lifestyle he wanted. Nobody got paid to surf in those days, no matter how good he was. So Dora had to hustle. You might say Mickey Dora was the professional surfer of his era.

One day when a bunch of us were in Honolulu, Dora grabbed me and said, "Come on, Doyle, let's go to dinner."

I figured we'd run down to some hot dog stand, gag down a few tubesteaks, then get back to the beach. But Dora had something else in mind. He took me to the Royal Hawaiian, one of the grand old hotels on the islands—very beautiful and very expensive. As we walked into the lobby, with huge candelabras hanging from the ceiling, I started thinking to myself, This place is way out of my league. It wasn't anything at all like the Busy Bee Cafe, where I usually ate in Honolulu and where two dollars would buy you all you could eat.

But Dora was right at home. He'd been groomed very early to feel at ease in that kind of place. He said, "Excuse me for a second, Doyle, I've gotta go see if somebody's here." He walked over to the registration desk and asked if Mr. So-and-So had registered yet. While the woman at the desk checked the registration book, Dora peeked over the desk and scanned the names in the book.

We took a table laid out with white linen and crystal and real silverware. Dora just glanced at the menu, then ordered a full dinner, with hors d'oeuvres, fine wine, dessert, and a liqueur.

After dinner the waiter brought the check on a leather tablet; it came to just over $200. Dora glanced at the check quickly, then looked up at the waiter and said, "I'll sign for it."

I had to gag myself to keep from laughing. But to my surprise, Dora signed the check, the waiter folded the leather tablet and said, "Thank you very much, sir."

I still didn't quite get it yet, but I knew enough to keep my mouth shut.

On the way out of the lobby, I looked over at the registration desk, and then the whole thing became clear.

I didn't say anything to Dora, and he never mentioned it to me again.

One night we had a big party at our house at Kawela Bay. We invited everyone we knew on the North Shore and told them we'd have the food, but bring your own beer. There were hardly any girls living on the North Shore then, so our party was mostly a bunch of guys trying to prove they could drink more beer than the next guy.

One of the guys who came to our party was a merchant marine named Henley, from Oceanside. He didn't really surf, but he hung around with the surf crowd when he wasn't out at sea. He was about 220 pounds, heavily muscled, crude, and pushy. The guys from Oceanside at that time were known to be very heavy partiers, and Henley was as heavy as any of them.

As soon as he walked in the door, Henley shoved his way through the crowd to the food, grabbed all of it he could, and started shoving it in his mouth. Nobody said anything, because the guy was really big, and besides, we didn't want to see our party turn into a brawl. When the food was all gone, Henley shoved his way into the kitchen, went to the refrigerator, and pulled out a beer.

Just then Ricky Grigg walked in. Ricky was six inches shorter than Henley, sixty pounds lighter and, unlike Henley, gentle by nature. But Ricky wasn't afraid of anything. He said, in a friendly way, "Hey, that's my beer."

"So what!"

Ricky looked him in the eye, then said again, "That's my beer." And he snatched it out of Henley's hand.

Henley grumbled something, then moved away. Ricky had backed that ape man down, and none of us could quite believe it.

Ricky Grigg was always doing things like that, which was why I was kind of in awe of him. He had won the Catalina-to-Manhattan Pier paddling race way back in 1955, he rode the hell out of the biggest Hawaiian waves, was a tremendous diver, and could hold his breath underwater for something like three minutes. But he was more than just a water jock. He seemed to have more focus in his life than most of us. He was going to school at Scripps Institution of Oceanography in La Jolla, he knew he wanted to be an ocean-ographer, and he went after it with energy and discipline. Although he was already one of the best big-wave riders in the world, surfing to him was still just a form of recreation. But everything he learned in school seemed to help his surfing, too. He had a real under-standing of the ocean, which gave him confidence and a power of survival in the water that I don't think any of the rest of us had. He understood how the ocean bottom affects waves, how rip currents could be used to the surfer's advantage, how the weather patterns can be used to predict surfing conditions. He really understood hydrodynamic design and was able to perfect his surfing equipment to complement his abilities. At a very young age, Ricky had become a master waterman.

Ricky had a sister, Robin, who was in Hawaii that winter, and I thought she was just as impressive as Ricky. She was blonde and lovely, athletic, had a pretty smile, and was a good surfer. She was about ten years older than I was, a nurse, and a lot more sophisti-cated than most of the people I knew.

Robin took a personal interest in me. She used to ask me what I wanted to do with my life, other than surf. What kind of books did I read? What kind of music did I like? She drew me into her circle of friends, which included people who didn't always have salty eyebrows and sun-bleached hair. Most of them were well educated and, to my surprise, they seemed to like me and accept me, even though I was a water jock with some pretty rough edges.

At first our friendship was a brother-sister thing—or so I thought. Robin was probably always one step ahead of me. One evening Robin and I were down at the beach in Kawela Bay, having a good time goofing around together. There was a full moon that night, and we swam out to a raft in the bay. . . . That was the beginning of an affair that lasted the rest of that winter. It was my first romance in Hawaii—a thrilling experience in itself, but even more so for a twenty-year-old kid lucky enough to have a beautiful and mature woman to teach him the proper way to have an affair.

Robin used her age and wisdom to influence me in a positive way. "Suppose that within the next ten years you become the world's greatest surfer," she said. "What happens in the ten years after that? There's a whole new generation of little gremmies back there in California learning to surf. Ten years from now, they're going to be surfing better than you. Do you want to spend the rest of your life proving you can still keep up with them?"

I think I was fortunate to have somebody like Robin help me see what my future might be like. She helped me understand how important it is for young athletes, no matter how good they are, to resist the tendency to let sports become their whole identity.

Halfway through that winter, just before I turned twenty, I came back to California and enrolled at Cabrillo Junior College in Santa Barbara, becoming the first person in my family who had ever attended college.

In those days, when you enrolled in college you were supposed to choose your major the first day. I didn't have the vaguest idea what my major should be, but because of Ricky and Robin Grigg, I wrote on the registration forms that my major would be biology. But the thing that really interested me the most in school was art. It had always been that way, even back in elementary school. Yet somehow I didn't think of art as a serious reason for going to college—maybe because I enjoyed it too much.

So I settled into the drudgery of English composition and Math 101. After the excitement of surfing twenty-foot waves in Hawaii, everything in college looked pretty tame to me. I had way too much restless energy, not nearly enough self-discipline, and I didn't have even the vaguest idea how to go about studying.

Luckily, I had an English teacher, Mr. Blankenship, who was a great help and gave me the confidence to continue with school. He was a very emotional fellow, very sensitive, and an innovative teacher. He would stand on top of his desk to get his students' attention, beat on the wastebasket, anything to communicate with us. He had us read *The Grapes of Wrath*, and I immediately became a John Steinbeck fan. I could visualize each scene in the book, and I understood the meaning and emotions behind them; but when the day came for the essay exam, I found I just couldn't put my thoughts down on paper. It was very frustrating. I knew that Mr. Blankenship was open to different approaches and that he really cared about helping his students, so I went to him and asked if he would consider taking the time to do an oral exam for me. He agreed, and after the rest of the class had finished, he and I sat down together. I found I had no trouble at all explaining out loud what I'd learned from the *The Grapes of Wrath*. In fact Mr. Blankenship said it was the best analysis he'd ever heard a student give, and he gave me an A on the exam.

I believe that was the first time I realized I had the ability to be a good student, I just needed to learn self-discipline and to focus my thoughts and energy.

One day later that semester, when I went to Mr. Blankenship's class, there was a graduate student standing in his place. He explained to us that Mr. Blankenship had had an emotional breakdown and would be taking a rest.

It didn't really surprise me. The man put so much energy into his teaching, he was so emotional and so caring, I could see that he was vulnerable.

Going to college didn't mean I was ready to give up surfing. In fact, one reason I chose to go to school in Santa Barbara was that I knew how good the surf was at Rincon, just down the coast a ways.

I settled into Summerland, a nice little town just south of Santa Barbara, and rented a house on Butterfly Lane with four other guys: Garth Murphy, Bill Engler, Lance Carson, and Kemp Aaberg, who were also attending Cabrillo. It was a beautiful, Tudor-style house owned by the Music Academy of the West. They had about ten houses that were supposed to be for gifted music students, but we talked the academy into renting it to us anyway—a decision I'm sure they came to regret.

Each of the guys staying there at the Butterfly Lane house had a whole pack of friends who came up from the South Bay every weekend. They weren't in school; they just wanted to surf Rincon, hang out, get drunk, and act crazy.

Something gets into young people at that age—a real craving

for the outrageous and absurd. Maybe it's a normal and healthy reaction to two decades of education. I don't know what it is, but you see it today just like you did in those days.

One night we were having a big party at the house. There were probably 200 people there. Everybody got pretty smashed, and the party got more and more out of hand. At one point, Lance Carson threw a whole weightlifting set, dumbbells and all, over the upstairs railing and through the hardwood floor below. Eventually the cops came, and everybody went in different directions—out the doors and windows and into the night. I lived there, so I couldn't split. I went upstairs, locked myself in my room, and went to sleep.

About six o'clock the next morning, I woke up and saw what a disaster the house was. As I was walking around in the rubble, trying to figure out where to start cleaning it all up, I heard a tiny little voice crying, "Help! . . Help! . ." I followed the direction of the voice out behind the house, through the eucalyptus trees, to the railroad track. There was a big hole there that had been dug for some construction project—it was about fifteen feet deep and maybe thirty feet long. I looked down in the hole and saw Lance looking back up at me. He was tired and hung over, but there was still that glint of mischief in his eyes. "I was running from the police," he explained. "After I fell in, I couldn't get back out."

I found a rope and pulled him out.

Another time at the Butterfly Lane house, when Lance had an audience of maybe thirty people, he went into some kind of self-induced fit. He starting breathing deeply, hyperventilating, until the veins in his neck bulged out. Then he smashed his fists into the walls and started breaking windows with his bare hands, yelling, "I'm gonna kill myself! I'm gonna do it this time!" Lance didn't really want to kill himself. It was just a strange mood he used to get into from time to time.

Just then we heard the train coming down the tracks toward our house. Lance's eyes opened wide, and he started chanting, "I'm gonna throw myself in front of the train! . . . I'm gonna throw myself in front of the train!"

The train track was only about sixty feet behind the house. Lance dashed out the back door and ran to meet the train. A bunch of people who didn't know Lance's mood's ran out after him, shouting, "No Lance! Don't do it!" A bunch more of us followed, mostly just curious to see how far Lance would take it this time.

With his audience all in place, at the very last second, Lance threw himself in front of the train.

From our perspective, it looked awfully close. Maybe Lance made it all the way across the tracks, or maybe this time he became the victim of his own joke. At any rate, there was nothing we could do until the train had passed. So we stood there for two or three minutes, saying, "Should we call the ambulance, or do you think he made it?"

"I don't see how he could have!"

As the last car finally rattled on by, we were ready to dash across the tracks and rescue whatever was left of our mangled friend. But instead of blood and gore, what we saw was even worse. Lance had his pants down around his ankles, and he was bent over showing us his hairy butt, using both hands to spread his cheeks as wide as they would go.

One of Lance Carson's biggest rivals when it came to wildness was a guy named Jim Wicker. He had a beautiful old woody that would be a real collector's item today, but Wicker had no regard for it at all. It was really embarrassing to drive with him. One day when we were coming back from the beach, Wicker knocked down a stop sign, drove over the curb and down a whole block of yards, across fences and hedges, peeling over lawns and rose gardens, smashing sprinklers and tricycles. When he got to the end of the block, he drove over the curb again, then continued driving slowly down the street without even looking back to see the damage he'd done.

One time Wicker went into a little market to buy a Coke. When the cashier, an Asian woman, told him how much it was, he reached into his pocket for the change, but his pocket had a big hole in it. He reached through the hole, grabbed his weenie and pulled it out of his pocket. "No," Wicker said, "that's not the right change." And he stuffed it back into his pants.

Another time three of us were riding in Wicker's woody to Baja, where we were going surfing for the day. We passed a carload of girls, so all three of us lined up against the rear window and gave them a bare-assed moon shot. We laughed and laughed, thinking what a wild bunch of guys we were. But a few minutes later, the carload of girls came roaring by us, and all of them except the driver had their pink little butts pressed up against the windows. We didn't think it was funny—in fact it kind of scared us to think there were girls that crazy driving around on the highway.

We pulled in at the Long Bar, in Tijuana, which was a mandatory stop-off for surfers. Inside the bar was a guy who had a hand generator—you would hold two wires while the guy cranked the handle, and a meter showed how many amps you were getting. It was a macho thing to see who could take the biggest shock. Wicker held onto the wires so long he fell over and passed out. I don't know if it was cardiac arrest or what, but we just poured a little beer on his face and shook him for a while until he came to.

That summer I went back to L.A. to work as a lifeguard. One day when I was in a nostalgic mood, I drove down to Manhattan Beach, where I'd hung out as a kid. I stopped at the Surf Right Inn, this little hole-in-the-wall burger joint that used to serve the greatest hamburgers. Everybody was dressed for the beach—surf trunks, bikinis. I was waiting for my burger, looking around, and way in the back I spotted Art Carnero, the *cholo* gang leader who had carved up my leg with his pocket knife. He was still wearing his khaki pants, black T-shirt, and square-toed shoes—exactly the same look he'd had in high school. And he was all alone.

In a way I was happy to see Art; he reminded me of a misery I'd overcome. I walked over to Art and stood beside him. He didn't look as big as I remembered him. In fact, now he was about six inches shorter than I was. He had these skinny little arms dangling out of that big black shirt. I said, "Hey, Art."

Art looked up at me. I could see the recognition in his face, and then I could see the fear in his eyes. He glanced around for an escape, but in that tiny little restaurant there was nowhere for him to run. Then he looked back up at me, anxious to see what I was going to do.

I said, "Do you remember me?"

"Yes," he said flatly.

"Do you remember the time on the football field when we played tick-tack-toe?"

"No. I don't."

Art looked around again for a way to dash out, but I moved over, blocking the only escape.

I didn't know what I was going to do. I just stared at him for a moment or two, making him squirm. Then I said, "I hope things are going well for you, Art."

And I left.

I was at a little surfing contest in Doheny one day, talking to Benny Merrill. Benny had been surfing since the early Thirties and was one of the San Onofre regulars I admired most. I knew he had done some tandem surfing back in his younger days, and I told him, "You know, that tandem looks like fun. Some day I'd like to give that a try."

The next thing I knew, Benny had me out in the water on a tandem board with his daughter, Linda.

Linda Merrill was about five-foot-two, with an hourglass figure. She was a very good surfer and paddler, and she was able to help me maneuver that big board into the waves. Also, she was a goofy foot, so when she stood up it was easy for me to reach around her arm and lift her into a shoulder swan.

Linda and I had a great time that day, and we even managed to learn a few of the traditional tandem moves. The last event of the contest was the tandem, so Linda and I entered it. We finished dead last, but we didn't let that discourage us. We made a promise to each other that we would keep practicing tandem surfing together as often as we could.

The next tandem contest Linda and I entered, we placed fourth, which we took as encouragement. By now I was beginning to discover how talented Linda really was. Not only was she extremely agile and graceful, but she was fearless. When she did one-legged shoulder stands, she kept her composure and trusted me to hold her. And when the surf got large, then we really excelled. In eight-foot surf, when the wave broke, she didn't panic; she would dive off, I'd ride the board through, then I'd come back to get her. So we were able to catch more waves than most tandem teams.

I had a few natural talents at tandem surfing, too. I was bigger than most surfers—about 6-foot-2 and 190 pounds—which made it easier for me to do the lifts. I was a strong paddler, I appreciated the ballet-like grace of tandem, and I got along well with the girls. There weren't a lot of surfers my age who would compete in tandem contests. Tandem wasn't macho enough for them. But that's exactly what I liked about it. Tandem surfing was a good excuse to get away from the chest-pounding guys and go play with the girls for a while.

Linda and I kept practicing our tandem surfing, and in our third tandem contest, at San Clemente, we placed first against top competition. After that, she and I won almost every tandem event we entered.

In those days, top competition in the tandem meant Pete Peterson. Pete, who had a number of tandem partners over the years, was in his late fifties by this time. He was bald and very fair skinned—neither are great assets for anybody who spends all his time in the sun—but he was a brilliant all-around waterman. I really admired Pete, and it was my goal to keep surfing as long as he had. He'd been a legend as a surfer before I was even born and knew far more tandem moves than I could ever learn. The only way Linda and I could beat Pete and his partners was to rely on our youthful strength.

Another great tandem competitor in those days was Hobie Alter, who had a very successful surf shop in Dana Point. Hobie was a good friend of Phil Edwards, and was an important innovator in surfboard design. Hobie was a bit small for tandem, but he was wiry and strong. He could pick up girls as big as himself and press them over his head. Oddly, Hobie was a chain-smoker. In his van the ashtrays were always full and spilling over onto the console, seats, and the floor. He smoked Kents, the ones with the fiberglass filters. Just the smell of them reminded me of the sanding room in a surfboard shop. I couldn't believe anybody who made surfboards would inhale something that smelled like that. But Hobie was a great tandem surfer, and some people credit him with revitalizing tandem surfing in the Sixties.

I used to make a lot of trips up to Santa Cruz in those days. Santa Cruz at that time, before the University of California was built, was a beautiful little retirement town. A lot of the old folks there owned immaculate, thirty-year-old cars that had spent most of their lives parked in the garage. There weren't any used-car lots in Santa Cruz in those days, but every gas station in town had half a dozen classic cars for sale. The old folks had always bought their gas at that one station, so when the husbands passed away, their widows would take the cars down there to sell.

Over a period of a two or three years, I made something like twenty trips to Santa Cruz to buy old cars. I'd fly to San Francisco and hitchhike down the coast. Sometimes I'd stay with my friend Jack O'neill, the wetsuit maker, who had a little shop on the pier. I'd spend a couple of days looking around for the best car deal in town; then after I'd made my choice, I'd take it to Pleasure Point, one of the best surf spots in town, and wax it down. After a few days of surfing, I'd drive down the Coast Highway with my new car, through Carmel and Big Sur, all the way home. I'd keep each car for a few weeks, sell it for twice what I'd paid, then go back and get another one. Eventually the Department of Motor Vehicles sent a notice warning me that if I sold any more used cars, I'd have to buy a dealer's license.

During the spring of 1962, I was in Santa Cruz during Easter vacation, hanging out, surfing at Steamer Lane, and sleeping in a car I'd bought there—a 1936 Buick with beautiful mohair seats. I happened to run into Mike Zuetell, one of the guys from the old 22nd Street Gang in Hermosa Beach. He was in the army at Fort Ord, near Monterey. He introduced me to a chubby-faced army buddy of his, a guy named Don Hansen, who had a crash pad in Santa Cruz. Hansen was from Redfield, South Dakota, and his teeth were stained brown from some mineral they had in the water back there. He'd been surfing in California for a few years before he joined the army, and sometimes he shaped surfboards for Jack O'neill.

Zuetell and Hansen told me that almost every night they would go AWOL, jump the fence at Fort Ord, party at their house in Santa

Cruz, and be back on base by reveille. They said they'd never been caught.

"Hey," they said, "we're having a big party at the house tonight. Why don't you come?"

It turned out to be one of the craziest parties I'd ever seen. The house was packed full of people getting drunk and wild, and as the evening went on they became more and more out of control. At one point Don Hansen took a ceramic mixing bowl, threw it as hard as he could at Mike Zuetell, and hit him square in the forehead. Mike had a crescent-shaped scar on his forehead for the rest of his life.

When I saw things were really getting out of hand, I retired to one of the bedrooms to get some sleep. But I'd only been asleep for a few minutes when I heard a terrible commotion in the front room. All of a sudden the door swung open, Hansen ran through the room, dived over the bed, through the screened window, hit the ground outside, and kept on running into the night.

Then, not far behind Hansen, came a great big cop. He looked around, but when he couldn't see Hansen, he became furious; he came over to the bed and started hitting me over the head with his flashlight. I tried to protect myself with my arms, saying, "What's going on?"

Somebody turned on the lights, and I saw that the cop was even bigger than I'd thought. Then a woman ran in and stopped the cop from beating on me. I looked up long enough to glance at his name tag. I'll never forget it—Wablinsky.

I recognized the woman. She'd been with Hansen earlier that evening. Now I found out she also happened to be Officer Wablinsky's wife. As I understood it, earlier that evening two police officers had been beaten up, supposedly by out-of-towners who had thrown one of the officers over a cliff. The officer was in the hospital in serious condition. So the cops were on the rampage, and Wablinsky was using that as an excuse to go after Hansen. I just happened to have been caught in the middle of it.

That was my first experience with Don Hansen, South Dakota farm boy, soldier, and future pillar of the surf industry.

In 1962 there was a big Surfarama trade show at the Santa

Monica Civic Auditorium. It was for surfboard manufacturers and others in the surfing industry to show off their latest products. The surfing craze hadn't really hit the country yet, although surfing was getting to be a big sport in Southern California, and the surf industry was just starting to become aware of its influence. As I walked around the trade show, filmmakers Bud Browne and young Bruce Brown were there showing their movies, and there were bands like Dick Dale and the Deltones playing a lusty rock 'n' roll some were calling surf music.

Tom Morey had a booth at the trade show, too. Since the old days when I used to see him surfing at Malibu, Tom had gotten out of aircraft engineering, had teamed up with Carl Pope, and had opened up a surfboard shop in Ventura called Morey-Pope. Together they started coming out with a lot of innovative products: They invented Slip Check, an abrasive material in a spray can that you could spray on your board for traction. They came out with the first molded polypropylene fin and fin-mounting system—until then fins had always been made of wood, which was much less flexible. And they came out with Tri Sec, a collapsible, three-part surfboard that folded down into a suitcase. (In those days surfboards were eleven feet long, and some airlines refused to accept them as baggage.)

When I stopped at the Morey-Pope booth, Tom Morey was standing in front of a small crowd describing a new surfboard he'd designed. At that time the rails on all surfboards were rounded symmetrically, what we used to call "egg rails," and the nose always turned up so the board wouldn't pearl. Well, on Tom's board the rails turned down and were flat on the bottom, and the nose turned down as well. It didn't make any sense to me, but Tom, who still looked more like an engineer than a surfer, was whooshing his hands through the air like a little kid flying a paper airplane, trying to explain to us how his surfboard worked. "See, if the top of the nose curves down, while the bottom of the nose is flat, then the water has to travel farther and faster over the top, and that creates a vacuum which automatically lifts the nose, just like an airplane wing. The same theory applies to my turned-down rails, as well."

At the time, I didn't really understand everything Tom was

saying, but he definitely stretched my mind. We were used to making surfboards in the same old way, and if we experimented at all, it was more in the outline of the board, rather than with the rocker or the rails. And rather than working from theoretical concepts, we were still plodding along with trial and error, which was a lot of fun, but slow. We didn't even realize that nobody really knew how to design a surfboard. Tom Morey at least understood that when it came to surfboard design, the whole thing was still wide open. (And he was certainly correct about the turned-down rails, because that's the way all surfboards are made today.)

Sometimes on the weekends, I liked to drive down to Laguna Beach and stay with Marge Calhoun and her two daughters, Candy and Robin. I first got to know the Calhouns at Malibu, where they were regulars, and over the years I became pals with all three of them.

Marge was a statuesque woman, extremely strong, with broad shoulders, narrow hips, beautiful skin, and penetrating blue eyes—just an amazing looking woman who radiated health and beauty. Marge got her first lesson in surfing from Buzzy Trent at Santa Monica in the early Fifties and went on to win the women's Makaha International Surfing Championships in 1958. Even though she was strong, she was still very feminine, and it was a wonderful thing to watch her on a surfboard.

Her oldest daughter, Candy, was strong, too, with beautiful golden hair, blue eyes, and lovely brown skin. She was great on a surfboard and won the women's West Coast Surfing Champion-ships in 1963. But her real love was bodysurfing. She swam like a seal. When you saw her dive into the water and come up with her wet hair slicked back, you just knew this person was meant to be in the water. Some people are like that—they're more at ease in the water than out.

The youngest daughter, Robin, was great in the water, too. She was taller—all legs, with long, elegant hands. She, too, had the most gorgeous, penetrating, blue eyes.

Their hair color, their skin, their physical strength and athletic prowess—the Calhouns were like ocean goddesses to me. Over the years, at one time or another, I had a crush on each of them, though it never amounted to anything more than wrestling around in the back of the car and a few friendly kisses.

The Calhouns and I became a tight little clique. When I came to Laguna Beach, I would stay at their little house on Glennaire Street, where they always made me feel welcome. It was a white beach cottage, very pretty, and decorated with sea shells and driftwood. We would surf all day at San Onofre, then go back to their house and make a big salad dinner, drink beer, laugh and tell stories until we fell asleep on the floor with our arms aching. What a wonderful feeling that was. Then we'd get up the next day and go do it again.

I loved being with the Calhouns. Over the years, I somehow lost touch with them, though I still miss them a lot.

The fall of 1962, I was back in Hawaii to compete in the Makaha International Surfing Championships. The Makaha was the oldest and most prestigious contest in surfing, but there was a lot of talk, particularly among California and Australian surfers, about how the thing was rigged, that you couldn't win it unless you were Hawaiian, or at least *haole* Hawaiian. If you looked at the contest results, you could see there was some truth to that. Since 1954 the contest had been won by Rabbit Kekai, and Buffalo Keaulana, both Hawaiians, and by Wally Froiseth, Peter Cole, and George Downing, *haoles* who now lived year-round on the islands. Personally, I didn't think it was rigged. It was just that the judges were all local guys from the Outrigger Canoe Club—they knew all the local surfers, knew their families, had watched the surfers grow up, had even taught some of them how to surf. Naturally, the judges wanted to see their local boys win. The judges *couldn't* be impartial.

Makaha was the first place where surfers rode really big waves, years before the surf spots on the North Shore were pioneered. It's on the lee side of the island, so when the North Shore gets blown out, Makaha can be sunny and tranquil. It's also drier there, with lots of cactus and thorn bush, and the water is usually a calm aqua blue, while the water on the North Shore is often a turbulent shade of green.

Even though it was a fine surf sport, very few of us *haole* surfers ever went over to Makaha because we knew we were going to get shafted there. The communities near Makaha, like Nanakuli, were almost entirely native Hawaiian, and a lot of the people were unemployed, living on welfare and food stamps. A lot of the locals at Makaha made their living stealing from *haoles*, breaking into cars. They had spotters up on the hill above the parking lot, and as soon as you got out of your car and hit the water, your car was stripped. Sometimes haoles would get beat up for even trying to surf at Makaha. So, like most *haole* surfers, I hung out on the North Shore. But I knew that if I was going to compete in the Makaha International, I would have to surf Makaha at least a few times beforehand.

The first thing I did when I went to Makaha was befriend the king of Makaha, Buffalo Keaulana. Buffalo, who was sort of a folk hero in the islands, had grown up around Nanakuli and knew everyone who lived there. He was a great surfer, a big guy with massive shoulders and sun-bleached hair. He looked like one of the drawings you see of the old Hawaiian kings.

I went to Buffalo's house and presented him with a case of beer. A lot of the locals liked to gather at his house in the afternoon to have a few beers, so I knew it was a gift he would appreciate. I mentioned a few friends he and I had in common, and he invited me to stay awhile. When I left, Buffalo let me know I was welcome at Makaha, and none of the locals hassled me while I practiced for the contest.

Later though, I was at Makaha with Dick Barrymore, a photographer and filmmaker. Within the first twenty minutes, our car was broken into and a bunch of camera equipment and surfboards were taken. Altogether, probably $15,000 worth of stuff was gone. So I went to Buffalo and told him what had happened. I knew if anybody could get our stuff back, he could. Buff said, "Don't you worry. You go surf and have a good time."

When we came out of the water the second time, everything that had been stolen was back in the car.

Joey Cabell won the Makaha that year, continuing the tradition of a Hawaiian, either white or native, always winning there. Nobody could deny, though, that Joey surfed brilliantly and deserved to win. Linda Merrill and I won the Makaha tandem event, in what some people told us later was one of the best tandem events they'd ever seen.

In 1963, almost overnight it seemed, everybody in the whole country wanted to be a surfer. Or, failing that, to look like a surfer. That has always been a great mystery to me, why people who had never even seen the ocean before would want to bleach their hair, put on a pair of baggies and blue tennies, and tell everybody how stoked they were. You could say it was all just a California fad, maybe one of the first California fads, but it's been going on for thirty years now, and a billion-dollar clothing industry has grown up catering to nothing but the average American's desire to look like a surfer.

I remember the first time I heard the Beach Boys song "Surfer Girl." I was riding in my car with Kemp Aaberg. When we heard that whiny, cornball music, we started hissing and hooting because we thought it was so hokey. It was a rip-off. The Beach Boys were stealing our culture. And they didn't even know how to surf!

To be fair to the Beach Boys, I have to say that when I hear their music today, I like it because it takes me back to that era. I think they really did capture some of the fun of surfing in their music, and I think the way they portrayed teenagers growing up in Southern California during that period was accurate: the cars, the beach, the awkward love, the obsession with being accepted by your peers. But at the time, we felt like our territory was being violated. The Beach Boys were pretending they had already made it down the stairs at Malibu, when we knew they hadn't.

Of course, the Beach Boys were geniuses compared to the dolts who made the first beach movies. *Muscle Beach Party* was probably the most ridiculous of them all: everybody dancing on the beach at Malibu, wearing bun-hugger swim trunks; all of a sudden somebody yells, Surf's up! Everybody grabs his surfboard and runs out to Waimea Bay breaking with twenty-foot sets.

Those beach movies were the first glimpse most people in the country had of the surf culture, and I think because the movies were so badly made, so phony and just plain dishonest, the image of surfing, at least in the mainland U.S., was forever stamped as being silly, adolescent, and superficial. There were authentic surf movies being made, too—by Bud Browne, John Severson, and Bruce Brown—but they were never distributed outside the relatively small beach communities of California, Florida, Texas, and New Jersey, and were rarely seen by anyone who wasn't a surfer.

That summer we started hearing rumors that Bruce Brown was working on a new surf movie that was going to be something special. Bruce had made his first surf films with a 16-millimeter camera while he was in the army in Hawaii. Later, when Bruce spliced those home movies together, Dale Velzy showed them at his surf shop in San Clemente, charging surfers twenty-five cents admission. I remember Bruce as short and wiry—he probably never weighed over 130 pounds—very blond and very fair skinned; he was always stoked, and he always smoked like a fiend.

For his new surf film, Bruce had taken a couple of well-known surfers, Robert August and Mike Hynson, and was traveling all around the world with them—to Japan, Senegal, Ghana, Nigeria, South Africa, Australia, New Zealand, and Tahiti—in pursuit of the perfect wave. Based solely on the rumors we heard about the movie, we couldn't wait to see it.

Also in that year, 1963, *Surfer* magazine came up with an interesting idea. It probably came out of the frustration almost everybody felt about the Makaha and other so-called international surf contests, which always seemed to favor the local heroes. The idea was, instead of having another surf contest, why not just ask the surfers themselves who they thought were the best surfers in the world? Most surfers had seen the surf movies, which tended to highlight the best surfers giving their best performances on the world's best waves. By letting the surfers decide for themselves, you could eliminate the hometown advantage, inexperienced or senile judges, and ridiculous rules. In fact, you could do away with contests altogether.

So *Surfer* conducted its first Surfer Poll, and the results that year pleased just about everyone. The winner was Phil Edwards, the California style master whose smooth, understated way with a surfboard and a wave had inspired every surfer in the world. What made the award seem even more just and fitting was the fact that Edwards had rarely participated in surf contests, believing they were irrelevant and meaningless. Edwards had won the poll entirely on his reputation among other surfers.

As a minor sidelight to Edwards winning the first Surfer Poll that year, I was ranked the 13th-best surfer in the world.

In the fall I transferred down to El Camino College, in the South Bay, where I could be with my on-again, off-again sweetheart, Marsha Bainer. She and I were both too restless to settle down yet, but we really liked each other a lot, and continued to spend time together. Marsha had adopted a lot of my training regimen—working out every morning, eating a low-fat diet, yoga—and she had grown into a healthy, vibrant, fun-loving young woman.

One morning, Marsha and I were in the parking lot of the college, fooling around in the back of my VW van. I had the radio tuned to a jazz station, and turned down softly. Suddenly there was an interruption, and the announcer said to stand by for a special bulletin. Then we heard the words everyone in my generation would remember for the rest of their lives: "President Kennedy has been shot."

Mickey Dora used to say that a curse fell over this country when President Kennedy was assassinated, and he predicted that a major cataclysmic event would soon follow. Mickey was becoming sort of the gloomy prophet of Malibu, and sometimes it was hard to tell how serious he really was. For example, as proof of the assassination curse, he claimed that many of the best California surf spots didn't break as big or as regularly as they had a decade earlier. But in spite of his eccentricity, Dora could be very perceptive at times, and I think he was correct in foreseeing the end of an age of innocence.

One day a few years earlier, I'd been surfing down at Trestles and was driving home along the Coast Highway, when I stopped to pick up a young surfer hitchhiking with his board. The kid looked about twelve years old, with a sweet little sun-kissed face. He had curly blond hair and blue eyes, and as he climbed up in the seat, the first thing he said was, "Are you Mike Doyle?"

"That's me," I said.

"Bitchin'! I saw you in *Surf Happy*. I surf, too!"

"No kidding," I said. "Where do you surf?"

"At Surfside! It's the greatest place! Nobody knows where it is. You gotta come and see it some time!"

"Okay," I told him. "I'll do that."

"Bitchin'! Wait'll I tell my buddies Mike Doyle's gonna surf with us!"

It was so funny to hear this hyperactive little surf rat hammering me with these stories about his favorite spot, which just happened to be right in front of his house. I knew the surf there was lousy, but for him it was as good as Rincon.

About a month later, I was reading the letters to the editor in *Surfer* magazine, when I saw a black-and-white photo of a little blond kid standing in front of mushy, three-foot waves. It was the kid I'd picked up hitchhiking, and his letter was all about how great this secret surf spot was right in front of his house. "I been surfing since 1956, and I never seen more than thirty guys in the water there!" the letter said. It was signed Corky Carroll.

Over the next few years, I started running into Corky at surf contests. He was still competing in the boys' division, but he was very good and very competitive. He was just a skinny little rail at the time, but he had huge pectoral muscles and was a great paddler. I got to know him and his parents pretty well.

Corky's folks were old. His mother had gotten pregnant with him when she was in her fifties, so when Corky was sixteen his parents were already in their sixties. He was their only child. Corky's father was a big Irishman who spent most of his free time in the local bars. His mother was a short, Old World kind of woman who said she didn't understand Corky at all. Neither of them did. So Corky more or less raised himself.

Corky's parents knew that Corky looked up to me and respected me, so when they learned I was going to transfer down to Long Beach State, they asked me if I would move in with them. They told me Corky had a hot temper, which I already knew, and that he was always getting into fights at school. They figured that if I would move in with them, I could be a big brother to Corky, and maybe that would help him find his way. The deal was that I would share a room with Corky, and in return I would get free room and board.

I didn't see how anything I could do or say would help Corky very much, but I was a struggling college student, and I could have used the room and board. So when Corky was sixteen, I moved in with him and his parents at their small house at Surfside, just south of Seal Beach.

Living with Corky was a real trial for me. He was an intelligent kid, but he had a tremendous amount of energy that could run rampant at any time. And his temper was the hottest I've ever seen. All he wanted to do was argue. Also, Corky had trouble with his eyes, and that aggravated his other problems. He wore Coke-bottle glasses, his eyes were always inflamed, and he was very self-conscious about the way he looked (something I had no trouble relating to). He always thought of himself as the underdog, like everybody was picking on him. If anybody tried to tell him what to do—his parents, his teachers, the law, or me—he'd just tell them to fuck off. He wouldn't accept direction from anybody.

I don't think I did a lot to help Corky during the time I lived with him. I wasn't old enough or mature enough to understand him. I definitely wasn't the big brother he needed. He always saw me as a competitive peer. Even after I'd lived there a while, if I crossed him at all, he'd throw everything down and say, "Come on, let's fight!"

But Corky and I did go surfing a lot, and we had some great times together.

Corky Carroll became one of the hottest competitors in small waves that surfing has ever seen. He would go out and do whatever it took to win. He'd take off in front of you, spin around backward, or stand on his head. Corky was a showman. Even after he'd already won the contest, on his last wave, he'd do a one-legged frog or some other wild move, not to get any more points—the contest was already over—but because Corky thought of a surf contest as his stage.

And Corky was a brilliant stylist. During a time when older guys were getting into an easy kind of soul surfing, Corky was aggressive and mechanical, bringing in the modern style of surfing we see today. I think Corky actually changed the direction of surfing.

One time at the West Coast Surfing Championships, at Huntington Pier, Corky threw a temper tantrum that a lot of people will never forget. Corky was almost unbeatable at Huntington; he was aggressive, dynamic, in great physical shape, and he could ride the nose like nobody else. He was also goofy foot, which is perfect for Huntington's left-breaking waves. In fact, he'd already won the West Coast Surfing Championships there five times in a row. But during this particular contest, there was a disagreement over the rules, and it looked like it was going to work against Corky. If he had kept his cool, he probably could have pleaded his case. But Corky was convinced there was some kind of conspiracy to keep him from winning. It was the world against Corky. So he did the worst thing imaginable. He stomped up and down in front of the judging stand, screaming, "You fat-assed old farts! You don't know a fucking thing!"

His attitude only antagonized the judges, and when the results were announced, Corky had lost. *Like John Macenroe*

Across the street from Corky lived Nancy and Walt Katin, who had a business making boat covers out of heavy-duty industrial canvas. Walt was a classic boat guy. He was short, robust, and wore powder-blue jumpsuits zipped up to the neck. He had a big salt-and-pepper beard and always wore a captain's hat with a gold anchor on the black plastic brim. And he was happy all the time. Nancy was a little eighty-nine-pound lady who chain-smoked—very nervous and excitable, but clear as a bell and the sweetest woman I ever met. Like her husband, she was happy all the time.

The Katins had no children of their own, but they loved kids, and they always made Corky feel welcome at their place. One day

Corky asked Nancy if she would make him a pair of surf trunks out of boat canvas. He explained that swim trunks wouldn't hold up to the stress of surfing—usually they would just rip out in the seat or the crotch.

Nancy had heavy-duty sewing machines and used hundred-pound-test, waxed-nylon thread. She knew how to sew things that would last. So she said, "Sure, Corky, let's give it a try."

Nancy sewed him a pair of red trunks out of sixteen-ounce drill canvas. She sewed them the same way she sewed her boat covers: with zigzag stitching, double and even triple seams. Corky loved them, but they were so stiff that every time he took them off, he just stood them up in the corner of his room. He wore them for two years before they broke in enough that they wouldn't stand up by themselves. And after three years, he was still wearing them.

Before long, hundreds of local surfers were coming to Nancy Katin and asking her if she would make them a pair of surf trunks just like Corky's. The Katins' boat cover business was rapidly turning into a surf trunks business. It was all word of mouth, no advertising, a walk-in business, no mail order. They called it Kanvas by Katin, and there wasn't anything else like it in California. Over the next four years, Nancy and the two Japanese ladies who worked for her made thousands of pairs of surf trunks. For surfers, Kanvas by Katin was legendary.

In December of 1963, I was back in Hawaii again, getting ready for that year's Makaha. The morning of the contest, I was surfing at a little beach break at Pokai Bay (south of Makaha), just warming up before heading over to the contest. As I came out of the water, Dave Rochlen came walking down the beach. Dave, who was about fifteen years older than I was, had been a lifeguard at Santa Monica, was a respected big-wave rider and somebody I'd always looked up to. He'd been kind of a playboy in his younger days (he dated Marilyn Monroe before she became a famous movie star), but when he went to the islands he fell in love with a Hawaiian woman. I remember him telling me that when he saw her surfing one day, he just knew he had to have her. He ended up marrying the woman, having kids and settling down there in the islands.

Anyway, what really caught my attention on this particular day was that Rochlen was wearing these great big, floral-patterned surf trunks, like big baggy sacks with a draw string. They were like a cross between a Hawaiian muumuu, and extra-large boxer shorts. I liked them right away—they really made me laugh. So I called out to him, "Dave, what the hell are you wearing?"

Rochlen looked at me, then down at his baggies. He had a funny way of talking with gestures—rolling his head, squishing his neck, tilting his shoulders—like he had to feel every word before he could let it out. "These are my new jams!"

I'd never heard the word before—jams. "Well, those are really cool," I said.

Dave acted surprised. "You really think so?" He stripped them off right there—he had a pair of briefs on underneath—and handed them to me. "Here, they're yours. First pair I ever made."

I wore Rochlen's jams around for a long time. They were comfortable, and they were so wild they made an anti-fashion statement, which I believe was the beginning of surf fashion.

Not long after that, Dave created one of the first surfwear companies, and called it Surf Line Hawaii. He registered the trademark, Jams, and came out with an entire line of his floral baggies.

An unbelievable thing happened at the Makaha International that winter: Midget Farrelly, an Australian, only seventeen years old and almost unknown, won. Even more incredible was the fact that almost everyone who saw the contest thought he should have won. Maybe, we thought, the judges were finally getting sensitive to the criticism that the contest rules at the Makaha were outdated. Maybe the judges were ready to put down their pencils and just watch for a change. But nobody expected the winner to be an Australian.

The friction between Hawaiians and Australians had been growing for years. The Californians, because they had grown up surfing in crowded conditions, had evolved an ethic about not hogging all the waves and not cutting off another surfer—it was a matter of survival to try to reduce tensions in the water. The

Hawaiians were generally easygoing by nature and were used to having plenty of waves for everybody. But the Australians tended to be very aggressive in the water. They were rightly proud of the great advances their surfers had made in recent years and were eager to demonstrate that they were now equal to any surfers in the world. But sometimes they pushed things a bit too far.

At any rate, Midget Farrelly's performance was brilliant. The surf was usually big at Makaha, but that year it was only four or five feet and breaking on the inside reef. So Midget just stayed inside. I was in the finals, too, and while I rode maybe five outside waves in an hour, Midget rode thirty inside waves, just ripping and tearing upside-down and sideways. He didn't score a lot of points on each wave, but he got so many waves that after a while he burned an impression in the judges' minds. He did everything wrong to win, everything against the rules, but it set him apart from the rest of us, and he ended up changing the rules.

That proved to everybody that it was possible for an outsider to win at Makaha. You had to have a few extra points sliding in your favor to beat the Hawaiians, but if you really outshined them, you could win.

My strongest memory of that winter of '64, though, was not the Makaha contest; it was of one huge day when the whole North Shore completely closed out, and even the waves at Makaha, over on the lee side of the island, got up to thirty-five feet. A group of us drove all around the island, but we only saw two guys out that whole day: Greg Noll and George Downing. After watching anxiously from the shore for a while, I finally decided I would go out at Makaha, even though it was by far the biggest surf I'd ever tried. And I was totally terrified.

I paddled out past the bowl, and watched as one massive wave broke in front of me, smoking and spitting froth out the barrel. I paddled over to the point and caught one of the first waves of a set. I had a screaming ride across the top of the wave, dropped down, then had enough speed to go out and around the bowl into the deep blue water.

I did that over and over that day. Everything went perfectly, like I had some kind of magic, like I was in a dream. I was adrenaline-pumped, but at the same time I was so relaxed and had such smooth control. I had learned to control my fear and to relax in the most critical situations. Although no trophy was awarded, and very few people even saw me surf that day, I knew I'd done something important. I'd made a major breakthrough in my understanding of how the mind and body can work together to accomplish great things. I felt like some kind of Zen master.

Every winter I'd spend a few weeks on the North Shore, skipping the winter semester of school, then heading back to California for the spring semester and my summer lifeguard job. A lot of people have asked me over the years why I didn't choose to live in Hawaii, like so many other surfers from that era.

One reason is what we used to call "rockitis." Unless you grew up on an island, it could be very difficult getting used to a world that small. It makes you feel uneasy. It's kind of an unconscious thing, but still very real.

Another reason is that, even in those days, Hawaii was way too crowded. Everybody thinks of Hawaii as a surfer's paradise, but on the North Shore there are only about ten good places to surf. As surfing began to grow worldwide, surfers began to flock to the North Shore. It never occurred to us that big-wave surfing would catch on the way it did. We thought there would always be just a few hard-core crazies on the North Shore. At first there had been just one house full of surfers, then it was five houses, then twenty houses, then fifty houses. All of a sudden, every surf spot had fifty or a hundred guys scratching for the takeoff zone. It had become a very aggressive crowd, and there were a lot of fights.

But the biggest reason I chose not to live in Hawaii was because of the racial tension. There were a lot of different races living on the islands, and they didn't always get along that well. Mickey Dora used to say he'd rather live in Selma, Alabama, than on the North Shore, because there was less racial tension in Alabama. In a way, he was right. If you were white, you had to get used to being called a *haole*, which, if said in a certain tone of voice, could be as offensive as "nigger." You had to understand there were neighborhoods where white boys couldn't go and that even looking at a Hawaiian woman could get you beaten senseless.

It was fun to read and fantasize about what a paradise Hawaii had been a hundred years earlier, but it just wasn't like that anymore.

Another thing that really changed the surf scene in Hawaii was that mainland girls started showing up. Until then, a winter on the North Shore was almost like taking a vow of celibacy. Living without women was one of the ways you proved how dedicated you were to the sport. Even in the Sixties, very few girls rode big waves, but a lot of girls decided the surfing lifestyle was cool. We called them the "Downey No Bras" because so many of them were from Southern California. At the start of the season, there'd be just a few hanging around, but they liked the North Shore so much, they'd call their girlfriends back in Downey and tell them to come on over. It seemed like overnight the female population on the North Shore would double, then double again. It was great, in a way, but very distracting and not at all what we were used to.

In May of 1964, the first World Surfing Championship was held in Manly, Australia. It's difficult to explain to people the excitement that event caused. Today there are major surf contests held almost every week somewhere in the world, but at that time, there was only the Makaha, held once a year in Hawaii. So when the Australians announced they would be hosting a world championship, we were thrilled. This was going to be the first truly international surf contest.

I was invited by the Australians to compete in the contest, based on my performance in contests in Hawaii and California. At first I didn't know where I would get the money to make the trip, but Hap Jacobs, Dale Velzy's old partner, offered to give me the money I needed for the plane ticket. It was my first real opportunity for world travel. To get away from school for a while, to see a new country, to see different customs—it was magic for me.

In the previous decade or so, surfing in Australia had grown to a level of importance it has never reached in the United States, and the Australians took their role as hosts for the contest very seriously. Australia is a water-conscious country: Almost everybody there lives along the coast, everybody swims, and almost everybody surfs or at least bodysurfs. The Australians were very proud of their watermen, and hosting a world surfing contest was an opportunity for them to show the rest of the world what Australia was all about. An American equivalent might be a baseball world series, but with every baseball-playing country in the world invited to compete.

The contest was sponsored by Ampol Oil, a major corporation in Australia. They not only covered the costs of organizing the event, but they paid for the hotel accommodations for all the foreign competitors. The contest was covered live by three Australian television stations that had helicopters hovering above the water. In addition, 65,000 people turned out to watch from the beach.

During the contest, surf conditions were only fair, getting up to five feet on the biggest sets, and the beaches were windy and cold in the mornings. But the Australians put on a first-class contest. To make sure the judging would be fair, they flew in judges from around the world.

When it was over, the winner was Australian Midget Farrelly. Once again it looked like favoritism, but I don't think it was. Nobody could outshine the hometown boy on his waves, and he truly did surf very well. Afterward, speaking to the Australian press, Midget paid me a great compliment by saying he had seen me surfing in one of Bud Browne's films that had played in Australia and he'd imitated elements of my style.

I took second place in the contest, and Joey Cabell placed third. Some observers thought Joey had outsurfed both Midget and me but was given third place because he'd been too aggressive, dropping in too many times in front of other surfers. The Australians had emphasized that this contest was going to strengthen the international brotherhood of surfing, and I suppose the judges felt Joey's aggressiveness had to be penalized.

After the main competition was over, Linda Benson (the top woman surfer in the world at that time) and I put on a tandem demonstration that was covered on national television. Many Australians had never seen tandem surfing before, and they were fascinated by the grace of the sport. In fact several Australians told us later they thought our tandem demonstration had been the highlight of the contest.

The next month, Bruce Brown's new film, *Endless Summer*, was finally released and started playing in California beach towns. Surfers knew right away that it was the best surf film ever made, but a lot of us were surprised by how popular it became with non-surfers as well. I think the movie captured people's imaginations by demonstrating the pure freedom of the sport. There were no bells, no stopwatches, no starting gates, no referees—just you, a surfboard, and the water. The surfers in the film weren't hurting anybody or anything. They were just doing something they truly loved, something as simple as looking for the perfect wave.

When Bruce Brown saw how the film was received by popular audiences, he decided to distribute it to regular movie theaters. He blew the 16-millimeter print up to wide-screen 35-millimeter. Then he took a big gamble by borrowing $50,000 to rent the Kips Bay Theater in New York City for the first showing of *Endless Summer* in 35-millimeter. The reviews were fantastic. *Newsweek* called it "breathtaking . . . a sweeping and exciting account of human skill pitted against the ocean." The New York *Post* said, "Something very special . . . anyone who can't see the beauty and thrill of it hasn't got eyes." And the New York *Times* said it was "buoyant fun, hypnotic beauty and continuous excitement."

In the next few years, *Endless Summer* broke box-office records all over the country, and the movie that had cost Bruce Brown something like $50,000 to make—an enormous amount for a surf film in those days—grossed $30 million worldwide.

That fall I was in North Hollywood, visiting Marsha Bainer. I knew Mickey Dora was living in Hollywood at the time, still trying to work his way into the movies, so I called him up and said, "Hey, Mickey, let's play some tennis."

I wasn't much of a tennis player myself, but I knew that Dora liked the game and played like a pro. He said, "Sure, Doyle, meet me at the public court in Beverly Hills in an hour."

Dora had grown even more eccentric in recent years, and in some ways his behavior had polarized the world of surfing. While some were calling him a creative genius and a cult hero, others were calling him hypocritical. On one hand, Dora was constantly attacking the commercialization of surfing; he hated what he called the "nauseating phony endorsements," which he said were "perverting integrity for grimy handouts from promoters." But on the other hand, Dora himself was endorsing Greg Noll surfboards and appearing in movies like *Gidget Goes to Rome*, and *Ride the Wild Surf*. Nothing had done more to pervert the integrity of surfing than those awful movies.

I couldn't figure out where Dora was coming from, myself; I just knew he was an old friend, and I enjoyed seeing him.

I was already at the tennis court when Dora drove up in a tiny, green Lotus convertible. As he climbed out from behind the wheel, I saw that he was wearing a full-length trench coat with an iron cross and other war medals pinned all over his chest. He also had a swastika on a chain dangling around his neck, a Nazi cap, and white tennis shoes. Dora reached behind the seat of the Lotus, pulled out a thick steel chain, dragged it under the front axle of the Lotus, and wrapped it around a telephone pole. Next he pulled a big padlock out of his coat pocket and locked the ends of the chain together. I suppose he was afraid somebody would pick up his Lotus and carry it away like a bicycle. Then Dora tucked his tennis racket under his arm and strolled onto the court, all smiles and charm.

It was a warm fall day, but the whole time we played tennis, Dora wore that big wool trench coat, with the swastika swinging around his neck. He wouldn't take either of them off. You have to understand that there are a lot of Jewish people at the public tennis court in Beverly Hills. Most people tried to ignore him and his Nazi medals, but still, as they say in Hawaii, there was "a lotta bad stink-eye."

After tennis we went back to Marsha's apartment. A hot Santa Ana wind was blowing that day, and brush fires were flaring up all around the L.A. basin. We could see the smoke from Marsha's window, and we were watching the news reports on TV.

Little by little, Dora started getting panicky about the fires. His face muscles started twitching, and he rolled his head around nervously, like he could already feel the heat on the back of his neck. He kept saying, "This is it, Doyle. It's all coming down . . . like Armageddon . . . just like I told you it would."

I think that was the first time I realized that Dora didn't go through all his bizarre antics just for our amusement. Maybe it had started out that way, but now it was different.

Finally he said, "You gotta get me outa here, Doyle!"

I said, "Sure, Mickey," and I told Marsha we were going out for a drive.

I put Mickey in my car and started driving south, out of the fire zone. After an hour or so on the freeway, Dora started to calm down.

The Makaha International was held on Christmas day that year, in big, rough surf. The old-fashioned point system still hadn't changed: Thirty points were awarded for the length of ride; only ten points were awarded for performance. And there was even more grumbling about how ridiculous it had become. Somebody pointed out that under a judging system like that, you could win without even standing up, just ride on your belly all the way to the beach.

Fred Hemmings, who had played center on Honolulu's Punahou prep school football team, surfed aggressively all through the contest, muscling other surfers off the waves, trying to intimidate with his strength. Hemmings wasn't much of a stylist, but he excelled at riding big waves, and he was extremely competitive. And being a local boy certainly didn't hurt his chances at Makaha, either. Nobody was surprised when he won that year.

Afterward, the L.A. *Herald-Examiner* ran an article in its sports section titled, "Is Hawaii Fixing Its Surf Contest?"

One of the surfers in Hawaii that winter was Don Hansen, the AWOL soldier who had nearly gotten me beaten up by a jealous Santa Cruz cop. He was married now and living at Kawela Bay, where I liked to stay every winter. Don and I became friends, and we spent a lot of time that winter talking about our plans for the future.

Don was thinking about moving to northern San Diego County,

to Encinitas or Cardiff, and opening up a surf shop. He'd spent some time there living in his panel truck, surfing at Swami's, and he'd grown to love the place. He'd gotten to know another North County surfer, Bob Driver, whose father owned a big insurance company in San Diego. Driver had promised Don $1500 in start-up money, in exchange for a partnership in the surf shop. Don thought it sounded like a pretty good deal and asked me if I would be interested in going to work for him, shaping and promoting my own signature-model surfboard. "Why don't you come in with me?" he said. "We'll join forces."

After spending so many winters in lush, green Hawaii, the prospect of going back to overcrowded and smoggy L.A. didn't look good to me. I knew that San Diego's North County offered more choice surfing spots than anywhere in California—I'd spent many happy days surfing them with my friend Rusty Miller. I also knew that North County still had a quiet, laid-back, country life-style. It was mostly retired people living there. The pace was too slow for young people, so as soon as they graduated from high school, they got out. But the area still had wide-open spaces, plenty of room to move, miles and miles of empty beaches, lots of good waves, and hardly any surfers.

So I decided to take Don up on his offer. I told him I would move to San Diego in the spring.

After I came back from Hawaii, in January 1965, I traveled with twelve other surfers from the Long Beach Surf Club to Lima, Peru, to compete in the Peruvian International. Our team was sponsored by Catalina Swimwear, which was eager to capitalize on the growing popularity of surfing.

The Peruvians had a beautiful clubhouse they called the Club Waikiki, at Miraflores Beach, just outside Lima. It was more like a polo club than any surf club I'd ever seen. It had two swimming pools, a restaurant, bar, squash court, locker rooms, lots of pretty girls lying around, masseuses, and white-jacketed waiters running all over the place. Everyone who surfed in Peru at that time was wealthy. There weren't any peasant surfers—no surf rats, no beach bums. Surfing was a gentleman's sport in Peru, and almost all the surfers were very, very rich. They would work for a while in the morning, tending to their business affairs, then come down to the club for the rest of the day. They would surf for a couple of hours at the little beach break in front of the club, shower, then have lunch and cocktails on the terrace.

At the Club Waikiki, guests weren't allowed to carry their own surfboards down to the water—the servants did it for you. One of the Australian surfers, Nat Young, didn't like that. When they tried to take his board from him, he snatched it back and said, "Goddamnit, leave me alone! I'll carry my own board!" Which is how most of us felt, too. But Nat only insulted the servant, and probably our hosts as well, and in the end the Indian carried his board anyway.

The servants waxed your board for you, too. If you lost your board, they would run over and shag it for you before it hit the rocks. You could surf right up to the beach, step off and walk away—the servants would run out, grab your board, and carry it up to your locker. If you happened to ding your board, at night a little Indian came out of a hole in back of the club and patched it for you. The whole scene seemed unnatural, and it made me uncomfortable. But the Peruvians were such great hosts, and they took the whole thing so seriously, we had no choice but to go along with it.

Most of the young Peruvian surfers were bored rich kids, like spoiled princes. They loved playing the role of Latin lovers, and they were outrageous partiers. But the older guys who sponsored the contest were active surfers, too. They'd paddle out, catch a wave and stand up, just to show they still had the old animal prowess. Then they'd come in, have cocktails and lunch, and play a few rounds of *paleta*, which is a paddle-and-net game, kind of like badminton.

We stayed at a hotel in town, and a bus would pick us up and take us to the club every day, or to one of the many social events the Peruvians had planned for us.

One afternoon they got us all drunk at the club, then took us to a bullring. They gave us all capes and said, "Here, it's time to fight the bulls." I didn't want to fight any bulls. Most of us didn't. We tried to get out of it, tried to politely decline, but the Peruvians wouldn't have it. It was a big macho deal to fight a bull, and everyone had to do it. The bulls had their horns trimmed so we wouldn't get gored, but it was still dangerous. Several guys got flipped around, and we could have been badly hurt. I really hated that, but I did it.

On another occasion, the president of Peru at that time, Fernando Belaundé Terry, invited the whole Long Beach Surf Club to a banquet at the presidential palace. We all filed by in our blue blazers and shook his hand. We were honored—imagine, a president who wanted to meet surfers! We drank huge pitchers of *pisco* sours, which are like the national drink, and had a great time.

One of the contest sponsors was Pancho Wiese, the president of a big bank chain in Peru. He surfed and had even won a few local contests back in his prime. Another contest sponsor and organizer was Carlos Dogni, in his eighties at the time, who had been one of the first surfers in Peru and had helped start the Club Waikiki. The skin on his face was taught and almost translucent, as if he'd had several face lifts. He was still in great shape, though, and he always had two or three young girls on his arms. Dogni never seemed to work, but he had a huge house, and he invited us all to come over there for a big party. I remember he had a big bowl of photographs sitting on a table where everybody could look at them. They were all pictures of Dogni in swim trunks flexing his muscles, Dogni lifting weights, Dogni on the beach with young girls on his arm. I remember thinking some of them were pretty wild photos to be leaving around for the guests to see. But that's the way he was, eager to project an image of great sexual vitality.

I was on a strict training regimen at the time. I was a vegetarian and trying to stay away from any hard booze. I figured if I'd traveled all that way to compete in a surf contest, I owed it to myself and to my sponsors to try my best. My roommate at the hotel was Reno Abellira, a great Hawaiian surfer who was teaching me some yoga postures. Reno and I would get up early in the morning and do some yoga, then go practice surfing on the Peruvian waves, trying to get ready for the contest.

But the Peruvians didn't want us to train. They wanted us to drink and party with them. Before lunch every day, they'd all start drinking. One guy would stand up at the club, wave his drink at the rest of us, and say, "Salud!" Then he would insist that we all lift a glass with him. As soon as he sat down, another Peruvian would stand up and say, "Otra salud!" And we'd all have to drink another one.

The contest was held at a place called Puntas Rocas, about thirty miles south of Lima, on a desolate point. There were some sharp barnacles that grew on the rocks there; the Peruvians called them *chorros*, and they could punch holes in your feet if you weren't careful, so some of the surfers wore tennis shoes. There was heavy fog on the morning of the contest, but the waves were ten to twelve feet and well shaped. The waves at Puntas Rocas reminded me a lot of Swami's, back in Encinitas, so I felt comfortable riding them.

Linda Merrill and I won the tandem event using only a regular-sized surfboard—nobody had thought to bring along a tandem board.

For the men's big-wave event, the best surfers in the world were there: George Downing, Mickey Muñoz, Paul Strauch, Buffalo Keaulana, Fred Hemmings, and Joey Cabell, just to name a few. In my first heat, George Downing dropped in ahead of me, and I had to bail out to avoid hitting him. The wave plucked my board away and carried it all the way to the rocky shore, about a mile away. I was able to bodysurf all the way to shore, grab my board and paddle back out. I placed second in that heat and eventually went on to the finals.

A handsome young Peruvian, Felipe Pomar, won the contest, with Nat Young taking second and Paul Strauch third. Some people thought favoritism in world surfing had stretched all the way to South America. Personally, I thought Pomar outshined us all on his home waves and deserved to win.

After the contest was over, the Peruvians wanted to party even harder. They took us all to dinner at a Chinese restaurant in Lima, where everybody got drunk. Little by little things started to get out of control, until eventually everybody was throwing food around the place and smashing their plates on the floor. George Downing, who had been coming to the Peruvian Invitational since 1955 and was sort of the Hawaiian ringleader, started breaking chairs and smashing them over the tables. I suppose he figured that was what the Peruvians expected us to do, so he did his best to make them happy. The Americans started throwing food at the Hawaiians, and the Hawaiians fought back by throwing plates at us. The crazier it got, the more the Peruvians loved it.

What really confused me was that the Chinese who owned the restaurant didn't seem to mind the demolition. They weren't thrilled about it the way our hosts were, but they accepted it in good humor. Later, when we all finally staggered out of the place, the Peruvians handed the restaurant owners a big stack of cash.

One of the Peruvians involved in the contest was Pitty Blocque (he pronounced it "Peetie Block"), a wealthy race-car driver who had competed on the international Grand Prix circuit. He was a bit heavy, dressed well, and always had a wild look in his eye. He made his living from a very successful body shop in Lima. All the Peruvians who were in the surf club drove the fastest American cars—Corvettes, GTOs, Trans Ams—and they all drove like madmen, which meant their cars were always in Pitty Blocque's body shop getting fixed.

The night after the dinner at the Chinese restaurant, Pitty asked me and a couple others to take a drive with him. He had a Jaguar XKE, and we all crammed into it. Right from the hotel, he started driving about eighty miles an hour through the narrow side streets of Lima, I suppose to demonstrate his skill as a race-car driver. An Indian peasant pushing a little cart full of oranges couldn't get out of his way, and Pitty splattered that cart like a cartoon. I was scrunched down in the back of the Jaguar, thinking we were going to get thrown into jail. But Pitty just screeched to halt and told us, "No problem." He got out, walked over to the little Indian, who was terrified, pulled out a roll of cash, and handed him a few bills. The Indian nodded agreeably, but then pointed to the wrecked cart. So Pitty handed him a few more bills for the cart. Now the Indian was elated! He couldn't believe his good fortune. Not only had he sold all his oranges, but he would get a new cart, as well. Getting run over by Pitty Blocque was probably the luckiest thing to happen to him in years.

Pitty laughed, gave us a nod that everything was alright,

hopped back into the Jag, revved the engine a few times, and we were off again at eighty miles an hour.

Before long we were way out in the country. I heard Pitty say something about a whorehouse, but I already knew there were several whorehouses right around the corner from our hotel back in Lima, so I couldn't understand what we were doing out here in the country.

We finally pulled up to an old, colonial-style mansion surrounded by rows and rows of new American cars. Pitty explained that this was an "official whorehouse." As near as I could tell, that meant the place had been set up by the ruling class, for the ruling class. That way there would be no blackmail, no bad rumors leaking out, no embarrassment to the men or their families. They controlled everything.

Inside, it was like a huge barroom. All the Peruvians from the Club Waikiki were there—they'd just moved the whole party out to their whorehouse in the country.

Most of the Hawaiians were there ahead of us and already in great form. They knew the routine, and they were primed for it.

I was amazed to see that every girl in the place was absolutely gorgeous. There were mulatto girls, Asian girls, Peruvian girls, American girls. They were all exotically beautiful.

Pitty pointed toward the girls, then asked me, "Which one do you want?"

I felt a little uneasy. I was twenty-three at the time and not exactly naive when it came to sex, but I'd never seen anything like this before.

"Don't worry about the cost," Pitty said. "I'll take care of it."

I pointed to a Japanese girl and said, "She's nice."

Pitty smiled and rubbed his hands together. "Okay, come on."

He led me over to the girl, nodded, and she immediately took me to a back room. We had a couple of drinks and talked for a while. She waited until I was relaxed and comfortable before she initiated the sex. She was a real professional.

When I rejoined the others, Pitty asked me, "Did you enjoy yourself?" When I nodded, Pitty pointed toward the girls again and said, "Do you see another one you like?"

Mike at Redondo
Beach, 1952

Tiki Mike with the totem board at Malibu, 1955

Mary and Mike with
the sixty-four-ants
board at Malibu

Mike in the Messerschmidt, 1956

The yellow Cadillac hearse

*Phil Edwards,
early Sixties*

Ron Church

Johnnie Fain and Mickey Dora at Malibu

San Onofre in the early Sixties

Lifeguarding at Santa Monica

Marsha Bainer, 1964

Mike with the Trestle Special at Santa Monica, 1960

Kemp Aaberg and Mike at the start of the Catalina race, 1959

Sunset Beach, on the North Shore of Oahu, early Sixties

Ron Church

Ricky Grigg, early Sixties

Ron Church

Bud Browne, 1962

Pat Curren, 1963

Leroy Grannis

Bruce Brown at Malibu, 1963

The Calhouns: Robin, Marge, and Candy, at Makaha, 1962

Kemp Aaberg, Lance Carson, and Mike, 1963

Corky Carroll

Ron Church

Nancy Katin, 1969

Leroy Grannis

*Mike with Linda
Merrill at the
Peruvian
Invitational, 1965*

*Mickey Dora
accepting praise,
1966*

Leroy Grannis

Leroy Grannis

Don Hansen, 1963

The Hermes Street house, Leucadia

An ad for New Food

Mike and Jamie,
wedding day,
July 31, 1966

Bill Engler pouring wax bars, 1967

Rusty, Joey, and Mike planting mango trees on Kauai

Mike cutting back at Sunset, 1966

*The treehouse on
Hermes Street*

Mike, Rusty (on top of the packard), and J

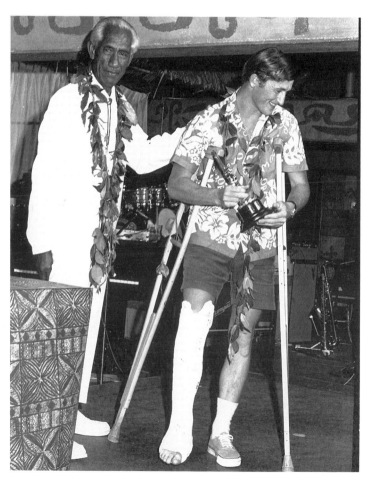

*Duke Kahanamoku
and Rusty Miller, 19*

Leroy Grannis

Mike on the winning wave at the 1969 Duke

Below: Ricky Grigg, Mike, and Fred Hemmings at the 1969 Duke. Mike is holding the first check ($1,000) ever awarded at a professional surf contest.

*Bill Engler with a lobster at
Punta María*

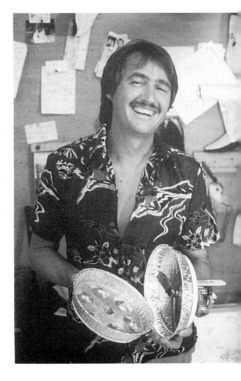

*Tom Morey with an early space
driver*

*Yvon Chouinard modeling a
Patagonia trenchcoat while
slapping lobsters with a spatula at
Punta María*

*John Robertson on
the single ski*

Mike and Diane, wedding day

Mike with the dory

Howard Benedict and Mike with an eighty-five-pound sea bass Howard speared off the coast of Cabo

I must have looked shocked, because Pitty laughed out loud. I'd been thinking this was a one-course meal—I didn't know it was a smorgasbord. But looking around, I began to notice that some of the older Peruvians disappeared with a different girl every few minutes. And when Pitty went into the back rooms, he took two girls at a time.

Sometime that night, I came to the realization that the Peruvians couldn't have cared less about the Peruvian International Surfing Contest. They just loved watching the rest of us go berserk in their country. They had already indulged themselves with every kind of pleasure imaginable, and the only new pleasure for them was watching us indulge ourselves. Officially they were our hosts, but actually we were there to entertain them.

That spring, 1965, I moved to San Diego to go to work for Don Hansen. His new surf shop was in a small building on the Coast Highway, just across the street from Cardiff Reef, one of the best surfing spots in San Diego's North County. That stretch of beach was practically deserted, except for one restaurant and one big, pink, two-story house with white trim. Along with L.J. Richards and a few others, I rented the pink house for $150 a month. It was just a funky board-and-batten beach house—so old the plumbing had been added onto the exterior walls—but upstairs there was a long panel of windows that looked out over the ocean and a long white sandy beach.

Every morning we would get up early and surf at Swami's, Cardiff Reef, or else the shore break right in front of our house, which we called the Proving Grounds. (To work for Hansen you had to "prove" yourself there first.) After surfing, I would walk across the street to Hansen's shop, where I would shape four or five of my signature-model boards. Don paid me twenty-five bucks a board, so I could make about $100 in just a few hours of work.

Also, I took the state's lifeguard test, passed it, and began working at Moonlight State Beach in Encinitas on the weekends. I also enrolled at San Diego State, where I planned to finish my degree in biology.

Later that spring, I got a letter from *Surfer* magazine inviting me to the awards banquet for its second annual Surfer Poll. The ballots for 1964 had come in from all around the world, and the results were going to be announced in June.

I drove up to Dana Point for the awards banquet and was surprised by how many people were there and what a lavish affair it was. Duke Kahanamoku, now in his seventies, had flown in from the islands, along with Fred Hemmings, who I figured would be the most likely winner, based on his performance in the contests that year.

After dinner they showed surf movies to get the crowd pumped up; then the master of ceremonies, Hevs McClellan, started going down the list of the ten finalists: Phil Edwards . . . Joey Cabell . . . Corky Carroll . . . until finally there were only two names left, Fred Hemmings and me.

"And now," Hevs said, "The most competitive and versatile surfer in the world today: Mike Doyle."

I was truly surprised and very emotional. I considered it a greater honor to be recognized by my fellow surfers than to win any surf contest in the world. To make the occasion even more memorable, the award was presented to me by Duke Kahanamoku, my boyhood idol and the man I considered to be the greatest surfer who ever lived.

On the Fourth of July, Tom Morey and his partner, Carl Pope, sponsored a nose-riding contest at Ventura Point that turned out to be what a lot of us thought was one of the best surf contests ever held. The concept was simple but innovative: Twenty-four surfers were invited, and each surfer put up a twenty-five-dollar entry fee to be used as part of the prize money. There were two divisions, regular and goofy foot. Each surfer would paint the front twenty-five percent of his surfboard red, and he would be awarded points based on the amount of time he stood in that area. The rider with the most nose time won his division.

The contest inspired some bizarre innovations, which is what Tom Morey wanted all along. Some people showed up with really long boards, so the front twenty-five percent was a huge area. Rusty Miller fiberglassed some bricks to the tail of his board, as a counterweight when he was standing on the nose. My board, which I called "the Stinger," was only eight feet long but with an additional eight-foot tail. Tom Morey disqualified it, saying it wasn't in good faith with the rules of the contest. But I didn't really care. I got to sit on the beach and watch the greatest nose-riding performances of all time.

Mickey Muñoz got a phenomenal ride of 9.9 seconds. Corky Carroll, a goofy footer, nearly matched him with 9.6 seconds. With their accumulated time, those two ended up winning their respective divisions and taking home cash prizes of $750 each.

Nose riding was only one element of surfing and, looking back on it now, maybe not a very important one. But at least we had a contest with some objective standards to judge it by.

When I first started surfing there was no such thing as surf trunks. We used to wear boxer shorts. We thought it was really cool to buy them about ten-inches too big in the waist so when we stood on the nose of the board, our shorts would fill up with air like big balloons. I don't know why we thought that was cool, but the point was we were making our own fashion statement. When I was a kid surfing at Malibu, my mother made my surf trunks out of awning canvas. They were nearly indestructible and way ahead of their time: purple and black, with diamonds down the side, or quarter panels in different colors. Other surfers were always asking me, "Where'd you get your trunks?"

Years later Steve Pezman, who was the publisher of *Surfer* magazine, told me, "You know, OP made millions of dollars selling surf trunks, and all they did was copy the trunks your mother made for you on her little treadle machine."

The first modern-style surf trunks I ever saw were made by a little Filipino who had a tailor shop at Waianae, south of Makaha. His name was M. Nii. The surfers at Makaha were always going in there to get their torn trunks mended, and this fellow realized there was a market for a better surf trunk. So he started making his own. In the island tradition of colorful silk shirts, he started experimenting around with bright and exotic colors, different panels in varying colors, a wax pocket in back, and surfer stripes down the sides.

Before long the M. Nii trunks became famous. Every surfer who went to Hawaii had to have a pair of M. Nii trunks, and more often than not, he had a whole list of orders for M. Nii trunks from his friends back home.

The first mass-manufactured surf trunk was made by Hang Ten, started by Duke Boyd, an advertising man who was one of the first to realize that the whole surf trend had marketing power. He advertised his first trunks in *Surfer* Magazine, and I was one of the models.

Hang Ten started out selling their clothes in the surf shops until they'd established an identity in the surf community; then they expanded to bigger clothing stores and, finally, to the major retailers. Hang Ten became a very big company by springboarding off the surfer image.

Of course, surfers were into anti-fashion, and as soon as Hang Ten become popular with non-surfers, surfers stopped wearing their trunks. But Hang Ten didn't care. They came out with matching tops and bottoms, which surfers wouldn't be caught dead in, and used their surfing image to market a whole line of clothes in the Midwest and the East.

After that, surf trunk manufacturers started popping up all over the place—Ocean Pacific (or OP), Surf Line Hawaii, Quiksilver, Gotcha, Instinct, Maui and Sons—and eventually dominated the casual clothing industry. You can go to any beach resort in the world now and see men in their seventies wearing baggy, neon-green surf trunks with bright floral patterns. Before surf trunks caught on, grown men wouldn't be seen in something like that. I've spent a lot of time wondering why people all over the world want to dress like surfers. Some sociologist could probably write a doctoral thesis on that subject. But I think the basic reason is pretty simple: Surfing is fun, and surfwear helps remind people of all ages that life is *supposed* to be fun.

But the surfing image wasn't always the path to riches. Some beachwear companies failed miserably at trying to capitalize on it, and for several years I worked for one of them.

Catalina Swimwear was an old, established company that had been into casual clothing for years. Their market had always been the older, East Coast, mom-and-pop crowd. They had what they called a cruise line, which was the kind of thing retired people would wear on a two-week cruise through the Caribbean. Catalina realized early on the potential that the surf trend had in the clothing industry, and they were determined to try to stay with the times, which meant designing for younger people.

Catalina got their foot in the door of the surf trend when they sponsored the Long Beach Surf Club at the Peruvian International. After that, Catalina started looking for a surfer to promote their swimwear, and they eventually chose me. Right away they started making Mike Doyle-model surf trunks. At first I had no say in the design process—I just wrote a little blurb for the hang tag and signed my name to it.

In the spring of 1965, after I'd moved to Cardiff, Catalina sent me on a promotional tour called "Make It with Catalina." They put me on a fat salary with an expense account and hired Bruce Brown, the maker of *Endless Summer*, to create a seven-minute promo film. I spent the next four months traveling through California, the Midwest, Texas, Florida, and the East Coast, bird-dogging for Catalina, going around to all the big department stores that carried the Catalina line. The deal was, if the local buyer gave Catalina a big order for beachwear, Catalina would throw in Mike Doyle and his seven-minute movie as a freebie. The more appearances I made, the more orders Catalina got. It was a good promotion— it really worked.

A lot of California surfers who did East Coast tours in the Sixties to promote surfboards or beachwear hated every minute of it. They hated being away from the beaches in California, and they hated having to smile and shake hands with people they didn't know or want to know. But for me, the Catalina promo tours were a lot of fun. I've always liked to travel, and on those tours I got to see a different town every two or three days. And every situation in every town was totally different.

In Atlanta, the Catalina rep happened to be a real swinger. Everybody who came to his town had to have a good time. He set me up with this woman who was about thirty. He had his own girl, too, and we all went to dinner way out in the country someplace where they served fried chicken, and black kids danced on the tables.

The next morning I was at some department store in downtown Atlanta, giving away autographed eight-by-ten glossies of myself and showing my seven-minute surf film. The parents walking by would grab the free photo and say, "Here, sign this for my kid. He loves surfing." They had no idea who I was or what surfing was about.

Three days later, in Miami, I was right in there with the Goldbergs, a husband-and-wife rep team. They took me home to meet their kids, I ate at their table, and slept in their back bedroom. We all went to the movies together, and I held their daughter's hand in the dark.

A few days later, I was in Cincinnati, where the local rep was a single guy, about twenty-four, driving a sharp El Camino. He didn't know Mike Doyle from Arnold Palmer. It was about eight in the morning, but behind the driver's seat he had a big ice chest full of beer; he handed me a cold one and said, "Hey, Doyle. . . . Is it Doyle? Today we're surfin' the Ohio!"

I laughed and said, "You gotta be kidding me!"

He downed his beer in two swallows, then crushed the can on the dashboard. "Nope, I got a forty-foot boat lined up. Macy's is puttin' up the money. We got a restaurant here in town to cover the food. Channel 8 and Channel 10 are both gonna be there. Surfing's a big deal in this town, Doyle!"

Next thing I knew, I was on the Ohio River, riding the wake behind a big yacht, smiling for the TV cameras, and doing my best to dodge things in the water that looked a lot like floating turds.

My next stop was New York City, where the young mayor, John Lindsay, had just seen Bruce Brown's *Endless Summer*, and was all stoked on surfing. As soon as I got to town, Lindsay arranged to meet me at Gilgo Beach, on Long Island. He flew in on a police helicopter and, in front of a big crowd, awarded me the key to the City of New York. It didn't look to me like it fit any real locks, but I figured if I got stopped by the cops, it might get me out of a ticket. Then Lindsay and I climbed in his helicopter, and we took a fifteen-minute flight around the mayor's kingdom while he pointed out the landmarks.

A couple of days later, when I hit Galveston, Texas, the taxi bringing me from the airport passed four huge billboards plastered with the message "World Famous Surfer Mike Doyle Is Coming to Galveston Beach!" As if that weren't enough, the local radio station repeated the same message every twenty minutes: "The famous big-wave rider Mike Doyle is coming to surf Galveston Beach! Be there to witness this once-in-a-lifetime demonstration!"

The local rep put me up at some glitzy, Las Vegas-type hotel with mirrors on the ceiling, red carpets, and gold doors. For the rest of the day I was treated like royalty, with a free haircut, manicure, and facial, and that night I was the guest of honor at a banquet for the town bigwigs.

The next morning, when I got out of bed, the beach in front of the hotel was lined as far as I could see in both directions with cars full of Texans waiting to see me surf. Looking out onto the Gulf of Mexico, I could see clear to the horizon, but the only waves were from a six-inch wind chop. I pulled on my flowery Catalina Big-Wave Riders, made with "Dependable Du Pont Nylon!" and the matching nylon wind shell, grabbed my surfboard, and made my way through the hotel lobby to the beach. I greeted the crowd with a wave, waxed up my board, and waded into the lukewarm water, which was the color of chocolate milk.

I walked 150 yards into the gulf, but the water was still only three or four feet deep. So I climbed on my board and paddled another 150 yards. Hundreds of people waded out with me. One of the local TV reporters, who was wearing slacks and a white shirt, slogged over beside me, leaned his elbows on the nose of my board, and said into his microphone, "For our viewers at home, this is the world-famous surfer Mike Doyle." He stuck his microphone a little closer to my face, then said, "Tell us, Mike, how do you like surfing here in Texas?"

"Well, the waves are a bit small today. But other than that, I'd say the surf conditions here are just about ideal."

After a few minutes, the wind chop picked up to maybe a foot, and I figured that was the closest thing to a real wave I was going to see. So I got up to my knees and started paddling. Just as I bent over, my Catalina Big-Wave Riders ripped out from the crotch, through the seat, clear on around to the waistband. As I rose to my feet on a cleanly shaped twelve-inch wave, with my bare ass hanging out, the cameras began clicking all around me, and the crowd parted to let the world-famous surfer pass.

As soon as I got back to Cardiff, I called up the president of Catalina, Chuck Trowbridge, and told him I didn't think Catalina's surf trunks were any good. I told him they were using cheap zippers and flimsy nylon, and the seams wouldn't hold up to the stress of knee paddling. I told him it was a lousy product that would rip out in the ass every time. And I tried to explain to him how their sense of design was killing them with surfers—that only kooks would wear matching trunks and shirts.

Trowbridge listened to me, then said, "That's interesting, Mike. Come on into the office, and let's talk."

So I went up to the City of Commerce, and Trowbridge called a meeting of the Catalina board of directors to hear what I had to say.

I told them everything I'd already told Trowbridge, then I said, "I know you can make a strong pair of surf trunks, because Nancy Katin is doing it right now."

Later on, Trowbridge drove down to see Nancy Katin. Not long before, Walt Katin had passed away and Nancy had been devastated. Nancy survived the loss of her husband because the young surfers who came to see her every day had become her children, her extended family. Anyway, when Chuck Trowbridge saw what Nancy Katin had done with her business, he liked it so much he offered to buy her out. And Nancy, perhaps thinking it was time for her to retire, agreed to sell Kanvas by Katin to Catalina.

I spent that summer and fall concentrating on school and lifeguarding on weekends at Moonlight Beach. But as soon as winter arrived, I was back in Hawaii competing in the Makaha International one last time.

The tandem event that year was interesting: There was some

confusion over what day the tandem event was to be held. The organizers changed the day at the last minute, and my tandem partner, Linda Merrill, who was in Honolulu, didn't know about it until they announced it on the radio. She jumped in her car and drove as fast as she could for Makaha. I waited for her as long as I could, but as the heat was about to begin, I still had no idea where she was. So I started looking around for an alternate partner. I found Margie Stevens, a local *haole* girl who weighed about 100 pounds. I asked her, "You wanna go tandem?"

She said, "Yeah!"

As we paddled out, Linda came running down the beach, but it was too late—the contest had already begun.

It was Margie's first time on a tandem board, yet she and I won the event. I felt bad for Linda, who had missed the event through no fault of her own, but it was also fun and exciting to win it the way Margie and I did. It was my third Makaha tandem title, something nobody else had ever done.

George Downing, a *haole* Hawaiian, won the men's event for his second time.

The biggest surf contest in Hawaii that winter wasn't the Makaha International, though. In fact, after that winter, the Makaha never again held the prominence it once had. This was the year of the first Duke Kahanamoku International.

I thought it was fitting that a surf contest be held in honor of the Duke. I'd always had a tremendous amount of respect, and even reverence, for him. When I was a boy, I'd seen pictures of him riding the old redwood boards at Waikiki. I'd read about how he'd been a three-time member of the U.S. Olympic team—even though he'd never had any formal swim training—and won two gold medals in the freestyle, one in 1912, and one again in 1924. He became a hero to all Americans and a legend in Hawaii. Back in the Twenties, when he was in Hollywood acting in movies, he introduced surfing to California and was among the first to surf at Malibu. I always saw in Duke Kahanamoku a living connection to surfing's history.

I met the Duke on several occasions. He was always a quiet gentleman, very congenial. He always stood very erect, always walked with dignity, and had a strong handshake. Sometimes at the awards ceremonies, he would get a little sleepy and start to nod out. His body had started to shrink a little, he was starting to get old, but he had that beautiful dark skin and gray hair, those beautiful Hawaiian features. He had lived a good life, and you could see it in his face.

In 1965, at the age of 74, the Duke was still a wonderful personality—a big, warm-hearted man who charmed people wherever he went. Though he still occasionally surfed, his health was in decline, and in spite of his worldwide fame, he had never really achieved the financial security he deserved.

The Duke had taken on a personal manager, Kimo Wilder McVay. McVay wasn't a surfer or much of an athlete. He chain-smoked cigarettes, and I remember his handshake as being cold and mushy. But McVay had a real talent for promotion. He bought the Duke a Rolls-Royce and mounted surfboard racks on top, so that everywhere the Duke went, he was recognizable, like a rolling advertisement for himself. Some people said McVay was using the Duke, but I don't think that was true. He was an unabashed hustler, but I think he wanted to see the Duke acquire, in his final years, the stature all Hawaiians knew he deserved.

Kimo McVay organized, sponsored, and promoted the first Duke Kahanamoku International. What we heard about it before-hand, most of us liked. Unlike the Makaha, it was to be held on the North Shore, at Sunset. The judges would be different, too. Some of them would be the *haoles* who had pioneered big-wave riding on the North Shore. A lot of them had married local Hawaiian girls, had settled in Hawaii, and were now Hawaiian *haoles*. So we knew a *haole* at least had a chance to win the thing.

But most important of all, the judging system itself would be different. Instead of just the longest ride, like at Makaha, it would be based on the biggest wave, the longest ride, and the most critical positioning—meaning way back in the wave, close to the curl. The judging system would be much more relevant to the modern style of surfing.

The first Duke was held in twelve-foot surf, and a CBS camera crew with a helicopter was there covering the contest from the air.

The excitement level was so high, all the surfers tried to give the best performance they could. When it was over, Jeff Hakman, a seventeen-year-old Californian who now lived in Hawaii, had won it. Hakman was only about five-foot-two and 120 pounds; but he was strong, gutsy, and he surfed very aggressively.

A lot of people said later it had been the greatest exhibition of surfing they'd ever seen, and the TV program itself was nominated for an Emmy. The Duke Kahanamoku International immediately became the most prestigious contest in big-wave surfing, the highlight of the surfing season and, in a way, the world championship of surfing.

That spring I did the Catalina East Coast promo tour again. They paid me about $100 per day, which was good money then. I lived on my expense account, so when I got home I had about $6,000 in my pocket—more than enough to pay my expenses to surf in Hawaii the next winter.

After I got back from the Catalina tour, I talked to Chuck Trowbridge again and explained how I thought Catalina could improve their line of swimwear to appeal more to young people. He seemed interested in my comments, and that summer he hired me to help Catalina design their swimwear. Two days a week I got on the Amtrak and rode up to the City of Commerce. Meanwhile, I kept shaping surfboards for Don Hansen and lifeguarding at Moonlight Beach on the weekends.

Though I enjoyed the challenge and the creativity of working for Catalina, I found out right away how frustrating it could be. One day I went in to see Catalina's pattern maker. I took along a pair of M. Nii surf trunks because I wanted him to see how well they fit. The M. Niis were patterned after what's called a "young man's fit," meaning the front of the waistband is about an inch and a half lower than the back, like a pair of jeans. But the pattern maker was sort of an Old World tailor who had been doing the same gentleman's cut for so long he couldn't change. I'm sure he understood what I was talking about, he just wasn't willing to consider doing things any differently. Swimwear *had* to have a waistband like a pair of baggy trousers. It was my first lesson in corporate paralysis.

I didn't like the idea of surf trunks made of nylon, which was what Catalina was using at the time. Nylon might have looked like a space-age fabric, but surfers knew it felt awful in the water. So I found some great industrial-grade canvas. It was made of 100 percent cotton, had a nice texture, and felt comfortable wet. Best of all, it was so strong you could make a pair of surf trunks that would last forever.

When I showed the fabric to Chuck Trowbridge, his response was, "How much does it cost?"

"Forty cents a yard."

"We don't buy that cheap," he said. "We usually spend four times that much."

"But if it's better quality, why not buy cheaper?"

"We just don't do things that way."

That was my second lesson in corporate paralysis.

I had more success getting Catalina to beef up their stitching. But I had no luck trying to explain why surfers would never buy matching trunks and nylon jackets. I wrote a twenty-page analysis of where the youth movement was going and how that would affect the clothing market, how young people were wearing natural fibers because cotton looked and felt real, while nylon had something phony about it.

Trowbridge told me, "But, Mike, our matching nylon trunks and jackets are selling in the Midwest."

"But surfers are just a little bit ahead of them," I said. "Believe me, the Midwest is going to like cotton trunks, too."

"Uh-huh. . . . Well, thank you, Mike. We'll talk it over, and let you know what we think."

By this time I'd begun to see that Catalina didn't really want me involved in the design of their swimwear. What they wanted was to be able to *say* they had a real surfer involved in their design. It was just a marketing angle. The problem was that I really *did* become involved. I got interested in the fabrics and the design process and the quality control and the marketing—I craved the creativity. And I felt an obligation to help deliver an honest product to the surf community.

After several months of work, I went before the Catalina

review panel to show them the line I'd designed. They were all sitting there smoking cigars. Chuck Trowbridge said, "What have you got for us, Mike?"

I showed them how I'd changed the cut on the trunks for a younger man. I showed them how I'd double-stitched the seat and used overlocking stitching in the crotch. I showed them how I'd switched from nylon to cotton.

They all gave me a screwy look, then Chuck said, "Gee, Mike. It looks a little wild."

I took a deep breath and began pleading my case. "Surfers are open to new ideas," I said. "They don't care what middle-aged men in New York or Miami are wearing. They're going their own way."

Then Chuck Trowbridge spoke the words that ended my corporate career. "Mike," he said, "there's something you have to understand. We aren't really selling to surfers. That's not our market. What we're doing is selling the surfer image."

I knew then it was hopeless. Not only did they fail to understand what I was trying to tell them, that the surf market would lead them to the future of their industry, but they were using my name to promote an inferior product. I said, "Well, you've got the wrong guy then, because all this time I've been trying to design a real product for real surfers."

And I walked away.

A lot of people in the surf industry thought I was a fool for leaving Catalina. It was a pretty sweet job for a young man just twenty-four years old, and if I'd milked it for ten years or so, I might have become fairly wealthy. I liked the money, all right—it bought me a lot of freedom—but I found the corporate environment to be stifling. I didn't like being used as a glitter boy to sell their product, and I didn't like having my creativity choked back. When I left Catalina, a pattern began in my life: Given a choice between money and freedom, I'll always take the freedom.

Catalina swimwear, which had been a giant in the industry, went out of business eventually. When authentic surfwear companies started popping up out of garages all over Southern California, pushing tough, creative, innovative beachwear, Catalina got eaten alive.

Back at the time when Catalina bought out Kanvas by Katin, I considered that deal to be a good thing. It gave Nancy Katin a good retirement after years of hard work, and it helped the Catalina label, too, by associating it with a quality product. Eventually, though, I realized that Catalina wanted the Katin name for the same reason they wanted my name: as a marketing gimmick. Right away they started making junky trunks and putting the Kanvas by Katin label on them. To surfers everywhere, Katin had meant quality, and almost overnight Catalina trashed the Katin name.

Nancy Katin was heartbroken when she realized what had happened. Her husband was gone, her business was gone, the kids who had come to her from the beach were gone. Even her name was gone. She had nothing left. But that gutsy little woman surprised us all. She paid Catalina double what they'd paid her, just to get her name back. Then she went back to making quality trunks. Before long the kids started coming back, she had her extended family again, and she was happy.

A lot of surfers in those days were beginning to get interested in skiing. We saw that surfing and skiing had a lot in common, not only in the physical mechanics, but in the way they used gravity and the elements of nature for fun and self-expression. Surfers began to talk a lot about the "surf/ski synthesis." I didn't know anything about skiing, mountains, or the snow, but I decided I wanted to learn. So I started taking trips to Mammoth Lakes, in the eastern Sierra Nevada.

One day while I was on the ski slopes at Mammoth, I happened to see a beautiful young woman, a ski instructor, teaching kids how to ski. She had long, curly, golden-blonde hair (her hair looked like it weighed ten pounds), a lovely cherub face, and a striking figure. I found out she was from Palos Verdes and her name was Jamie Robertson. I arranged an introduction, she seemed as attracted to me as I was to her, and we became very close, very fast.

Jamie was a tomboy who had grown up to be a very curvaceous woman. Somehow, though, she had never become comfortable with that. When she was thirteen she got kicked off the school softball team because she was a girl—a real trauma for her. She was very buxom and tended to be self-conscious about her body. At first she wouldn't surf because of that, so I designed a swimsuit that made her feel more comfortable in the water, and together we had a lot of fun.

Jamie's mother was involved in politics in San Diego County. Before Jamie and I met, her mother had married a man named Pete Wilson, who at that time was a state assemblyman. Pete Wilson was a thin, neatly dressed man with a lot of self-confidence and a lot of ambition, even in those days. I was impressed by his speaking ability, and I used to say he was going to become president of the United States. Later, of course, he became the mayor of San Diego, a U. S. senator, and the governor of California.

I was twenty-four at the time, and Jamie was just eighteen. Looking back on it now, I can see that we didn't really get along that well, but there was an intensity to our relationship that was irresistible. On July 31, 1966, a few hours after I'd competed in a surfing contest in Redondo Beach, Jamie and I were married in Palos Verdes.

That fall, from September 26 through October 2, the third World Surfing Championships were held in San Diego, at Ocean Beach. It was the biggest surf contest ever held on the mainland, with 80,000 spectators. More important, though, it was the first time the U.S. media covered surfing as a serious sport, rather than just a wacky California fad.

That world contest shook up California surfing. At the time we were all riding ten-foot surfboards with trash-can noses, and we were still into an old-fashioned style of surfing where you stomp on the tail to kick the nose up, let the wave build-up go in front of you, then you either run forward and crouch down inside the tube, or else you stand on the nose and arch back in a kind of pose. We had all these stock poses we did over and over—el Spontanéo, Quasimodo, Nose Tweaking, Bell Ringing. They had originated back in the goofy Malibu days and had been a lot of fun over the years. But they had also stifled the creation of new styles. It was time to move on to other things.

The real agent of change that year was Nat Young, who came

over from Australia with an old, beat-up, nine-foot log that looked like hell. But it was shaped like one of the old pig boards—a shape that had mostly been forgotten.

I should back up a few years: The pig board had gotten started by accident at Dale Velzy's shop in Venice back in the Fifties. In those days, all the boards were wide in the front and narrow in the back. The guy who glassed Velzy's boards accidentally glassed the fin on the wide end and left a narrow nose. But Velzy, to his great credit, was always open to new ideas. When he saw what had happened, he just laughed and said, "Ah, hell, don't knock it off, let's try it in the water and see what happens." The first time they put it in the water, they were amazed to find that it turned wonderfully, with all the width in back as a planing surface where the rider's weight is, and the narrow nose to trim in close to the wave. In a very short time, that became the hottest new shape in surfboards—a wide tail and a narrow nose—and became known as a pig board.

But over the years, with all the experimentation that had taken place in surfboard design, (and mostly because the nose-riding style of surfing required a wide nose) the pig board concept had been forgotten.

Then Nat Young, with his born-again pig board, made a quantum leap in style. Instead of nose-riding like the rest of us, Nat was making lines and patterns on the faces of the waves. And that board of his, which looked like a piece of junk to us, was really pretty sophisticated. Besides being small (nine-foot was small to us then), it had a continuous-curve outline and continuous-curve rocker. While we were riding long, straight, cigar boards, Nat's board was much more suitable for doing cutbacks and what I call S-turn surfing.

At the world contest that year, Nat gave us all a lesson in the future of surfing. While we would cut back or stomp on the tail to stall, Nat would cut back by compressing his body and pushing out with his legs, driving to get more power off his fin. He came out of a turn with more power than when he went into it, which allowed him to keep the board moving all the time, cutting a much bigger pattern in the water. He would accelerate way out into the flat of the wave, cut way back into the curl, then drive way out in front again. The waves at Ocean Beach were small and mushy, but Nat was still carving all over them.

It was the first time most of us had seen anything like Nat's style, and it set him so far apart from the rest of us and impressed the judges so much, it was impossible for him not to win the contest.

It was the first time a world championship had been won by a surfer from a country other than the host nation.

And by the way, all modern surfboards today follow the pig-board concept—wide in the tail and narrow in the nose.

After the world contest, Jamie and I settled into a nice house on a hillside in Del Mar. Money wasn't a problem—we had everything we needed. Actually, we had more than we needed, which made me feel uncomfortable. I was beginning to see how the pursuit of wealth and the accumulation of possessions could weigh you down. Like a lot of other people in the Sixties, I was starting to think about finding a simpler lifestyle.

This was a major turning point in my life. I could have kept going the corporate route, working for some company like Catalina, doing marketing and promotional work. I might have done very well at that, and today I would be entrenched in some fortress-like mansion in Del Mar, with a huge mortgage, high blood pressure, and a job I hated. But I didn't want to be a high roller in Del Mar. I wanted to own my own little house free and clear, grow as much of my food as I could, surf whenever the waves were good, have fun with my friends, and be as free as I could be in a world where freedom was rare.

I heard about a small house up the road a couple of miles in Leucadia that was going to be auctioned off at an estate sale. I stopped by and looked at the house, which was on Hermes Street. It was a clapboard shack, only 700 square feet. The glass in all the windows had been broken out, and the place was badly run down. But it was on three-quarters of an acre, in a section of Leucadia that had deep, black soil that was perfect for an organic garden. There were some large fruit trees on the property, as well as some great shade trees. Best of all, the house was only a couple blocks from a

145

good surf spot at Beacons, and about a mile from a great surf spot at Swami's.

I loved the place. I thought it was perfect. But when I took Jamie by the house, she wouldn't even get out of the car.

I could understand her point of view, in a way. Leucadia is a high-priced neighborhood today, filled with professionals commuting to San Diego, but at that time it was rural funk—nothing but avocado orchards and nursery workers. To Jamie it must have looked like things were really going downhill for us. Her husband, whose prospects had looked pretty good when she'd married him, wanted to live in some trashy shack and grow tomatoes.

I went to the auction in San Diego, bid $7500 on the Hermes house, and got it. That was the turning point in our marriage. From then on, it was constant fighting and arguing.

Actually, our marriage had been a disaster from the start. I never had an affair during our marriage—I was faithful to Jamie—but while I was busy working, Jamie had all the free time in the world. She didn't work, and she wasn't going to school. I think she was kind of intimidated by my success. At any rate, she wasn't happy and we fought a lot.

Before we even moved into the Hermes house, I could see that the end of our marriage was inevitable. One day, in a fit of anger and frustration, I took everything I owned—furniture, books, old surfing trophies—and threw it all over the bluff behind our house in Del Mar. The peace that came over me after that was amazing.

My friends John Baker and Rusty Miller drove around to the bottom of the bluff, backed up their cars, and started hauling off all my things to their house. They couldn't believe their good fortune—it was like finding a swap meet where everything was free.

Later my mother went down and gathered up all my old surfing trophies, dusted them off, wrapped them in Saran wrap, put them in boxes, and stored them in her garage.

I moved into the Hermes house by myself, grew a beard, planted a garden, and went to work fixing up my new home.

One day I was working at Hansen's shop in Cardiff, when a guy named Hoyle Sweitzer stopped in to see us, carrying a big tandem board. I recognized the tandem board because I'd shaped it. It was twelve feet long and twenty-eight inches wide. But he had a flimsy sail mounted on a collapsible mast in the middle of the board—I'd never seen anything like that before. Hoyle didn't know what to call the thing. It was a big, awkward-looking monster, and he wasn't even sure what to do with it. He wanted our opinion— would Don and I like to invest in his idea and help him develop it?

Hoyle left his board with us, and I thought about taking it out in one of the lagoons and giving it a try. But I was a surfer, not a sailor. And besides, I couldn't see how an idea like that could possibly work.

About a week later, Hoyle called the shop. "What did you think of it?" he asked.

"Oh," I said, "I don't think we're interested."

Later Hoyle found his investors, designed a molded polypropylene board, and improved the mast pivot and sail. Eventually it became the first sailboard.

About this same time, a guy named Jim Jenks started working for Don Hansen. He'd been the manager of an auto parts store for a long time, so he had good practical experience running a business, and he soon became Hansen's right-hand man. He did all the ordering for the shop, organized the sales force, and kept things going smoothly.

Jenks started talking about organizing a company and making beachwear, following the same trend as Hang Ten. When Hansen heard about that, he was afraid he would lose Jenks, who he'd come to rely upon, so he said to Jenks, "If you're going to start a beachwear company, why don't you do it right here in this office? I'll help you with it. Let's do it together."

So that's what Jenks did. Hansen got his old partner, Bob Driver, to throw in some start-up money, Don threw in some money, they found a fourth partner, and together they started a little beachwear company called Ocean Pacific, or OP.

OP started out making just a corduroy walk short and sold it to the surf shops. Before long they expanded their line and moved their offices out of Hansen's shop to a factory in Oceanside. It

wasn't very many more years before OP became the most successful beachwear company of its era, worth hundreds of millions of
dollars.

In Hawaii, 1966 was the year of the comeback, beginning with
Joey Cabell. After a phenomenal start in his surfing career, Joey
had left Hawaii and moved to Aspen, Colorado. There he'd teamed
up with Buzzy Bent (not Buzzy Trent), a surfer from La Jolla who
had been in an underwater demolition team in the navy, and with
something like $800 between them, they'd opened a restaurant
called The Chart House. It was modeled after Mike's, in Hawaii, a
place where you could cook your own steak and serve yourself at
a salad bar. Joey had a notion that a place like that would work in
Aspen, and it did. But Joey had moved back to the islands that
winter to concentrate on surfing again. He was determined to make
a comeback, and he pursued his training with an intensity of
concentration that only Joey was capable of. And it paid off for him.
In the Makaha, which everyone realized had lost much of its luster,
Joey Cabell took the first-place trophy.

In the second annual Duke, Ricky Grigg, who was in graduate
school at the Scripps Institution of Oceanography in La Jolla and
hadn't surfed on the North Shore for two years, surprised a lot of
people by taking first place. In some ways, though, his win wasn't
so surprising. The surf was big during the contest, about twenty
feet, and there weren't many surfers in the world who'd had as much
experience riding big Sunset as Ricky.

I had an acceptable winter: I managed third place at the
Makaha and second place at the Duke. But for my buddy Rusty
Miller, the Duke that year was a disaster. He took a terrible wipeout
on a huge outside wave, hit the bottom hard, and broke his leg. A
lot of people said it was one of the most horrible wipeouts they'd
ever seen.

I didn't make it to the Peruvian International that winter, so I
only heard about it. While training in Peru for the contest, Corky
Carroll came down with a terrible case of dysentery. It was so bad,
he'd gone into convulsions and was taken to the hospital, where he

was in critical condition for two days. (Mickey Dora, who'd never gotten along that well with Corky, visited him in the hospital. Dora was embarrassed later when people found out—he didn't want people to think he'd turned soft.) The day of the contest, Corky pulled the I.V. tubes out of his arm, staggered out of the hospital, and somehow made it to the Club Waikiki. He was so weak and dizzy, he could hardly carry his board, but once he was in the water he was able to paddle out. He only caught eight waves, but his performance was good enough to win it. Like I said, Corky Carroll was one of the toughest competitors surfing has ever seen.

After my frustrating experience with Catalina Swimwear, I was soured on the idea of working for another big company, but I started thinking I'd like to try my hand at running my own company. Two of my old buddies, Rusty Miller and Garth Murphy, had been thinking about doing the same thing, so back in Leucadia that spring, we decided to join forces and start a company together.

Rusty had changed a lot since his tweed jacket days, when he was studying to be a professor of history. He was still a bit of an intellectual, but more of a rebellious intellectual. He had traveled all around the world as an assistant instructor of the College of the Seven Seas, which was as much a floating party as it was a college. Rusty knew a lot about history and was more politically astute than any of us, which tended to make him a bit cynical at times. And of course he was still a fantastic waterman and a world-class surfer. Hamm's Beer put out a great billboard of Rusty taking a huge drop at Sunset, down in a crouch with his arms out and with a monstrous wave curling up behind him. It was one of the most beautiful surf photos I've ever seen.

Garth Murphy, who had lived with me in the Butterfly Lane house when I was going to school in Santa Barbara, had grown up in Hawaii and La Jolla, where his father was a marine biologist. Garth was an excellent surfer and for the past couple of years had been working for Don Hansen doing East Coast promo tours.

Rusty, Garth, and I hired our friend Bill Engler as our first employee. Bill had grown up in La Jolla, where he'd been a high school football star. We called him "Biceps Bill" because he had huge arms and was extremely fit. He was blond and had deep-set eyes that were a bit crooked in spite of an operation to correct the muscle problem. Because he had those deep-set eyes and because he was sometimes very quiet, people who didn't know him thought he looked mean. But he was really a very gentle soul, extremely trustworthy—the kind of friend you could always count on.

Just across the highway from Hansen's shop, we started what we called Surf Research, and our first product was a surfboard wax. Until then surfers had just used paraffin—the kind little old ladies used to seal their jelly jars. But paraffin didn't always work that well on surfboards. If the water was too cold, it was just like rubbing a rock on your board, and if the water was too warm, it came right off. Steve Knorr, who was a third-generation candle maker, helped us formulate a custom surfboard wax. We fooled around with different formulations—soft waxes for cold water and harder waxes for warm, adding different elements that made the wax sticky. We

added purple coloring and a scent to the wax, and just for the hell of it, we put a fortune in each bar.

After our wax proved to be popular and profitable, we started making surf trunks out of a stretchy, lightweight, quick-drying net material—like what Speedo swim trunks are made of. I'd recommended that material to Catalina as a kind of sexy surf trunk, but when it got wet the net material showed a bulge in the crotch, which greatly offended the Catalina approval committee. Surfers loved it, though. When you were in the water, it felt like you were naked. Our surf trunks were a big success from the day we put them on the market. We were making them by the hundreds, in purple only, and shipping them all over the country.

My little house on Hermes became the center for activity, and at one time or another, all my business partners and dozens of other people lived there. We were vegetarians, living mostly on brown rice and veggies. In North County you can grow some kind of produce in every season, so along with the fruit trees in the yard, we grew tons of organic fruits and vegetables. Everybody helped with the gardening. The house had a small kitchen, but we shared the cooking chores. We decorated the house with driftwood, hand-woven alpaca rugs, and secondhand furniture, including a big overstuffed couch and two great old rocking chairs. We made a fireplace from a fifty-gallon drum.

I really loved that house. Not only was it the most relaxing, soulful place I've ever lived, but it gave us the freedom and the security to experiment with new lifestyles. Today it makes me feel good to see young surfers coming up with goofy clothing styles and new ways of talking, making weird music and new toys, because they remind me of my own youth and all the fun we had at the Hermes house.

I was still keeping a very strict training regimen. I would get up early in the morning, do an hour of yoga, then go surfing at Swami's. For cross training, I would sometimes go jogging. One morning while I was jogging down the Coast Highway, a sheriff's deputy started following me. After a mile or so, he pulled up alongside and ordered me to stop. He got out of his car, sidled over to me with a suspicious look on his face, then said, "What are you running from, son?"

"Nothing," I said, "I'm just taking a workout."

He looked at me like I was crazy—he'd never seen anybody jogging before. Nowadays, of course, North County is like one big fitness class, with people in multicolored outfits jogging, biking, and power-walking everywhere.

At Surf Research we used to make all our own advertisements for the surf magazines. They were simple and crude, but they were always fun and creative, and they usually brought a good response. For one of our ads in *Surfer*, we ran a picture of me with a T-shirt pulled over my head—like an Egyptian pharaoh's hood—blowing smoke over a bar of our surf wax. I don't even know what it was supposed to mean, some goofy, mystical notion we had.

Not long after that ad appeared, Bill Engler was making wax bars in the back yard under a big mulberry tree, pouring the hot wax into the molds. While he was working, mulberry leaves kept falling into the molds. Bill didn't let that slow him down, though—he had to get to Swami's while the surf was still glassy.

Later that spring when I flew back to Florida on a promo tour for Hansen Surfboards, I took along some of our wax, thinking I would give out free samples to the surf shops. But apparently some redneck surf shop owner in south Florida had seen the ad of me blowing smoke over the wax, and when the bars arrived at his shop, he'd seen Bill's leaves embedded in them. He was sure we were putting marijuana leaves in the wax so kids could scrape it out and smoke it. He informed the police that I was smuggling marijuana, and on his tip I was stopped at the airport in Miami.

The police were convinced I was from some California-Egyptian marijuana surf cult. When I finally figured out what they were talking about, I started laughing so hard I couldn't answer their questions. So one of the cops whipped out a bar of our purple surf wax, pointed to the leaves, and said, "What's this?"

"It looks like mulberry leaves," I said.

The cop gave me a long, cynical stare, then said, "Well, we're going to have it tested in our crime lab, and we'll let you know how it comes out. Now get outa here."

I never heard from them again.

I spent the next few weeks touring the East Coast again, from Florida up to Maine and back. The East Coast at that time followed the West Coast in surf fashion. They weren't making their own surfboards, and they weren't making surf clothes. There was surf madness on the East Coast, and I was back there riding that wave, stoking the local surf shops, surfing with the guys, partying with them, doing whatever it took to get them excited about Hansen Surfboards. Of course I'd leave and two weeks later the Dewey Weber crew would come in and get them all excited about Dewey Weber surfboards. (By this time, Dewey Weber had become hugely successful as a surfboard manufacturer, and people were calling him "the first millionaire of surfing.")

When Joey Cabell's Chart House in Aspen turned out to be a success, he and his partners opened up a second Chart House in Newport Beach and a third one at Shelter Island in San Diego. But in spite of his success, or maybe you could say because of it, Joey moved back to the islands again, this time to Kauai. All the action

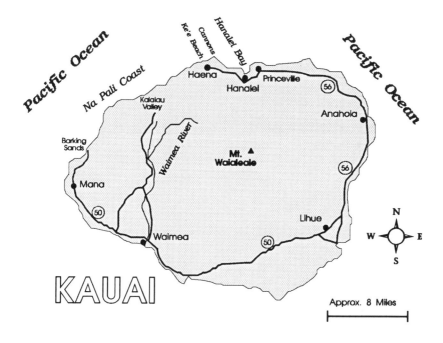

KAUAI

Approx. 8 Miles

was on the North Shore of Oahu, but Joey had grown up on Oahu and had seen the incredible changes it had gone through. Kauai, on the other hand, was still kind of a lonely outpost in those days. Kauai was the last island in the chain, and the most untouched. Joey bought himself five acres near Princeville, $40,000 worth of clear redwood, and built a simple country house with a tin roof.

Over the years, Joey, Rusty Miller, and I had become close friends. When Joey moved to Kauai, he invited Rusty and me to spend some time with him getting ready for the Makaha and the Duke. Rusty and I thought that sounded like fun, so we arranged for Garth to look after our business, and we took Joey up on his offer.

When it was time to head to Joey's place, in the fall of 1967, I had just spent three months touring the East Coast for Hansen Surfboards. I had some money in my pocket, but I hadn't surfed any real waves in weeks. It was hard to stay in shape on the promo tours. The schedule just didn't allow time for much of a workout. Plus, a lot of the job was going out to dinner with people. Normally, I was a vegetarian, but in those days it was hard to eat in restaurants if you were a vegetarian. So with the change of diet and the lack of exercise, I was starting to gain weight and feel out of shape.

From the East Coast I flew straight to Kauai, where I'd never been before. Rusty picked me up at the airport, and I could see just by looking at him he was already in great shape. "Hey, br'ah, how was your trip?" he said. "Today we're gonna surf the most incredible place you've ever seen."

Rusty tossed my bags in Joey's car, and we drove straight to a place called Cannons. The surf there was breaking ten feet, in an incredible tube, right on the rocks. It was the most dangerous place to surf I could imagine.

Joey was already there, too. He was in great shape, as usual, and had a devilish twinkle in his eyes, like he was operating on a different level. Joey was always naturally wired anyway, but this look he had now was more than that. To surf at the highest level, on the fastest waves, you have to be in a state of mind that isn't quite normal. You have to be quick, relaxed, and spontaneous to be able to interact with the wave in a creative way, like jazz musicians jamming. This was a time when a lot of young people were experimenting with marijuana and other drugs, but our experience had been that drugs didn't improve your surfing ability, they hindered it by tangling your thoughts up and slowing down your reaction time. We believed there were natural ways to get high, to clear our minds and to tap into a higher energy level without using drugs. The best way, we found, was to go on long juice and fruit diets. We used to call that "papaya consciousness," because when we were really wired we lived mostly on papayas. All I had to do was look at Joey and I could see he was already there, tapped into that pure energy, balancing on a fine line between exhilaration and disaster.

"Come on, br'ah," he said. "Let's get to it!"

There had always been a lot of love between Rusty, Joey, and me. They were stoked I was there, and they really thought they were turning me on to their favorite surf spot. But I wasn't ready for it at all. When I tried to pull on my old pair of surf trunks, I found I had gained so much weight I couldn't even get them up. Rusty handed me a pair of bigger trunks, and I was out of excuses.

As I paddled out at Cannons, I watched Joey take off on a wave—I was shocked! I'd been surfing little dribblers in Florida, and now all of a sudden I was looking at Joey down the tube of a ten-foot grinder breaking right on a reef. As he whistled by me, the wave sucked out and exposed the bare rocks. I could see the whites of Joey's eyes and his big happy smile.

Just as I reached the line-up, Rusty took off on the next wave—and WHAM!—he dropped right in there and was down the line before I even knew where he went.

Then I was sitting all alone.

I paddled for the next wave, but my consciousness was so far from being ready for it, the wave just gobbled me up. I caved in at the knees, got sucked over the reef and into the flat. Amazingly, I didn't get cut up. I dragged myself up to the beach and found my board. I said to myself, I gotta get in shape if I'm gonna hang with these lunatics.

I sat on the beach for a while, studying the line-up, mapping out the reef in my mind, watching Joey and Rusty, trying to bring my reflexes up to speed with theirs. I got back on my board and paddled out, but I just couldn't focus on surfing. I sat there bobbing up and down while the waves passed me by. Finally, I paddled back to shore and lay there in the sand, trying to understand what the problem was.

The East Coast promo tour had left me exhausted, both mentally and physically. I had started to really dislike all the schmoozing, all the dining out with the local businessmen. Even though it paid my bills, it seemed like such a waste of time and so superficial. I wanted a simpler life. I wanted to surf with my friends, work in my garden, and make things with my hands. I didn't care anymore about the money!

As I sat there in the sand, I stared at my hands. I was wearing a spun-gold ring with three little emeralds in it—a little bauble I'd picked up on the East Coast. It was the kind of thing people wear to impress people they don't know. It represented everything I didn't like about my life, a direction I might have taken at one time but now made me sick to my stomach. The ring was just a piece of phony crap that was a barrier between me and my water brothers.

I jerked the ring off my finger and threw it in the ocean.

When I paddled out the third time, I knew I was at least mentally prepared.

I made the next wave, barely, and rode it all the way to the beach. Rusty and Joey went berserk, screaming and hollering because their friend was in there again. I was with them.

Back at Joey's house, I found that Joey had a new girlfriend. Her name was Gail, she was about 5-foot-10, blonde, strong and healthy, feminine and flirty. I liked Gail right away. She was easy to talk to and could be very funny when she wanted to be.

Every morning at Joey's, we did a seven o'clock surf check. If the waves were any good, we'd surf three or four hours, then come back to the house and work in Joey's garden.

Joey had the energy to make every day special. He never quit moving, and he never ran out of ideas. I think that's why Joey was so successful with the Chart House. He would be up at four in the morning, drawing up plans, calling people on the phone, making things happen. Joey always did everything to the best of his ability. He wasn't necessarily brighter or more talented than anyone else, and he wasn't a complicated person, but he had such intense focus that he captured people who didn't have it.

The other side of Joey was that he had a limited ability to communicate with people. He had tunnel vision. Everything you said to him, he would repeat back the way he wanted to hear it.

Joey wasn't a loner, though. He liked to have playmates along on his adventures, it was just that he ran out of playmates real quick. Joey always played hard, and there just weren't very many people who were willing to risk as much as he was, all the time, every day. When Joey was on that high-energy level, that papaya consciousness, hardly anybody could keep up with him. Rusty and I were about the only ones who would even try.

A few weeks later, Joey, Rusty, and I went on a five-day fast, living on nothing but fresh coconut and papaya juice. While we were sitting around Joey's house listening to music, Joey had an amazing idea. He had maps of the islands pinned all over his walls, and he'd been lying on the floor looking up at them. All of a sudden he said, "Let's swim around Kauai."

Rusty and I looked at each other. "You mean *all* the way around?"

"Why not?" Joey said. "I think it can be done."

It sounded to me like another one of Joey's ingenious schemes for dying young. And Rusty, who was usually one of Joey's prime playmates, wouldn't have anything to do with the idea. I said, "I don't know, Joey."

But Joey wouldn't give up on the idea—he just sat on it for a while. A couple of days later, he said, "Okay, then, let's just swim the Na Pali Coast."

I looked at one of Joey's maps and saw that the Na Pali coast was about twenty miles of the most rugged and pristine coastline on Kauai. Sometimes people hiked above the coast on the Kalalau Trail, and some of the beaches could be reached by boat if you swam the last mile or so, but most of the coast was totally inaccessible.

It didn't sound that great to me. Oh, it sounded exciting in a way, but I knew it would be very dangerous. But what could I do? I was Joey's guest. I couldn't say, "I'll be right here. See you when you get back in a week."

"It's the wrong season," I said. "The water's too rough. We'd have to do it in the summer when there aren't any waves."

I thought that would put an end to it, but to my surprise Joey just nodded and said, "How about July?"

In spite of my concern, over the next few weeks Joey's idea started to intrigue me. Without even knowing it exactly, I started to wonder how you might go about a swim like that. One day, I asked Joey, "What would we take?"

Joey had already thought it out. "We'll keep it real simple. Just take swim trunks and goggles. No food, no tools."

"Swim fins," I said.

But Joey shook his head. "No, if you do that your legs will get tired. It's better to just use your natural body."

Of course, Joey was right. The human body is designed for

land or water. If you modify the way your legs naturally move in the water, you throw everything out of balance and end up with leg cramps or some other problem.

Still, I didn't commit myself to Joey's plan.

The greatest day I've ever had surfing was later that winter at Hanalei Bay, near Princeville, on the north shore of Kauai. Up to about twelve feet, Hanalei Bay was like a long Malibu-type wave and was one of our favorite places to surf. But on this particular day, after a big storm, it was breaking twenty-five to thirty feet.

Joey and I stood on the pier watching huge, extremely fast barrels steaming through the bay, spitting water out in front of them. It looked like a huge Banzai Pipeline, not the way Hanalei Bay usually breaks at all, and we figured the waves were unmakeable.

We went up on the hill above Princeville, where we had a better view. From there we could see the swell breaking on a reef two or three miles out, where it usually didn't break, and then it would back off again before it reached the inside reef. That gave us an indicator of when a big set was coming. We could also see that a current was pulling across the point at about ten knots and drawing into the faces of the waves, which caused those huge, hollow barrels.

There were maybe thirty surfers on the cliffs watching all this. Nobody had ever seen Hanalei Bay breaking like that, and nobody would go out. Finally Joey and I grew impatient. We looked at each other and said, "Let's try it."

Joey was riding the board he'd used to win the Duke the winter before. He called it the White Ghost. It was a big, thick board—five inches thick—with hard-down rails and the first flat bottom I'd ever seen. It was so fast, it was hard to control—it wanted to spin out all the time—but Joey was so quick and agile, he could pull it off.

Joey got outside before me, and I watched him drop in on a thirty-foot wave; within seconds he was deep inside a monstrous, perfectly shaped barrel. The barrel was so big, Joey could stand up straight and not even be touched by the white water. I was looking down into the barrel, but Joey was so far back I'm sure he couldn't even see the beach. He started to inch out of it, then he dropped back in again. Finally he got so far back, there was no way he could get out again, and when the barrel finally broke over the top of him, Joey bailed off the rear.

The wall of water seemed like it broke forever, pounding and rolling, and when Joey came up, the White Ghost was broken in two.

I watched as Joey swam to shore. Then I realized I was out there all by myself now. Rain squalls were still coming in. Way outside I could see waves breaking on the reef Joey and I had spotted earlier. That meant a big set was coming, and I was sitting right on the point, where I was vulnerable. So I started looking for a small wave I could ride in. I finally picked a wave that looked like it had no line on it at all, thinking it would be small enough that I would make it for sure. But as soon as I took off, the wave reared up to a twenty-five-foot monster. My board and I fell the first five feet, then my fin caught, and I had a good solid drive down the line. The face of the wave was glassy, and the speed was incredible. I'd never gone that fast before on a surfboard. The board was slapping and chattering, and when I got to the end of the wave, I eased out of it as carefully as I could, yet I still flew twenty feet in the air.

Without even thinking about it, I turned around and paddled back out.

After an hour of watching and waiting, I picked a wave that looked like it might give me a chance. As soon as I dropped in, the water sucked out below me, and I was instantly inside a thirty-foot barrel, wide enough to drive a truck through. I know people won't believe me, but I'm sure that barrel was 200 feet long.

I slipped twenty feet back in the barrel, then thirty feet, then fifty feet. Then I started inching forward again . . . thirty feet back, ten feet back, until I finally edged all the way out of the barrel and emerged into the bay.

After Joey's wipeout, he realized he might never see a day like that again, so he jumped in his car and drove home—about a twenty-minute drive—got another board and came back out again. This time he got one great ride; then on his second wave he got too deep inside the barrel again and broke that board, too. Joey swam all the way in, got back in his car, and drove home for a third board.

I played it very cautiously after that. In about a five-hour session, I got maybe eight rides, and when Joey came back, we had a couple of good rides together.

Every now and then, I'll run into somebody who was on the cliffs overlooking Hanalei Bay that day, and they always tell me they've never seen anything like it—before or since. There were no pictures taken, nothing to prove it even happened. But it was definitely the highlight of my surfing career, and an experience I wouldn't trade for anything.

Later that winter, Joey won the Makaha for the second year in a row, and I managed fourth in the Duke.

Not long after the Duke, I was surfing at Sunset. I was in great shape by now, feeling like I could do almost anything. The waves were about fifteen feet that day, but after riding big surf all that winter, they looked small to me. As I was paddling out, a fifteen-foot wave came rolling in, and I realized I wasn't going to get outside fast enough to avoid it. In the days before leashes, we used to "turn turtle" on the smaller waves—we would roll over and hold onto our board while a wave broke over the top of us. But this time, as soon as I rolled over, the peak threw out and—BAM!—the lip of the wave hit the board about a foot in front of the fin and broke the board in two. Then the upper part of the board broke again over my head. That board had about four layers of glass, plus a one-inch redwood stringer down the middle. It was probably four times as strong as surfboards are today. And now it was in three pieces.

After the wave passed over me, I opened my eyes underwater and could see my arms flailing around in front of me like seaweed. I was completely numb from the neck down. I was still conscious, I just couldn't move. And I was thinking, This is it, I'm going to drown. It was the closest I had ever come to dying.

After half a minute of pure terror, I started getting a tingling sensation in my fingers. Then I could move my arms just enough to get my head above water long enough to catch a breath of air, but not enough to duck under water again before the next wave hit me. I knew from being a lifeguard that the most important thing with a spinal injury is to immobilize the area. So as the next wave broke over me, I was able to steady my head with my hands so the wave wouldn't thrash it around and do more damage. I still couldn't swim, but I could kick my legs a bit. Fortunately, the waves washed me toward shore, and I was able to drag myself up to the beach.

At first my friends on the beach didn't realize anything was wrong. I had to tell them, "I think I broke my neck." They helped me into a car and drove me to Honolulu. At the hospital, the X-rays showed that two vertebrae were crushed. The doctor put me in a neck brace, which I had to wear for four months.

Forget the Peruvian International—my surfing for that winter was over. Joey went on to Peru, though, and won.

I went back to California to recover from my neck injury. I finished a semester of school and worked on our business at Surf Research. But that summer, in July, I found myself back in Kauai at Joey's house, getting ready to swim the Na Pali Coast. My neck was healed, and I was in pretty good shape again.

Actually, there wasn't anything to do to get ready for a trip like that. We just drove to the end of the road, at Ke'e Beach, which was only about two miles from Joey's house, got out, and walked down to the sand, carrying nothing but a pair of swim goggles.

The Na Pali Coast is extremely rugged, with green 3,000-foot cliffs that are nearly vertical, and very few places to get out of the water. That stretch of coastline faces north and gets some of the biggest surf in the islands. In the summer it's usually calm there, but if a big swell did come along, we would have been battered against the cliffs.

As we started swimming, the ocean was nearly flat, and the water was crystal clear. Joey and I swam side by side for about two hours, staying about three hundred yards offshore. Then Joey started swimming farther out. I knew he was trying to avoid the chop coming off the cliffs by swimming out where the surface was calmer. But I didn't want to go out there because I knew the waters off Hawaii were full of sharks. I wanted to stay close enough to land that I could get back to it quickly if something happened.

About every half-hour, I would look up and try to find Joey. Even though I was probably a stronger swimmer than he was, he had pulled ahead of me because he was swimming in smoother water. After a while I lost sight of him, and the thought occurred to me that we might never see each other again.

The only diversion was in watching the ocean bottom, which was about sixty feet below, and extremely beautiful, with interesting patterns of light and shadow, and a great number of small fish. Some of the fish were following close behind me, and it was fun watching them play.

At four in the afternoon, after about six hours of constant swimming, I happened to look up and see Joey squatting on the rocks next to the cliffs, waving to me. I was ready for a break, so I swam in and joined him.

We were both hungry, so we made a dinner of the limpets (like miniature abalone) that live on the rocks. The Chinese really covet them, but they had become very hard to find on the islands. At this remote site, though, they were abundant. We pried them off with our fingers and ate them raw.

Joey knew the geography of the coastline better than I did. He knew all the points and landmarks, so he said, "Let's swim for about another half-mile, then go up to the Valley of the Lost Tribe."

It was about five-thirty and still sunny when we stopped at the beach below the Honopu Valley. According to Hawaiian legend, the Honopu Valley, or The Valley of the Lost Tribe, was the home of an ancient tribe of people known as Mu. There is evidence of an ancient settlement in the valley that supports the legend, but as we walked up into the valley we could see signs of a later settlement as well. We could see the terraces where the natives had cultivated taro fields and orchards; there were some old pieces of machinery lying around; and there were coffee trees, orange trees, and tangerines—all overgrown now but still producing fruit.

(Later I read about a colony of lepers who had refused to be rounded up and herded onto the island of Molokai with the other lepers. Under the leadership of a man named Koolau, they settled in these remote valleys where they held out for many years. Perhaps this settlement in the Honopu Valley was one of theirs, I don't know.)

We ate some of the oranges, then went back down to the beach.

The night was cool—too cool, really; but after seven hours of swimming, we were exhausted. The sand was still warm, so we just pulled it over us like turtles and fell asleep without any trouble.

We woke up at about five o'clock, when the sky was just starting to get light. We were both eager to get in the water. Not only did we know the water would be warmer than the cool air, but we working on papaya consciousness now, full of energy and eager to get moving. We slipped on our goggles, dived in the ocean, and started stroking for the west.

By now I felt more comfortable in deep water. There were still sharks out there somewhere, but I had become more like a creature of the ocean myself, and I was able to put them out of my mind. I swam even farther outside than Joey did.

There were long periods of time, hours, when nothing at all happened—just the steady pounding of my heart and the rhythm of my stroke. But then two ono, each about four feet long, started following us. At one point they pulled up right below us, less than twenty feet away. Having them there was almost like having someone to talk to. But after following us for a mile or so, they turned and went their own way.

I became totally at ease in the water, staying within my natural stroke, a pace I felt I could keep up indefinitely. I wasn't thinking about getting to the end of the swim, because I didn't even know where the end was. Only Joey did. Besides, I didn't really care anymore. I was totally enthralled with the adventure.

In the afternoon we edged closer to the cliffs. As we swam over a shallow reef, out of the corner of my eye I saw something big moving only three or four feet below the surface. Joey saw it, too. We immediately stopped swimming and started looking underwater. All around us was a churning mass of turtles, most of them about four feet in length. Some of them were swimming idly, but most of them were eating a type of green moss that grew on the rocks.

In the islands, if you see a turtle, that's considered a big deal. If you catch a turtle, that's an even bigger deal. It thrilled us to know there was a place on the islands the fishermen couldn't get to very easily and that turtles like these were thriving. Joey grabbed one turtle by the shell, I grabbed another, and we stood up on the reef, laughing and showing them off to each other. When we tossed the turtles back into the water, they went right back to munching the moss, as if we weren't even there.

Joey and I continued swimming until seven o'clock that evening; then, several hundred yards ahead of us, we saw a thirty-foot boat at anchor. As we drew closer to it, we saw a little cove. Inside the cove were anchored a couple more small boats.

We weren't happy to see signs of civilization. In a way, we resented anybody else being there. Joey said, "Let's just swim on by," and I quickly agreed. But we had only gone a few yards when we realized that was a foolish idea. It was already starting to get dark, and we might not find another good place to stop for the night. Without even saying a word to each other, communicating only by body movements, like fish, we turned and swam toward the cove.

Once we hit the beach, it took us a couple of minutes to get our land legs. After two days in the ocean, our bodies felt heavy and awkward. Also, neither one of us was in a state of mind to see other people. Not only were our brains oxygenated by the exercise—that in itself is enough to alter your consciousness—but we felt like we had reverted back to being some kind of sea apes, totally acclimated to living in the ocean and unfit for socializing with land apes.

As we started walking up the beach, we could see a campfire ahead of us, as well as the silhouettes of thirty or forty people. It looked like some kind of big family campout. As we got closer, we could see a block hut, and outside that were tables heaped with food. Until we saw that, we hadn't realized how hungry we were.

It was almost totally dark now. We stood just beyond the glow from the campfire, eyeing the table of food like dogs begging for scraps. After a while a little boy happened to look our way. He stopped, stared at us for a moment, then ran away. He must have said something to his friends, because two other kids came to stare at us, too. A few of the adults glanced toward us, but they couldn't bring themselves to actually see us. The only way to get to this place was by boat, and they knew very well that another boat hadn't arrived; therefore these two hairy men lurking in the shadows weren't really there.

Joey and I couldn't organize our thoughts into speech. So we just stood there, hoping somebody would offer us some food. Instead, the adults began to ease away from us, dragging their curious kids along with them.

Finally, after several awkward minutes, a Japanese guy with a goatee walked out of the block hut, carrying a platter of food. He took one look at us and said, "Hey, Joey!"

The Japanese fellow was a sculptor who had done all the wood carvings for one of Joey's restaurants—relief panels of old Hawaiian scenes. In the past couple years, he'd earned several thousand dollars from Joey.

Joey nudged me in the ribs and said, "Hey, br'ah, we're in there."

The sculptor grabbed both of us around the shoulders and gave us a big hug. Then he started introducing us. "This is Joey Cabell! He owns The Chart House!"

And all of a sudden the people recognized us as human beings. "The Chart House! We ate there. That's really a great place!"

"And this is Mike Doyle."

"Mike Doyle?" a woman said. "I saw you in the Makaha tandem a couple of years ago. I'm a big fan of yours."

Now they insisted we share their five-course Hawaiian luau, which of course we were more than happy to do.

After dinner we should have sat and talked with our hosts for a while, but as soon as our bellies were full, Joey and I started nodding off right there in the sand. Somebody brought us a couple of blankets, and we crawled off into the dark and fell asleep.

The next morning we were rested and full of energy from our meal. We entered the water at dawn and swam without stopping until four o'clock that afternoon. That put us at Barking Sands, the end of the Na Pali Coast and the place where the road coming from the other side of the island ends.

As we emerged from the water, a couple of Japanese fishermen watched us walk shakily up the road. Naturally, they were curious about how we got there. "Where are you coming from?" one of them asked.

"Ke'e Beach."

That only made them more curious. "By boat?"

"No," we said. "We swam."

"You what!"

When we asked them if we could hitch a ride into the nearest village, they quickly gathered up their fishing gear and hurried us into their car.

On the drive back, my body was so relaxed, it almost felt like I was sedated on morphine. I told Joey, "All I want to do is get back to your house and take it easy for a couple of days."

Joey nodded, but said, "First, I wanna stop and see this *haole* guy I know in Waimea. He's got a mango plantation, and he said I could have some seeds. Our senses are so keen, this'll be the perfect time to taste mangos."

That was Joey. The guy never stopped. He couldn't just plant any old mango seed—they had to be the best. So we went to the mango plantation, and I followed Joey up and down the plantation rows, sampling the fruit from maybe 200 mango trees, until he found what he thought were the perfect mangoes.

We didn't get home until long after dark.

Like a lot of other surfers in the late Sixties, I was growing more and more disgusted with professional surfing. I've already explained why I thought surf contests didn't have much validity, but the problem went deeper than that.

Since my early days at Malibu, the part of surfing I cherished most was the friendship and camaraderie I shared with other surfers. Even though surfing isn't a team sport, it isn't a solitary sport, either. The point, at least for me, was never to prove how great you were, but to have fun with your friends. If there was a competitive element involved, it was in challenging each other to do better.

But in competitive surfing, you have to screw your buddies to win. Too many times the contest comes down to you and another guy. You're sitting side by side in the water, there are the judges on the shore watching and waiting for you to perform, and here comes the perfect wave. Who gets it? I placed second in the Duke Kahanamoku in 1967 because I let the other guy take the perfect wave. They don't give you points for that, but that was the way I was taught by the older guys when I was a kid.

There were some professional surfers who turned into complete animals during a contest. They were out there to win. It didn't matter if you were their best friend or their worst enemy. And it didn't matter if they'd already taken six waves in a row and you hadn't had any yet. They would fight you for the next wave, and if you dropped in ahead of them, they would try to cut you off. They believed so much in the importance of contests, they would do anything to win.

A few other guys refused to act that way. Barry Kanaiaupuni was always brilliant in the water, and everybody said he was the best surfer on the North Shore. But in a big contest, when the perfect wave came, he would just shrug and say, "You take it, br'ah." The contest sponsors kept inviting him to every contest because they all knew how great he was. But he never changed his attitude, and as far as I know, he never placed in a major contest, even though he might have been the greatest surfer of his generation. Today a lot of people have never even heard of Barry Kanaiaupuni, but among his peers he is still very well respected. I think the respect of his peers meant more to Barry than winning a contest. To this day, I admire Barry more than I do some so-called champions.

But the way the contest system was set up, if you weren't aggressive toward the other surfers in the water, you weren't going to win. After the contest was over, nobody asked who was the most considerate or who should have won. They asked, Who won? It was that simple. That was why winning a surf contest could be such a hollow feeling. When you came out of the water, everybody would say, "You did it! You won!" But in the back of your mind, you knew you cut that guy off, and he knew it, too. Maybe he was cool enough that he didn't come over and give you a hard time about it. Maybe he understood that the whole situation was impossible. But in your guts you felt bad. And when the writers were interviewing you, and when your picture came out in the surf magazines, you still felt sick in your guts. Every time you thought back on winning that contest, it would never make you feel good, but would only make you feel sorry you ever had anything to do with it.

The situation wasn't getting any better, either. Every year the contests in Hawaii seemed to get a little more intense, and the competitors were enjoying the experience less. If you just put the Americans, the Hawaiians, and the Australians out in the water and let them surf together, they always managed to have fun. But make a contest out of it, and you had a war. I think a lot of the racial tension in Hawaii started when international surfing became intensely competitive. Competitive surfing was making life in the islands unbearable.

Also, even though nobody would admit it, more often than not the winner of a surf contest was chosen beforehand. It came down to politics. The winner was chosen based on who he was, what he'd done in other contests that year, what he'd said to the media, and how good his image was for the sport. I have to admit that this worked in my favor a few times. I could give a fifth-place performance in a contest and place second. My reputation was influencing the judges, and sometimes it was embarrassing for me to see that I had placed higher than somebody who had outperformed me.

The basic problem with surf contests, at least for me, was that I'd always thought of surfing as more of an art than a sport. Competing in sports can be fun, but only a fool will try to compete in art.

Like a lot of other surfers, I competed in surf contests because they were my free ride. All my trips to Hawaii were now being paid for, I was getting paid for endorsements and advertisements, the Ford Motor Company sent me a new van, the sales of my signature-model surfboard at Hansen's were directly related to my success in surf contests, and to some extent the success of Surf Research was based on my name. Competing in surf contests was my job, and like a lot of other people in all types of work, I didn't like everything about my job.

By this time, 1968, I was twenty-seven years old. Every year a new seventeen-year-old sensation appeared on the world surfing scene. One of the surf magazines had already called me the "old man of surfing." Most surfers stop competing in their mid-twenties, but I couldn't see why a person couldn't go on surfing, maturing like an artist or a musician. I knew I was in top physical condition, my body didn't feel old at all, and I felt I was still improving my equipment and my surfing style.

168

So I began to feel a real conflict: On one hand, I didn't want to compete in surf contests anymore; but on the other hand, I wanted to demonstrate that a surfer my age could combine the elements of experience, style, and creativity to perform at the highest level. I resolved that conflict by deciding I would get out of competitive surfing after one more round of contests, after one more year of giving it my very best.

I spent the rest of the summer and early fall of 1968 touring the East Coast for Hansen Surfboards, and during that tour I never saw a wave bigger than three feet. But I had learned that spending too much time in Hawaii getting ready for the big contests can actually work against you. You get so channeled into what the other guys are doing, both in board design and surfing style, that you stop improving. Alone on the East Coast, I spent a lot of time considering the changes that were taking place in surfing—mostly thinking about how the smaller boards were creating a quicker, more maneuverable style. I came to the conclusion that the smaller boards would give an advantage to surfers who were a lot smaller than I was, but I also figured that if I designed a board that was perfectly suited to my own size and style, I would still have a chance. So I put all my thought and effort into designing a new board to take to Hawaii that winter.

That November a world contest was held at Rincon, Puerto Rico. I flew down from Florida with one of my older boards—I still hadn't had the time to build the new board I'd been thinking about.

The waves at Rincon were absolutely perfect, about ten to twelve feet high, fast, and powerful. After seeing what Nat Young had been able to do on his short board at the world contest in San Diego, most surfers had started riding shorter boards, too. Fred Hemmings was the exception. He showed up with a monstrous board, a 10' 6", about four inches thick. You had to be in top physical condition to paddle the shorter boards, and as I said, they tended to favor smaller surfers. But Hemmings, the ex-football player, had gained some weight. He was a real moose now, with broad shoulders, a thick chest, big waist, and stocky legs. He didn't look like he'd been surfing much, and with that huge board, nobody figured Hemmings would do well in the contest. But he was such a talented athlete, we all knew he couldn't be dismissed.

Hemmings and I had never gotten along very well. He and I had always been rivals in the water, competing against each other time and again in the finals of the major contests. That was probably at the heart of most of our troubles. But there was more to it, too. He always seemed to think of me as a California hippie, and I tended to think of him as a redneck football jock. I recognized his athletic talent, but I didn't think there was any place in competitive surfing for his aggressive behavior in the water. He seemed to think surfing was a contact sport, and to win you had to knock your opponent down.

At Rincon, Hemmings and I both ended up in the finals. The takeoff spot for everybody riding short boards was on one boil (a shallow spot where the water churns up from the bottom). But with that big old paddler, Hemmings was able to sit farther out and get into the waves before the rest of the pack. Once Hemmings was in the wave, the interference rule prohibited anybody from taking off in front of him. So Hemmings was able to catch the best wave of the set, and then after each ride he could paddle back out quickly again and be in position for the next set. There were several other guys surfing with more style and innovation than Hemmings, but on that big board and in those big waves, he played the strategy just right, and he won the thing coming out of the blue—a real upset victory.

After the world contest in Puerto Rico, the action moved back to Hawaii for the fourth annual Duke. I flew home to California and stopped in Leucadia just long enough to throw together my new board. I picked up a new blank from Clark Foam, cut it in half and, using my old pipe clamps from high school wood shop, I glued it to a redwood stringer. I shaped the board and glassed it, then left immediately for the airport.

Two days later I was in the Duke.

The Duke Classic, as it had come to be known, was now the most prestigious event in all of surfing, overshadowing the Makaha and every other contest in the world. The sponsors, the contestants, and the observers all agreed that it had the best organization, the fairest judging, and usually the best waves. But the Duke was still an amateur contest. In fact, there was no such thing as professional surfing, although most world-class competitive surfers were getting some kind of support from commercial sponsors. Most surfers believed the future of surfing was as a professional sport and welcomed the transition to professionalism, since it was the only way surfers could afford to compete in contests all over the world.

So the night before the contest, Duke Kahanamoku's promoter, Kimo McVay, called a meeting of all the surfers and all the contest organizers. The meeting was held at the Hilton Towers in Honolulu, where all the competitors were staying. Kimo said, "We believe the time has come to establish surfing as a professional sport. Therefore, in this year's Duke Classic, we are offering a cash prize of one thousand dollars."

A thousand dollars wasn't much, but before McVay's announcement, we hadn't expected anything. So we were all pretty excited.

The morning of the contest, the waves were big: fifteen to eighteen feet. The news media were out in hordes, and ABC was covering the contest for *Wide World of Sports*.

I knew the first time I put my new board in the water, I'd made an equipment breakthrough: It was much lighter than anyone else's board, but because I'd used far less fiberglass than on the typical board, it was very fragile and could have broken at any time. It had a basic shape but an excellent rocker pattern and a V-bottom. It had good flotation but was still short enough that I could turn quickly. It had a new fin with a lot of flex. It had what I called a ball-bearing tail—a big round tail; I could stand back on that tail and turn so quickly. And I could do edge sets—weighting and unweighting, like in skiing, to get sharper turns. I was able to change directions constantly. While other guys were carving out their long, slow turns, I was doing four or five little zigzags, carving up and down the face of the waves, doing S-turns, and slow-rotation turns. I'd made a board that suited my style perfectly.

All through the preliminary heats, I could see that what I was doing was really catching the judges' attention, and I gained confidence with every wave.

In the finals it came down to Nat Young, Rusty Miller, Jock Sutherland, Felipe Pomar, Ricky Grigg, Eddie Aiku, Fred Hemmings, and me—the same bunch of guys who had been going head-to-head with each other for ten years.

The waves were big enough that day to keep everybody spread out. We didn't have to all sit on the same boil scratching for the same wave. It was a clean competition. There weren't any dogfights. Guys weren't snaking each other, and nobody was losing his temper. And it was definitely my day. After I'd catch a wave and paddle back out, the next set would come rolling in and I'd be the only guy in the right position. My timing that day was perfect, and it seemed like I could do no wrong.

As soon as the final horn went off, I knew I'd won.

I'd been banging on the door of the Duke for so long, I was relieved to have finally gotten in. But the most gratifying thing about that win was the way my friends reacted. Several of the other surfers came up to me and told me they were as happy as if they'd won it themselves. In an interview with one of the local papers, I tried to explain how I felt about that: "Surfing isn't about winning trophies, it's about sharing, about give and take with nature and with your water brothers." It may sound corny, but that really is the way I felt then, and it's still the way I feel today.

The awards ceremony was held at the Duke's restaurant in downtown Honolulu. Don Ho and his band were there. I remember they sang "Tiny Bubbles," and then the dancers ran out into the audience, grabbed the surfers who'd been in the contest, dragged them onto the stage, and made them hula.

Late that night, the Duke himself awarded me the first-place trophy.

Just a few days later we were all in Lima again for the Peruvian International. At Puntas Rocas the waves were about twelve feet— big and powerful. My magic board was still holding together, and I was tearing up the waves with it.

Fred Hemmings was there, and twice in the preliminaries we found ourselves on the same wave. Both times I stayed way out on the shoulder, giving him plenty of room, but he came up behind me, drove his board into my legs, then banked off of me, trying to knock me down. He tried to do the same thing to a Peruvian and an Australian surfer. His whole strategy seemed to be to intimidate and to win at all costs. On one wave he went so far out on the shoulder to try to knock off another surfer, he ended up ruining his own ride.

I'd never seen that kind of attitude in surfing before, and it really disturbed me. Hemmings had already accomplished as much in the sport as anybody ever had. His attitude seemed so unnecessary.

In the end, though, Hemmings's strategy didn't work. I won the contest and was presented the trophy for Campéon Olas Grandes.

Western United States

Mountain Dreams

*A*fter the Peruvian International, I never competed in a major surf contest again. It was over for me; I wanted to put my competitive career behind me and get on with my life as quickly as I could. I had a nagging suspicion that the whole game of playing a surf hero was a nasty trap. I was quoted that year in one of the surf magazines as saying, "Surf stardom interferes with your development as a human being." I still feel that way today. To allow your ego to be blown up by the media is just setting yourself up for a fall. They're going to find new heroes, and the new heroes are going to stand on your head. If you don't know how to step down from the winner's stand, sooner or later you're going to find yourself very unhappy.

When I see athletes in any sport trying to come back after their prime years, I feel sorry for them. To me it says that person hasn't developed as a human being. It says they haven't learned to deal with life as an ordinary mortal. They still want to be idolized and adored.

In later years I would run into surfers my age who were still competing, or trying to compete, and I didn't envy them at all. Even today when I talk to young professional surfers, a lot of them tell me how much they dislike the contest circuit. They're angry because of the way the sponsors are jerking them around; they're angry because they have to be at a certain place on a certain day, even though everybody knows the surf will be lousy; and they're angry because they don't have the freedom to go out and enjoy the sport they love.

All the hot young kids whose life dream is to become a professional surfer don't have any idea how disturbing that life can be. Surf stardom is an illusion, and if you're foolish enough to believe in it, it will only bring you unhappiness. Go for the joy and freedom of surfing, and for the satisfaction of sharing the good times with your friends. All the rest—you're better off without it.

While in Peru, I became friends with a surfer from Ecuador, a young woman named Dorothy Aguirre. She was a very kind person, with an open, energetic personality. Her family owned a ranch on the coast of Ecuador, and after the contest she invited Nat Young and me back to her home, where she promised to show us her favorite surf spots. It sounded like a wonderful adventure, but I was enrolled at San Diego State for the spring semester, and I only had a few more units to complete my degree in biology.

I'd started to have some doubts about going back to school. For years I'd been getting in a semester here, a semester a there, thinking that someday I would get a teaching credential and become a high school biology teacher. But to get a teaching credential would have required another year of school, and I had lost any desire to follow that career. In fact, all traditional workaday careers had lost any appeal for me: lifeguard, schoolteacher, fireman. I was ruined for all that. I had the notion that I could make a living by creating something of my own—I was already doing it at Surf Research.

So I decided not to go back to school, and I told Dorothy I would take her up on her offer.

Nat and I flew to Quito, then drove to Dorothy's ranch on the coast. I was a little worried that it would be a lavish place, with European cars and palatial mansions, but I was relieved to find it wasn't that way at all. Her family owned a lot of land and lived well by Ecuadorian standards, but they were hardly wealthy. The ranch was simple but comfortable, on open, arid rangeland overlooking the ocean. There were wild animals all over the place, and deer wandered freely in and out of the dining hall while the family ate. The place seemed like it was right out of California's Spanish rancho days.

Right in front of the ranch house was a hot little beach break, and we had fun surfing there every day. Then Dorothy took Nat and me on a couple of surfaris along the coast north of the ranch, where we found a few point breaks that had never been surfed before.

When the time came to leave Ecuador, Dorothy asked me if I

would make her a surfboard. Surfboards were hard to come Ecuador, even if the surfers there had the cash. So I agreed to her a board, if we could come up with the materials.

We didn't have any foam blanks, but the ranch had a stockpile of native balsa—much lighter and finer balsa than any we could get in the States. (The best balsa is as good as foam for making surfboards, and if there were an adequate supply of the stuff, surfers might still be making surfboards out of balsa.)

We didn't have any tools for shaping the surfboard, but there was a blacksmith on the ranch who repaired the farm implements, and I asked him if he could make me a drawknife. The blacksmith took the leaf spring from an old car and spent several hours grinding it down until it had the rough shape of a drawknife. He welded handles onto it, then filed one side until it was razor sharp.

Nat and I glued the balsa slabs together, but we didn't have any pipe clamps, so we cut up strips of old inner tubes and wrapped them around and around the slabs until there was a tremendous amount of pressure squeezing them together.

After the glued slabs had dried, I sawed out the rough shape of the surfboard, then used the drawknife to complete it. Dorothy had stockpiled some fiberglass and resin at the ranch, so we were able to finish the board. When I left Ecuador, my friend had a custom-made surfboard that had cost her just a fraction of what it would cost to ship one from the U.S.

I came back to Leucadia to find that a huge winter storm had dumped tons of driftwood along our beach. What a bonanza that was. Garth Murphy and I gathered up truckloads of the wood and built a fantastic tree house in my back yard.

There's something about tree houses that I've always loved. They're great places to withdraw to when you have some thinking to do. They elevate your thoughts, and they offer security from all the predators roaming around on the ground below. I strongly recommend tree houses to anybody going through a major change in life.

Garth, a quiet and resourceful person, supplied most of the inspiration for our tree house. He would come back after a morning surf session and announce that there was a telephone pole lying on the beach. So we would all march down there like a band of scavengers and drag it home. We used that pole as a kind of flying buttress to support one whole section of the tree house, which was about thirty feet in the air. We made it split-level, with a big bed about three feet higher than the main salon, and we added a ladder that could be pulled up after us so we could take our girls up there and not worry about being disturbed.

Life at the Hermes house was like a peaceful dream. I'd wake up at dawn every morning, begin the day with an hour of yoga, then drive my '57 Packard to Swami's to surf for a couple of hours. After a breakfast of fresh fruit and granola, I'd meet with my partners, Garth and Rusty, and our trusted employee, Bill. We'd pour a batch of wax or work on one of our new designs or, if the surf was good, we might spend the rest of the day surfing.

We started coming out with lot of new products. We made Spraymate, a spray-on traction that bonded to fiberglass surfboards. We made Noselifter, a polypropylene fin attachment for increasing nose-riding ability. We designed a new type of surfboard rack—most of the surfboard racks then were metal pipe racks, which were heavy and awkward, so we came up with a lighter and more portable rack. We also made a rescue device, a flexible tube a lifeguard could snap around a victim's waist to give him flotation; it became very popular with lifeguards up and down the coast.

Although it wasn't exactly an invention of ours, one of the most innovative marketing concepts we came up with was New Food. California at that time was just starting to become aware of health foods. The East Coast was behind the curve on that one, but they would go crazy over anything to do with the surf culture. So we packaged bulk granola into small packets, labeled it New Food, and advertised it in the surf magazines with pictures of me dumping a bowl of it over my head. A stupid ad, but it attracted a lot of attention, and we were shipping tons of this stuff to the East Coast surf shops. What we were doing, really, was selling the concept of California living.

We also had a lot of ideas that didn't work out so well. For a long time Rusty was interested in surfboards with no fins, or small three-inch fins. He called them "finger fins," so the board would spin out and side-slip. He liked the physical sensation of surfing on really squirrely boards. Unfortunately, that idea never caught on.

But we had so many successful products in such a very short time at Surf Research, none of us really took our achievements very seriously. We didn't really appreciate what a great success this young company of ours was starting to become. We were all excited that the business was working, that we could make a living and keep on surfing, but when the business started to cut into our play time, we didn't like that. Play time was our top priority.

I can remember how excited we were when the first answering machine came out. We thought that was going to be the solution to our playtime problems. We wouldn't have to hang around the office taking orders anymore. The answering machine would handle all our business calls, we'd go surfing all day, then sort it all out when we got home in the evenings. The money would just come in the mail.

The first answering machine was about the size of a typewriter. It was called Answer Phone. You'd slip the phone down into a slot inside the answering machine; when the phone rang, the machine would turn on, two arms would slide under the receiver and lift the whole thing up. But it never worked right. Sometimes it would flip the receiver about two feet in the air, and when we came back from surfing, the receiver would be lying on the floor going "Beep! Beep! Beep!" The salesman who had talked us into trying the thing came back so many times to fix it, we finally threw it at him and said, "Here, it doesn't work, we don't want it, we're not paying for it!"

In the meantime, my deal with Don Hansen, shaping my signature-model board, had gradually diminished to a minimum level. Surfers on the East Coast had finally gotten smart and started making their own surfboards, so the orders for all the shops in California dropped way off. Hansen talked to me about taking a cut in pay, but I was tired of mass-producing surfboards anyway, so I suggested we just stop making my signature-model altogether.

Rusty, Garth, and I knew we could easily double or triple the sales on almost every product we had at Surf Research. We could have sold twenty times as much purple wax. We couldn't keep up with the orders on our surf trunks, and that could have easily been expanded into a whole clothing line. But we'd watched Don Hansen go from a fun, fit, happy surfer living in his panel truck, to a . . . well, a businessman. We used Hansen as an example of what we didn't want to become. We didn't want to be surf moguls; we wanted to get our water time, be healthy and happy. Running a business had no appeal for us.

To be fair to Don, though, he worked very hard and deserved the success he achieved. He would look at our business and wonder what in the world held the thing together. He used us as an example of what he didn't want his business to become.

We hired a general manager for a while, John Baker. It was a pretty shrewd decision; he already had a wife and kids, so we figured he had no choice—he had to work.

Meanwhile, the whole country was going through some tough, gut-wrenching changes. Vietnam had turned into a bloody, full-scale war, and all of us had friends dying over there. A lot of us were becoming concerned about what we saw happening to the ocean and the rest of the environment. People my age and younger were beginning to feel isolated from the older generation, and a mood of anger and despondency was setting in. We all had those feelings, but none of us felt them more intensely than Rusty Miller. Rusty understood history and politics better than the rest of us, and at times, talking about politics became an obsession with him. He would talk and talk until he became so bitter and negative, it was tough being around him. We would try to show Rusty that the world wasn't such a bad place, he was just seeing it from an extreme perspective. But Rusty would resent that, thinking we were picking on him—which we were, but because we loved him.

Finally, Rusty said he was so disgusted with the United States, the only answer was to give up his U.S. citizenship and move to Australia. I tried to convince him there was no point in giving up his U.S. citizenship, that he could move to Australia and keep a dual citizenship, but he said he was so ashamed of his country, he wanted no part of it anymore.

That fall Rusty packed up his few belongings and headed for

180

Australia. After he left, the synergy of our little group fell apart. Without Rusty, Surf Research just wasn't that much fun anymore. Garth, Bill and I talked things over. We all agreed it was time for us to dissolve the partnership. We remained close friends—in fact, Garth, Bill and I became even closer—we just weren't business partners any longer. We sold the wax works to a guy in Colorado who wanted to make ski wax. He changed the name from Surf Research to Wax Research, and it was over. I had some money in my pocket, and it was time for a freedom run.

Maybe it was just the force of habit, but after ten years of heading for Hawaii every fall, I had the itch to go again. Even though I had no intention of competing in any surf contests, I still missed Hawaii a lot. So I flew to Honolulu, where I stayed with Joey Cabell.

Joey and Gail had gotten married by now. They had moved back to Oahu and were living in a small apartment above his restaurant on the Ala Moana harbor. The new restaurant had done well, and Joey was planning to build a massive new house on Kauai. Like everything else Joey did, he was totally absorbed with the details of the new house, with the marble floors, with making sure every nail was made of copper just like on a boat, and with the corrals where Gail would keep horses.

Joey had another love in his life now too, a new sailboat he called the *Hokule'a*. Joey had put something like $250,000 into this boat, but the first time he showed it to me, I couldn't see where all the money had gone. It was just two sixty-foot hulls thirty feet apart, and four spindles that came up off the hulls to support a little pod about the size of a Volkswagen van. The boat looked like a big waterskater—one of those bugs that can walk on water. It was built to go fast and nothing else. There were no comforts at all: no head, no showers, no galley, not even a radio. He stored coconuts and papayas in the hulls, but they were his only survival gear. Gail was terrified of the boat and didn't even want to set foot on board.

But the *Hokule'a* was Joey's pride and joy, and when he showed it to me, I started to get excited about it, too. As soon as Joey saw my enthusiasm, he said, "Hey, let's sail over to Maui."

I said, "Yeah! I've always wanted to sail to Maui."

We left Waikiki at three in the morning. As we were leaving Joey's house, I happened to hear a weather report on the radio saying there were strong winds in the Molokai Channel—maybe up to forty knots. I knew Joey had never tested his boat in heavy weather, but I figured he knew what he was doing.

Out of the harbor the *Hokule'a* was clipping along at fifteen knots, with smooth conditions; the boat was trimmed out perfectly, water was flying off the hull, and I was enthralled. I mentioned to Joey the weather report I'd heard earlier, but he just shrugged and said, "No problem."

I didn't realize until later that Joey had heard the weather report long before I had. It had been his intention all along to take the boat out in high winds, just to see what she would do. And I was his guinea pig, brought along to see whether or not the crew could survive those conditions.

As soon as we rounded the point of the island, off Diamond Head, and were in the open channel, all hell broke loose. The swells jumped up to twelve feet and were breaking completely over the boat. There was a little bit of moonlight that night, but all I could see was white froth. I'd been in thirty-foot surf, but I'd never been exposed to the open ocean the way we were that night. I was scared to death. I said to Joey, "Don't you think we should turn back?"

Joey got that grin of his. He had his toy in the open ocean, and he had me with him. "Naw," he said. "We're fine."

I kept thinking, Joey doesn't make a lot of mistakes, but when he does, they're big ones. What if this is the mistake of his life?

Joey was concentrating on sailing the boat, trying to get a feel for it in heavy weather. Once he pointed too high into the wind, backwinded, and—BAM!—the sail swung clear around and slammed into the stops. It was a wonder he didn't snap the mast.

I didn't know an awful lot about sailing in those days, but I knew we should at least be tied in just in case we got swept overboard. But the boat didn't have any tie-in lines. At the very least we should have been running a lifeline behind the boat so if one of us fell overboard we would have something to grab onto. So I asked him, "Joey, are we running a lifeline?"

"No, but you're a good swimmer. You should be all right."

But I wasn't all right. I was starting to lose faith in my captain. Every time I looked out at those huge rolling seas, I couldn't see how any boat this size could survive. "Joey," I said, trying to scream over the wind, "this is a bit too much!"

"Just don't think about it," he said. "Now go down on the hull and wind in that winch."

The pod was way up in the air, but the waves were breaking over the top of it. When I went down on the hull I was totally exposed to the sea, and there were very few handholds. But Joey had me. If I wanted to survive, I had to do whatever he said.

The wind was blowing so hard, the guy wires were whistling and howling. Even though I was wearing foul-weather gear, I got soaking wet and totally exhausted. I climbed back up to the hull and said, "Joey, this is no fun."

Joey just laughed at me. For him it *was* fun!

I crawled inside the little pod, seasick, cold, and frightened. I was just waiting for the inevitable. I fell into a kind of sleepy stupor for a while, which was probably an early stage of hypothermia.

At one point that night, I woke up, unzipped the door of the pod, and looked out. By the moonlight I could see Joey at the wheel, wearing his yellow slicker, with a scrunched-up grin on his face. A wave crashed clear over the top of him, and for a moment he was buried in white water. As the water peeled off, there he was again, smiling more than ever, his eyes all lit up. Every wave that hit him only excited him more.

Finally, about five in the morning, we came into the lee of Maui, and the ocean started settling down some. By now, though, my guts were rattling violently. I knew I had to get moving, so I crawled out of the pod and started helping Joey trim the boat.

And then, all of a sudden, the sun came out, and everything was warm and bright. We were stroking for Maui, and the whole world looked beautiful.

Rusty Miller, as it turned out, didn't move to Australia right away. First he stopped off at a hippie colony on Kauai owned by Howard Taylor, Liz Taylor's brother. After I survived the sailing ordeal with Joey, I went over to see Rusty for a few days, to rest and recuperate.

There were about fifty or sixty people living on the Taylor Camp, which was near the end of the road in a dense jungle. Most of the hippies were living in bamboo-framed houses covered with sheets of clear plastic. Almost everybody ran around naked all the time. Rusty had the only real house at the camp. It was in a clearing about 500 yards above the main camp. It was a nice spot, with a clear stream running through it.

My old surf buddy welcomed me into his little house. He looked happy to me. He didn't mention politics, and I certainly didn't want to get him going on that again. He had a daily pattern like a monk's. He practiced yoga, ate brown rice, and swept his floor. I think he was trying to put some order into his life. But I really upset his order because I'd forget to take my shoes off when I came inside, throw my clothes around on the floor, and generally make a mess. He took it with patience and good humor. Every time I came and went, Rusty would get out his broom and sweep the floor again.

I noticed one morning that every time Rusty had to relieve himself, he would walk out of his house and go shit in that clear little stream, which then flowed down into the hippie camp, providing the hippies with their drinking water. So I said to him, "Rusty, what are you doing?"

He just shrugged. "Shit dissipates in about fifty feet."

"Like hell!" I said. "That's really high consciousness, Rusty. You think you're living some kind of holy life here, all blissed out and organic. Meanwhile, you're sending other people your shit."

I realize now that Rusty was going through a major change in his life, and I probably could have dealt with it a bit more tactfully. But it really hurt me to see my old friend withdrawing from the world, and I felt like I had a responsibility to shake him out of it. At any rate, Rusty didn't appreciate my criticism of his hygiene, and before long I got the feeling my welcome there was over.

Before heading back to California, I stopped to see Joey again. Joey had put aside his toy, the *Hokule'a*, for a while. He was thirty-two years old now, but he wasn't ready to give up competitive surfing yet. He made himself a new version of the White Ghost, the favorite board he'd broken that day surfing with me at Hanalei Bay, and started training hard for the Duke.

Just a few days before the Duke, Joey was surfing at Sunset when he went over the falls in a crushing wipeout that shattered his new board and broke four ribs.

Everybody figured that was it for Joey's surfing season. The day of the Duke, he was so sore he could hardly lift his arms, and half his rib cage was black-and-blue. But Joey wouldn't even consider dropping out of the competition. He had Robin Grigg tape up his ribs and give him four shots of cortisone. The whole side of his body was numb, but Joey went out and won the Duke.

As much as I'd missed Hawaii a few months earlier, it only made me feel restless and uneasy now. It seemed like everybody in the world, surfer or not, wanted to hang out on the North Shore. There was constant racial tension, as well as hostility between the locals and the seasonal invaders, and for me the whole experience wasn't enjoyable anymore. Hawaii still had the best waves in the world—it always will—but that wasn't enough. I had to admit to myself that the Hawaii I had dreamed about as a boy looking at pictures in *National Geographic* just didn't exist anymore.

Every winter, after the best of the surfing season was over, Joey would go to Aspen, Colorado, to look after his restaurant there and to ski. I'd never been to Aspen before, and I didn't really know much about skiing. But when Joey started telling me about some of his ski adventures, I started thinking that skiing, and a life in the mountains, would be a welcome change.

In late January, Joey said, "Hey, why don't I fly back to California with you, we'll get in your old Packard and drive to Colorado? We can stay in my apartment there."

I said, "That sounds like a good idea to me."

From my very first day at Aspen, I loved being in the mountains, and I loved skiing. But skiing didn't come very easily to me. I had learned to surf at such a young age, I'd never really had to think about the fundamentals very much. Skiing, though, I had to learn step by step, and I became fascinated with studying and analyzing the body mechanics involved.

One thing I didn't like about the mountains. All my life I've hated being cold, and Aspen was colder than any place I'd been before. Also, I had trouble with the altitude. I'd spent almost my whole life at sea level, and I didn't understand that if you don't conserve your energy at high elevation, you quickly became exhausted. Joey and others tried to warn me about this, but I was so excited about learning how to ski, I just couldn't force myself to stop and rest. After skiing all day, Joey and I would work at his Chart House in the evenings; I would wait on tables, run errands, act as host—anything Joey needed me to do. We had a very active schedule, and before long it wore me out.

My old Packard and I quit at the same time. It had a powerful V-8 engine, but it just didn't like the high altitude and the cold. My Packard refused to start one morning, and I came down with pneumonia.

My doctor warned me that trying to recover from pneumonia at high altitude wouldn't be easy. He even suggested that I go back to California. But I didn't want to leave Colorado. I was determined to get back on my feet and learn as much as I could about skiing before the winter was over. So while Joey and everybody else was out having fun all day, I lay around the apartment by myself, trying to recover my strength.

Later that winter, Bill Engler joined us from California. After Surf Research broke up, he was looking for adventure and to get out of Southern California for a while. He was as excited about skiing as I was, and he attacked it with energy. But all I could do was sit around and listen to him and Joey talk about their adventures at the end of the day.

It took me about a month to get enough strength to ski again. I should have rested even longer, but I just couldn't stay indoors. The result was predictable: My first day back on the mountain, I overexerted myself again. But I kept skiing, even while I could feel my strength draining away. Finally, in the afternoon, I went back to Joey's apartment, turned the heater on full-blast, crawled inside my down sleeping bag, and fell asleep. When Bill and Joey came home that afternoon, I was unconscious. They had to take me to the hospital.

This time I had double pneumonia, and I was so sick I had no choice but to lie flat on my back until I was well again.

By the time I finally recovered my health, winter was almost over.

One day in late March, when I was finally feeling strong again, Joey, Tommy Lee (a photographer friend of ours from Hawaii), and I went looking for some powder skiing. It was a beautiful sunny morning, the day after a storm had passed through, dropping several feet of fresh powder. We took the ski lift to the top of the mountain, then hiked about two more miles. We wanted to get some photos of Joey skiing, so Joey picked out a steep slope and climbed to the top of it, while Tommy and I waited at the bottom.

At the top of the mountain was an eighty-foot cornice. Joey skied out to the edge of the cornice and waited while Tommy set up his camera. Tommy called out when he was all set, and Joey started skiing down the face of the cornice. But on the first turn the whole cornice cracked clear down to bare rock, and broke away from the mountain. The avalanche of snow and ice slid about 300 yards down the slope, before settling in a gully that was about fifteen feet deep.

And Joey was gone.

Tommy and I quickly skied down to the gully, then started digging where we thought Joey might be. All we had to dig with were our hands and our ski poles, but we dug frantically with those, knowing that each minute that passed lessened Joey's chances of survival. The crushing weight of the snow and ice could have suffocated him almost immediately, but if he were lucky enough to have an air pocket and the room to expand his lungs, he might last thirty minutes before he ran out of oxygen.

After digging for about twenty minutes, I finally found the tip of Joey's ski pole. I dug down the length of the pole until I found his glove, and when I squeezed the glove, Joey's hand was still in it. His body was all twisted around in the snow, but I dug down his arm until I was able to find his head. When I pulled the ice away from his face, Joey looked up at me with a big grin and said, "I knew you'd find me!"

As much as I liked Aspen, I was disappointed by how crowded it was. I had expected Colorado to be quiet and secluded. There was a lot of wild country surrounding Aspen, but all the crowds flocked to one small area, which made it feel about as crowded as Southern California.

That spring I got my Packard running again, and Bill and I drove back to Leucadia. Along the way, we talked about our plans for the next winter. Like a lot of young people at that time, Bill Engler and I had started feeling the need to be closer to nature. The ocean had filled that need for most of our lives, and now we wanted to make that same connection in the mountains. So we started talking about finding someplace more primitive.

Back in Leucadia, Bill and I bought a big flatbed truck and went to work building a wooden camper on the back of it. This was before the days of the good, used motor home or camper. There were a few new Winnebagos on the market, but their price tags were way beyond our reach. So we knew that if we wanted a camper, we'd have to build it ourselves. Our creation had a steeply pitched roof, shake-shingle siding, and a wood-burning stove with a big metal chimney coming out the top. On the inside, it had a big double bunk over the cab and a smaller bunk down below. We insulated the walls and ceiling, then lined the interior walls with madras bedspreads. It looked like a real gypsy wagon.

I didn't have a job, but I still had some money in the bank. So instead of going to work for somebody else, I spent a lot of time that summer thinking and talking about the comparisons between surfing and skiing.

What intrigued me most about skiing was that it felt so damned awkward. Obviously, this could have been due to the fact that I'd been surfing for nearly twenty years but had only recently taken up skiing. But I suspected otherwise. People learning to surf have a great deal of difficulty at first, but the technique soon becomes natural to them. Skiers, on the other hand, can spend years trying to master the fundamentals of parallel skiing and never really get

it right. There was something wrong with the mechan
something unnatural about it, and I kept wondering v

That fall Bill and I loaded our gypsy camper wi
clothes, and food, and said good-bye to Leucadia jus
winter surf was starting to roll in. We drove north to Mammoth
Lakes, where we stopped to ski for a few days; then, with a break
in the weather, we headed east across Nevada and Utah, to Jackson
Hole, Wyoming.

Our first look at the Grand Tetons left us dizzy and a bit
intimidated. The vertical drop at the ski area was 6,000 feet! But it
was a strikingly beautiful place, and still wild, with moose, elk, and
other animals wandering around. We felt we had found what we
were looking for. We parked our big camper at the ski area and
settled in.

The skiing at Jackson Hole was everything we'd hoped for. We
skied every day, then came back to our camper, lit a fire in the wood
stove, and huddled in our sleeping bags while we cooked supper.
We hadn't thought to insulate the camper floor, so with the cold air
flowing underneath us, we were miserably cold at night. We had
no shower, so every morning we'd go to the Mangy Moose, a bar
where they'd let us wash our face and hands in the restroom. But
before long we made friends with people who lived in the area, and
every once in a while they'd let us take baths at their houses.

There was a lot of camaraderie among the young people
working at Jackson Hole, and they welcomed us into their circle of
friends. Bill and I were being invited to dinner at somebody's house
almost every night. One of the people we met there was Dean Betts,
who owned the food concession at the ski area. Dean had been a
real estate broker in Newport Beach, a real suit-and-tie guy with a
Mercedes and all, before he chucked it all and went looking for a
simpler life. He was a very quiet, low-key person, who probably
had the lowest blood pressure of any living human being. I liked
him a lot.

Another person we met was Terry King, a rock climber and
mountaineer; in the summer he worked at the Great Pacific Iron
Works in Ventura, California. Great Pacific made climbing ham-
mers, bongs, chocks, and other innovative climbing gear. Terry kept

telling me that I should come to Ventura sometime and meet Yvon Chouinard, the guy who'd started the company. "You guys really have a lot in common," he said. "Yvon loves to surf, and I know he'd like to meet you."

I told Terry I looked forward to meeting Yvon, and I put it on my list for the next summer.

Late that winter, after skiing all day and coming back to the camper to sleep, I started having a recurring dream. In the dream I was surfing down a mountain of snow. At first I didn't think much about it. I knew the unconscious mind works at night to solve the problems the conscious mind can't solve in the day. But I had that dream so many times, it got to be almost an annoyance. I wanted to tell my unconscious mind that surfing isn't skiing and you don't ride surfboards in the snow. But when I really thought about it, it didn't seem all that absurd. I was forced to ask myself, Why can't you ride a surfboard in the snow?

The answer to that simple question kept me occupied for the next ten years.

The trouble with downhill skiing, at least the way I saw it, was that it evolved from cross-country skiing, which in turn evolved from walking. In northern Europe, where skiing was invented centuries ago, it was a functional form of transportation across the snow. In those early days, all skiing was cross-country, which required the ability to travel uphill, downhill, and over flats. A cross-country skier needed the independent motion of his feet. But after the invention of the ski lift, downhill skiing became an entirely different sport. Downhill skiing was no longer a form of transportation, it was a form of recreation. And using two skis to move downhill simply made no sense.

Because I was looking at skiing from a surfer's point of view, I could see very clearly that two skis were a hindrance. I knew that with a single ski you would have a much more natural and fluid motion, which could be mastered by almost anybody in a short period of time. And if you had a surfing or skateboarding background, then you had practically mastered it already.

One of the most important lessons I'd learned from surfing is that you can't maximize your potential until you've adapted your equipment to suit your own abilities. So I decided to make myself a surfboard for the snow.

That summer, back in Leucadia, I started working on a prototype. I designed the ski as if it were two skis joined together—a single ski. Because I'd been doing a lot of powder skiing and struggling to keep my feet parallel, I designed the bindings so the feet would face forward, parallel to the length of the board. This was a departure from the concept of surfing, where the feet are more or less perpendicular to the board. But an advantage to having your feet parallel to the ski was that you could still use ski poles to help you turn, to pole across flat ground, and to help you maneuver onto a chair lift. If your feet were perpendicular, poles would be useless.

I made five single-ski prototypes in my back yard, all of them from fiberglass. By the time I'd finished the fifth prototype, I thought I had a single ski that might work.

One day my friend from Jackson Hole, Dean Betts, stopped by to see me in Leucadia. He was on his way to Cabo San Lucas, on the tip of Baja California. Cabo was Dean's favorite place, and he was always raving about how beautiful it was, like the Sonoran Desert, but with warm, tropical waters.

I'd heard of Cabo, of course, but had never been there myself. I'd always wondered if there was any surf there, but the people I asked always said, "No, no surf in Cabo." I looked at a map, and thought, That's incredible! It's on a long peninsula with it's tip facing due south—there has to be surf there!

Dean wasn't much of a surfer, so he couldn't answer my question, but he did make me curious about the place. When he asked me if I wanted to go along with him, I couldn't resist.

It's about a 1,000-mile drive from San Diego to Cabo. We took Dean's van, filled with camping, diving, and fishing gear. Also, at the last minute, just in case everybody I'd talked to was wrong, I tossed in a couple of surfboards.

The first night on the road, Dean and I stopped at Hussong's, a famous saloon in Ensenada, and really cut loose. In those days, stopping at Hussong's was a ritual with surfers traveling in Baja.

We drank until late that night, slept in the van, then hit the road again at first light.

In El Rosario we stopped at Espinosa's Restaurant and had a big breakfast to settle our stomachs. From there on, the road was only partially paved, so we took it slowly, enjoying the Baja countryside. It was great to be out in the open again, away from all the stress and confusion in Southern California. It took us three days to get to the tip of the peninsula, and with every mile it seemed to become more beautiful.

I've always loved the desert. When I was in college, I used to drive out to Palm Springs and sleep on the golf course, just so I could watch the stars at night. I always thought that if I could find a place that had a desert as beautiful as the American Southwest, plus an ocean, that would be my paradise. But I didn't think such a place existed.

As soon as I saw Cabo, I knew I'd found my place. The colors of the water and land were so bright, and I couldn't believe how clean and dry the air was. My sinuses dried out, my ears popped, and my hearing became clear. It was like somebody who is nearsighted putting on glasses and being able to see things he'd never seen before.

We drove up and down the Costa Azul, and I soon learned that Cabo had excellent surf. The people I'd asked before had all been boat owners who sat in the harbor and never realized that just a couple of miles away there was great surf! I particularly liked a place called Zippers, between Cabo San Lucas and San José del Cabo. It broke on a reef, and when the swell direction was right, the waves could be fifteen feet.

We stayed at the only trailer park on the peninsula, Alfonso's, and every day we went surfing, fishing, or diving. Dean didn't surf much, but he loved to fly-fish. While the tourists in Cabo were going miles out to sea in charter boats to catch marlin and wahoo, Dean was fly-fishing for mackerel and bonita in the shore break.

Dean spoke very good Spanish, and he already knew a lot of the locals from previous trips. They greeted him warmly, took us right into their houses, and give us fresh fish, fruit, and vegetables.

After a couple of weeks, Dean and I had to head back to

California. But all the way home, we fantasized about how nice it would be to have a small place of our own in Cabo where we could stay a couple of times a year.

While I was struggling with the design of my single ski, Bill Engler started to get a bit bored. Bill always had a lot of restless energy, and he was eager to try something new and dangerous. So he started suggesting we try rock climbing.

Bill had never been rock climbing, and he didn't really know anything about it. The first time he suggested it to me, I told him I had no intention of hanging my ass by a rope over some cliff. But Bill wouldn't give up. He kept telling me I might be missing the greatest adventure of my life. Finally, I agreed to try rock climbing, but only if we went with somebody who knew what he was doing.

I remembered Terry King had told me I should get to know Yvon Chouinard, who was one of the best climbers in the country. So I called Yvon in Ventura, introduced myself, and explained to him that Bill and I wanted to try rock climbing. As an incentive, I told Yvon, "If you and your buddies will take Bill and me rock climbing, we'll take you surfing someplace you've never heard of before."

Yvon's response was, "Be here tomorrow morning. We're leaving for Yosemite at dawn."

Bill and I left at midnight and drove up to Ventura, where at dawn we piled into a van with Yvon and five other climbers, four or five dogs, several boxes of food, and half a ton of climbing gear.

We arrived in Yosemite Valley around noon and settled in at Camp Four, the traditional, walk-in campground for rock climbers. Then Yvon took Bill and me on an easy climb called After Five. It was short, not too steep, and not too scary. Bill and I both thought it was fun. We did a couple more simple climbs that weekend, but mostly Bill and I took it easy and watched Yvon and his climbing buddies show us how it was done.

Yvon was shorter than I expected him to be. I thought of mountaineers as big, strong, burly guys. Yvon was about five-foot-six, but he had very long arms and was powerfully built. And he wasn't a fashion dresser—this was before he started Patagonia, the

ear company. Yvon and his climbing friends weren't into
ʟ and Lycra yet. They were grubby and dirty, wore scruffy
_ˍ, stacked on layers of old wool sweaters, and liked to grovel
in the mud and charcoal with their dogs.

Yvon was quiet by nature. If you wanted to have a conversation
with him, you had to seek him out. But he was intensely focused.
I remember him describing how he loved to go rock climbing
barefoot and naked in the moonlight so he could feel the power of
the granite through his body. That made perfect sense to Bill and
me, because we liked to surf naked so we could feel the power of
the ocean through our bodies.

On the way home, Yvon said, "Next weekend we're going to
a place called Tahquitz, up behind Idylwild. Why don't you guys
come along?"

Bill and I looked at each other, shrugged and said, "Sure, that
sounds like fun."

So that next weekend Bill and I met Yvon and his crew at
Idylwild. One of the climbers with him was Doug Tompkins, who
in 1968 had started the clothing company Esprit.

There was a short hike into Tahquitz Peak, which is in the San
Jacinto Mountains. It was a pretty place, in the pines but overlooking the desert around Palm Springs.

The climb Yvon took us on was called Mechanics. As we
started up the mountain, there was a party of climbers next to us.
They were drilling holes in the granite and placing bolts, which
Yvon hated. He was a purist and didn't believe in damaging the
mountain with bolts or even pitons. He was a strong advocate of
using only hardware like bongs and chocks that could be placed in
the natural cracks and removed without chipping away the rock.

The climb up Tahquitz was much more difficult and frighten-
ing than anything Yvon had taken us on in Yosemite. After we'd
climbed about halfway up the mountain, one of the climbers in the
party next to us slipped and fell part way down the mountain. He
slid right by me, with his rope, pitons, and other gear flying in all
directions. He was belayed, and his partner broke his fall before he
got hurt too badly. But still, that really shook me up.

I stopped to rest on a rock overhang. Far below I could see the girls who'd come along with Yvon's crew. They were l; rocks, sunning themselves with their tops off. I thought What am I doing up here? That's where I wanna be!

After that I was ruined for rock climbing. My ⌐_ .. ⌐.. wobbly, and I almost fell a couple of times. Bill, who's a strong, athletic guy, slid a couple of times while I was belaying him. But we both managed to get to the top unhurt. Meanwhile, though, Yvon and his bunch were climbing casually up the thing, unaided. For them it was like surfing a little four-foot beach break.

That night we all went to dinner at the Chart House in Idylwild. Yvon said to us, "You guys did real well today. But just wait until you see where we're going tomorrow."

I looked at Bill, and Bill shook his head. "Yvon, there isn't going to be any tomorrow," I said.

Yvon looked surprised. I don't think he had any idea how badly he'd overloaded us. "That little fall you saw today shake you up?"

"I don't mind falling," I said, "but I wanna land on water."

Yvon only smiled. He'd fulfilled his half of the bargain.

About a month later, Yvon came down to collect on the other half of our bargain. He and his tribe drove down to Leucadia, where we all piled into vans and campers loaded with surfers, surfboards, dogs and food, and headed for Baja.

When we got to El Rosario, about 225 miles south of Tijuana, we left the main highway and turned west, following a narrow, badly rutted dirt road. There was nothing out there then except tiny fishing villages and miles of untouched coastline. We drove for a couple more hours, to a point below the village of San Carlos. We stopped to scan the coastline from the cliffs, saw some sloppy surf, and a lot of happy seals, but we decided to keep going.

A few years earlier I'd flown over that stretch of coastline, and I knew there was a series of four or five points north of the village of Santa Rosalía. The one I liked most, the one I thought showed the most promise for good surf, was called Punta María.

After hours of driving over dusty, tortuous roads, and even some sections where there was no road at all, we finally arrived at Punta María. There was a beautiful little bay on the south side of the point—a gorgeous setting that looked like parts of Southern California must have looked 200 years ago.

The diving there was incredible. We saw places that looked like nobody had ever dived there before: abalone stacked up on top of abalone, and lobsters two feet long walking all over the bottom. It was like what the old watermen from La Jolla and Palos Verdes had talked about years before. I'd never seen a stretch of coastline that pristine.

We camped at Punta María for ten days and had a wonderful time, diving for abalone and lobster. The surfers knew the ocean better than the climbers, so we had a few things we could teach them now, but the climbers knew camping much better than we did. They were experts at cooking over an open fire with a minimum of gear, and together we put together some great feasts. We'd found a place where surfers and mountain climbers felt equally comfortable, and the camaraderie between our two groups of friends is a memory I'll always cherish.

But the waves never got over two feet. That's surfing.

In late September, I took my single-ski prototype to Mammoth Lakes, where skiers were still skiing on icy snow packs from the winter before.

The first people to see my single ski looked at me like I was out of my mind, but they lined up to watch me try it. I was afraid to get on the chair lift, thinking it would be awkward with the single ski. I figured the T-bar might be easier the first time. So I put the ski on and hobbled over to the T-bar. As I stood there waiting, I could hear people in the crowd starting to laugh. But I didn't care. I felt something important was about to happen.

The T-bar swung around, hit me below the ass, I fell backward, and both toe bindings pulled out of the ski. Before I'd moved even six inches up the hill, the single ski was ruined. I was frustrated, embarrassed, and very disappointed.

I had a friend there at Mammoth, a Paiute Indian named Rhubarb. We had spent some time together when I skied at Mammoth the winter before, and he was now the manager of the ski repair shop there at the lift. Rhubarb had seen my disaster on the

T-bar. He walked over to me and said, "Don't worry about it, Mike. Bring it over to the shop, and we'll put your ski back together."

In Rhubarb's shop, we drilled holes clear through the ski and bolted the bindings in place with nuts and washers on the bottom so they couldn't pull out.

This time I rode the T-bar without falling over, and with Rhubarb's repairs, the bindings held. My first few runs down the mountain, I side-slipped some and spun out a few times, but after about an hour I started getting used to it.

At first I was afraid to really open it up, but to my surprise I found that, unlike double skis, the faster I went on the single ski, the more stable it became. I started gaining confidence with every run.

I knew by the end of the day that I had something exciting. Where to go with it, how to manufacture it, how to market it, how to get it into the hands of people who could have fun with it, I had no idea. The biggest problem, I knew, would be to get people to accept it. There was a huge industry built around the double-ski concept. Trying to convince the manufacturers, then the retailers, and finally the skiers themselves that there might be a better way—that would be a challenge.

I took what I'd learned from the single ski's first trial, went back to Leucadia, and started building stronger, better prototypes.

It didn't take long for word of my invention to get around the ski industry. The vice president of the Hexcel Corporation called me one day and asked me if I would come up to their headquarters in Livermore, near San Jose, to tell them about my invention.

I told him I'd be happy to.

The truth was, I was a bit nervous about talking to the people at Hexcel. This was a big, successful corporation that had developed an extremely lightweight, yet strong, ski made from an aluminum honeycomb. (Actually, their ski was just an offshoot of their real business, which was making an aluminum-honeycomb skin for aircraft.) Not only would their people be excellent engineers, but they would also be shrewd businessmen. I felt I needed some help.

Bill Bahne, from Cardiff, was a self-taught engineer who had designed and manufactured a revolutionary system for mounting surfboard fins and had become very successful with it. Bahne told me he wanted to expand his manufacturing business, that he liked my single-ski concept and wanted to help me develop it.

I liked the idea of working with somebody from the surf industry, and somebody I knew. So when I drove up to Livermore to the Hexcel Corporation, I took Bahne along.

At the meeting there were several Hexcel executives gathered in a conference room. One of them said, "Mr. Doyle, we hear you've made something that's very interesting, some kind of single ski. Could you tell us more about it?"

I showed them a short film of me using the single ski at Mammoth, and I could see by the look in their eyes they understood the potential. They immediately offered me $80,000 for the patent rights and diminishing royalties over about six years. They also offered to give me a brand-new van and to put me on the road promoting the single ski.

I was astonished. It was a great offer. I wish now I'd taken it. Instead I looked at Bill Bahne, who had scarcely spoken a word. Bahne was a very thin, quiet man—a total introvert. But even his normally expressionless face registered some excitement. I said, "Let me think about it."

As soon as we were out the door, Bahne said, "I'll bring in brand-new machinery from Germany. We'll set up a factory, and make our own single ski. But we'll own the company ourselves."

I liked the idea of building a company from the ground up. That sounded exciting and creative to me. Besides, I'd already learned from my experience with Catalina that good ideas have a way of getting lost in the corporate bureaucracy. This time I wanted to have control over it myself. So I agreed to Bahne's offer.

Bahne put me on a small salary—just enough to live on. Though I was also getting a small royalty from Clark Foam, for the next several years I lived mostly on the money Bahne sent me. Luckily, I owned my home in Leucadia free and clear, so my living expenses were very small.

We went back to Bahne's factory in Cardiff and spent several weeks experimenting with different single-ski designs. Our best prototype was one with metal edges, and as soon as it was finished, I took it to Aspen to test it.

In Aspen I stayed with Joey, who was eager to see how my single ski worked. On the first day, Joey and I took the lift to the top of the mountain. There was a layer of deep, fresh, ungroomed powder, and I wasn't sure how the single ski would perform. On the first run down, after about the fourth turn, I fell end over end. I had set the bindings too loose, the single ski came off, and it disappeared in the powder.

Joey and I spent at least five hours digging around in the powder, trying to find that damned ski. We probed up and down the hill with our poles, but with no luck. Then we dug a trench six feet deep and twenty feet wide, again with no luck. When it started to get dark, we had to go home without it.

That was the only prototype I had with metal edges. It was much more sophisticated than my older prototypes, so going back to test the older skis would have been meaningless. I was so depressed, I couldn't talk to Joey or anybody else. I went to my room, shut the door, and went to sleep.

The next morning, Tommy Lee (our photographer friend from Hawaii, who was also staying with Joey) came into my room, woke me up, and said, "Come on, br'ah. Let's go look for that ski again."

Tommy and I rode the lift back up the mountain, but instead of thrashing around in the powder like Joey and I had the day before, Tommy stood there at the top of the mountain, meditating like some kind of Hawaiian Zen Buddhist. Finally, after several minutes, he said, "Tell me again where you fell."

I pointed out the exact spot where I had gone down. Tommy stood there again, studying the mountain and meditating. Finally, after the longest time, he pointed way down the mountain and said, "See there?"

I looked to where he was pointing, about a hundred yards away. Following the line of fall, I could barely see the hump the single ski had made as it burrowed under the snow. We followed the hump, and sure enough, we found the single ski where it had hit a tree and stopped.

That afternoon I was ripping and tearing on the single ski, coming down the mountain faster, but with more control, than anybody on two skis.

People all over the mountain were talking excitedly about the guy on one ski. But there was also a lot of resistance. When I was waiting in line at the chair lift, people would say, "Hey, how do you pee with both legs together like that? Ha! Ha!" Or, "Surf City's that way, dude!"

I didn't let it worry me. I knew there would be a lot of people who wouldn't want to see the single ski work. They had put so much time into mastering two skis, they didn't want to see a drastic change in skiing equipment and technique. But I knew that if I could just get people to try the single ski, they would see for themselves how much fun it was.

After spending a few more days at Aspen, I went up to Jackson Hole, where I knew I could really open up with the single ski. Jackson Hole had long, wide-open runs that were perfect for it. But more important, Jackson Hole was where I'd first had my dream of surfing in the snow, and I couldn't wait to get back there and make the dream come true.

On my first morning at Jackson Hole, the ski patrolmen let me go along on the first lift as they checked for avalanche danger. I'd gotten to know some of the patrolmen at Jackson Hole the year before. A lot of them were old surfers from California, and they were used to the idea of seeing new toys coming along and technological improvements on the old toys. They knew I was kind of a kook at skiing, but they also knew my reputation as a surfer, and they respected my ability. They acted like they really wanted to see my single ski work.

At the top of the lift, the ski patrolmen tossed out a few of their bombs to release the snow build-up from a storm the night before; then we all headed down the mountain together. I took Rendezvous Bowl at about fifty miles an hour, and the faster I went, the more stable the single ski became. With just a flick of the wrist I could glide smoothly into a giant slalom turn. I was really surfing down a mountain!

Almost immediately I left all the ski patrolmen behind. They were all better skiers than I was, but they couldn't compete with my single ski. And right away their attitudes began to change. I wasn't just a kook anymore. I was on their mountain, doing things they couldn't do. Maybe they thought I was showing off. I know they felt threatened. Skiing was their whole life, and they'd spent a lot of time becoming good at it. To see a guy on a surfboard make everything they knew obsolete was more than they could take. But what they didn't understand was that I wasn't outperforming them, I just had a better piece of equipment. Using a single ski, any one of them could have done better than I was doing.

For the rest of that winter at Jackson Hole, there was friction between me and the ski patrolmen. For a while they tried to get my single ski banned from the mountain—they said it was a safety hazard to other skiers, which was just ridiculous. But I didn't worry about it. I was on a high. Now I could ski the steepest runs on the mountain with total confidence and control. I was even jumping off of cornices like the most expert skiers. I had conquered my fear of skiing steep chutes, and I had made my own equipment to do it.

Meanwhile, every few days I would call Bahne back in California, and say, "This thing is really working, Bill. Send me more!"

And Bill would say, "Okay, don't worry. You'll have a dozen of them in another couple of weeks."

Until then, we had just been making each ski by hand, using wood and fiberglass. But Bahne wanted to begin immediately with the highest technology in ski manufacturing. He'd gone to Germany and bought a lot of very expensive machinery to tool up for mass production. And right away he'd started to run into all kinds of production problems.

I didn't see another single ski all that winter.

That spring, when I went back to Bahne's factory in Cardiff, I found the place in disarray. Bahne, who always looked like he was under great pressure, like he was inside a vacuum tube and the world outside was pressing in on him, was sitting in the middle of a dozen half-opened crates of machinery, trying to set up the factory all by himself. So I went to work helping him get the machinery in place, rearranging the office so it would function more efficiently, then building more handmade prototypes—doing everything I could think of to help.

One day when I was at Bahne's factory working on the single ski, Tom Morey drove up with a big grin on his face. He opened up his trunk and pulled out a piece of blue foam. It was two feet wide, three feet long, and two inches thick—the size of a belly board. Tom waved the chunk of foam at me and said, "Look at this, Mike." He bent it, twisted it, punched it. "This is the neatest thing. You can ride waves on it, belly board on it, paddle on it, sleep on it."

I looked at his piece of foam and couldn't make any sense out of it. I said, "First of all, Tom, it's upside down." He had the rails (the edges) beveled up from the bottom. Years ago Tom Morey had convinced everybody in the industry that a surfboard's rails should be turned down. Now here he was doing the exact opposite.

"No, no," he said. "Without a fin, the turned-up rails hold it in the wave. I call them Vacuum-Track rails."

I should have known right then that Tom was onto something. Besides being a design genius, he had a natural knack for marketing. "Okay, so it's got Vacuum-Track rails. But what is it?"

"Well, I think I'm gonna call it a Boogie Board," he said. "I'm looking for three investors to help me get this thing off the ground. I'm going to start building them in my garage and expand from there. A couple thousand dollars, and you're in."

I knew that you couldn't ever dismiss any of Tom's ideas, but I also knew he'd spent a lot of time on Kauai, and maybe his thinking had gotten a little too fantastic. As long as I'd known Tom, he'd been working on the design of a spaceship he called "the space driver." Gravity really concerns him a lot—mostly how to get released from it, how to fly or skim over the water. Once Tom made a surfboard that was air-lubricated; it had holes on the deck and a step effect on the bottom, so when you moved over the water you would suck air down and shoot bubbles out the bottom to reduce the friction.

Once Tom designed a car made out of foam so you could crash without getting hurt. He also developed his own universal language, with his own alphabet, so people could travel to foreign countries and be able to communicate. Tom always had a bunch of theories about how this or that worked, and he could wear you out talking about things most of us can barely conceive of. So I always tried to keep our conversations on a level I could deal with.

Anyway, at that time I had enough worries with my single ski. Besides, I didn't have $2,000 to invest. So I looked at his Boogie Board and said, "Good luck with it, Tom."

Tom wasn't discouraged. He took the thing back to his garage and went to work. He made a few Boogie Boards by hand, gluing the skins on himself; he sold those, made a few more and sold those, until eventually he had to hire his first employee. That's the way the Boogie Board got off the ground—little by little.

That winter I returned to Jackson Hole with Bill Engler. I was still trying to promote the single ski, even though I was starting to wonder if Bill Bahne was ever going to get the manufacturing end of it together.

As much as I enjoyed skiing at Jackson Hole, I was tired of taking flak from the ski patrolmen there, who were still trying to get my ski banned from the mountain. Bill Engler and I started thinking about finding a new place to ski.

In those days, Jackson Hole didn't have many women, and the ones it did have were hippie mountain women—the perfect mates if you were planning a move to Alaska. But Bill Engler and I had heard rumors that just over the hill, at Sun Valley, there were women who shaved their legs and didn't look half grizzly bear. So one day we drove over to there to have a look.

Bill and I liked Sun Valley so much, we went back there several times that winter. On one of those trips I met a wonderful and very captivating woman, Diane Hall. I remember the first time I saw her. She was working at the Crepery, a restaurant in Sun Valley, and she was wearing a black Danskin top. She was a lovely, graceful woman with a very sensual nature. From the first time we saw each other, we started sending love signals back and forth with our eyes.

Little by little, I got to know Diane better that winter: I learned that she was originally from Oregon, where her father had been governor. She had been raised in the governor's mansion, was cultured and artistic, had studied ballet, and was a wonderful conversationalist. Even though Diane had a boyfriend at the time, she and I both knew that somehow we would be seeing more of each other in the near future.

When I got back to California that spring, I saw that Bahne still hadn't made any progress on manufacturing the single ski. I was beginning to worry that if we didn't get the single ski into production pretty soon, somebody else would steal the idea. I went to the Hexcel Corporation again to ask if they were still interested in buying it from me, but they said their new aluminum-honeycomb ski had been a great success, and they had all the production challenges they could handle at the time. I could feel the opportunity slipping away.

Besides the extreme frustration I was having with the single ski, I was becoming disgruntled with North County. It was changing very rapidly from a beautiful and quiet retirement area into the new place for affluent Southern Californians. The beaches were getting crowded, and real estate prices were exploding. After spending so much time in the mountains in the last few years, my thinking about open space had changed, and I felt the need to live in a place where the lifestyle was slower and more peaceful.

I wasn't the only surfer who felt this way. Although surfers from Texas and Florida were migrating to San Diego County, lots of native surfers were looking to get out. The trend was toward what we called "soul surfing," which emphasized the freedom and independence of the sport. It rejected organized and competitive surfing, as well too much commercialization. The idea was, instead of surfing to impress other people or to win a trophy or an endorsement, you surfed to satisfy your personal sense of creativity and for the feeling of being in harmony with nature. But it was hard to be a soul surfer in Southern California.

I sold the Hermes house (I needed the money by now), loaded up the flatbed truck, and drove north on Highway 1, through Malibu, Santa Barbara, and Big Sur. I almost settled down in Santa Cruz, where I had several friends, but I could see that the new University of California was having a drastic affect on that small community; in a few more years it, too, would be overcrowded.

I continued driving up the coast, through Mendocino and Crescent City. When I got about sixty miles north of the Oregon border, to the area around Port Orford, I figured I'd found what I was looking for. I bought ten acres in a small valley called Hubbard Creek, about a mile inland from the coast. There was a year-round creek on the property, an apple orchard, lots of firs and cedars, and plenty of peace and quiet. Down at the end of the road, just a few minutes away, there was a good surf spot. It seemed like this place really had it all.

I put up a tent for my first shelter, built a big barn to keep all my tools dry, then set about building a home. I cut down a few of the Douglas firs on the land, loaded them onto my flatbed truck, hauled them to the mill, and had them sawed into lumber. I had electrical power brought to the land, and I set up a pump in the stream. Then I began building an octagonal house, forty-five feet in diameter, with a big loft upstairs. I wanted to use as many recycled building materials as I could, so I went to an auto wrecker's yard and bought several automobile windows. I mounted the roll-up windows in plywood; the windshields I put in two-by-twelve casings and sealed with three-inch rope.

I bought an old claw-foot bathtub and used the inside of the tub to mold four fiberglass skylights, which I mounted in the roof panels. The lighting effect inside the house was gorgeous. I added a hardwood floor, put paste wax on it, and buffed it in until it had a beautiful warm glow. I installed a big eighty-gallon water heater, knowing when I came in from surfing I would need long hot baths.

There was a bend in the creek behind my house, so I screened off a big pond and filled it with trout, which I fed Purina trout chow.

At night there were always black bears out in the apple orchard. When you walked outside, you could hear the bears munching on the apples, and in the daytime you could see the claw marks on the trees. The bears didn't bother me other than that, and I wasn't afraid of them. But one of the locals told me I shouldn't let the bears eat my apples. He didn't say why, just that it was a bad thing to do. He said I should set up a trap and try to catch the bears. So one night I set up a bear trap, and a funny thing happened. As soon as I set the trap, I became afraid of the bears. Now the bears and I were at odds with each other, and I no longer felt comfortable going out at night.

I learned something from that: Fear has more to do with your own aggression than it does with the object of your fear. Once I understood what had happened, I put away the bear trap and let the bears have as many apples as they wanted.

Before long a couple of old surfing pals from California, Gary Bickler and Walt Phillips, bought land next to me. We all bought the best custom-made wetsuits available, and together we started cracking the southern Oregon coast.

Gold Beach was the nearest surf spot. Every time we went down there, the local fishermen would look at us like we were crazy and say, "Going out on that shingle again?" Or, "Feeding the sharks today, are ya?"

We surfed huge waves at Cape Blanco, the most westerly point of the contiguous United States. One time, during a powerful storm, the waves there were twenty feet. On one side of Cape Blanco, the wind was blowing so hard we could hear the telephone wires whistling. It was scary and very dramatic. But on the lee side of the cape, the weaker wind was blowing offshore, which improved the surf. To a Southern California boy though, the water was too damn cold. I got ice-cream headaches every time my head went underwater.

Of course it rained a lot there, more than I cared for, and it was windy much of the time. And the lifestyle was about as different from Southern California's as you could get—which, of course, was one reason I went there. The only social life was the one we created—there wasn't even a movie theater in town. On the days when it was too cold and windy to do much outdoors, we hung out together playing music. We had dinner at somebody's house almost every night. Somebody would kill a deer or catch a bunch of fish, and that would be reason enough to celebrate. We drank a lot.

Port Orford was a small town, with an economy mostly based on fishing and shrimping. At one time there had been a lot of logging, but most of the commercial timber there had already been cut down. Most of the people back in the mountains grew pot. I remember that when they got loaded, they liked to sing a magical incantation: "Grow 'em strong, grow 'em tall, thick trunks! thick trunks!" I don't know if it worked or not.

One of my friends bought some land down by Gold Beach and grew about a half acre of pot before he got arrested. He lost the property and spent about six months in jail.

Although I could have used the money, I didn't grow any pot. Because of the wind and the weather, I thought that country looked like a bad place to grow anything except trees. But growing pot also looked like trouble to me. I always imagined myself sitting in a chair in front of my mother, and she would be saying to me, "Michael, I told you this would happen if you didn't listen to me!" The fear of hurting my mother and having to deal with her anger has kept me out of serious trouble most of my life.

One of my neighbors there on Hubbard Creek had a mailbox with the words "El Ratón," the rat, painted on the side. Every time I drove by, I wondered who lived there. Then one day in town, somebody pointed out El Ratón to me and said his real name was Pete Lenahan. He was slightly built, with dark hair and a ruddy complexion, about ten years older than I was. He was a bit jaded, sort of cynically amused, and I thought he looked like somebody who'd had an interesting life.

I happened to be working outside one day when Lenahan came walking over the hill, hunting deer. I called him over, we started talking, and soon became friends.

In some ways, Lenahan became my idol. He could fell trees, build boats, hunt deer—he knew all the things I was just learning how to do. But the more I got to know him, I found that he was a very complex person. Among his many other talents, he had a passion for the jazz piano, which he played well. He'd been raised in a wealthy family in Pasadena, California, and his family had owned a house near Port Orford for years.

Lenahan had worked as a wooden-boat builder in Denmark for five or six years, and he was building boats for a living now. When I expressed an interest in boat building, he asked me to work with him. Together we built a pair of forty-foot commercial fishing boats out of Port Orford white cedar, which is a highly prized wood. We cut the trees down ourselves, took them to the mill, and had them sawed into planking. Everything you build on a boat has a curve to it, so the carpentry is very complex. Lenahan taught me how to work with compound curves, how to bend boards in steam boxes, how to move heavy logs around with fulcrums, and how to move boats down to the docks. He taught me the correct way to use woodworking tools. It was hard work, but I found it to be very rewarding. In return, I introduced Lenahan to the world of surfing.

Late that fall, as I was getting ready to go back to Sun Valley for the winter, I received an interesting visit from Diane Hall. Oddly, she brought along her boyfriend. They were traveling down the coast of Oregon to Southern California, and Diane made it sound as if their stop in Port Orford was just a last-minute whim. I'm sure she had convinced her boyfriend that was all it was. But Diane and I both knew she had come to see if there was still something between us.

There was, all right, but neither of us could find the right way to express it. She had a boyfriend, and I had a girlfriend at the time—we just couldn't figure out how to get things started.

When I arrived in Sun Valley that winter, Diane was still with her boyfriend. We started seeing a lot of each other, but it was awkward. We would see each other skiing or around town, but it was like we were right back where we'd started. I couldn't figure out what was going on.

I was still getting some money from Bahne, and I'd saved a little money from building boats with Lenahan, but I could see that wasn't going to last. Finding a new sponsor for my single ski was still my one big hope. I was certain it could still be very big, if only I could get it into production. I talked to the people at K-2, a ski manufacturer located on Vashon Island, in Washington; they liked my idea but said they, too, had more production challenges than they could deal with at the time.

Joey Cabell would come up to Sun Valley to ski with me from time to time. After trying the single ski, he loved it and did everything he could to support me with it. *Sports Illustrated* heard there were a couple of world-champion surfers out in the Rocky Mountains, surfing on skis. They sent a writer and photographer out to Jackson Hole, and they did a feature article on Joey and me testing the single ski. The story ran January 13, 1975, along with a beautiful picture of Joey and me jumping over the photographer. The publicity was great, I was lining up distributors, and people were constantly asking me, "Where can we get a single ski?" The whole thing was building to a peak, but with one big flaw—I had no skis to sell.

Corky Carroll moved to Sun Valley that winter. He'd given up competitive surfing, was married now, and had started a little band he called Corky and the Corkettes. He worked as a waiter in the day and played in the bars at night. His wife and three other girls wore little Hawaiian outfits and sang "Ooh La, Ooh La La." He tried hard, but Corky never quite made it as a musician.

The money from Bahne had dribbled down to nothing, so to pay my bills, I started working as a waiter in the restaurants. It was very difficult for me because I don't hear that well, especially in a crowded room where a lot of people are talking at once. A lot of the people in the restaurant were drunk, and I would have to ask them three or four times before I could understand what they'd said. It was depressing.

Later that winter I had to sell my place in Oregon to make ends meet.

I went back to Leucadia that summer, thinking I'd try one more time to help Bill Bahne get the single ski into production. It was one of those gray summers along the Southern California coast. The sun hardly ever came out, and that was about how my life felt at the time, too.

Bahne hadn't made any progress setting up the machinery for the factory, and as near as I could tell, he'd given up trying. Finally his brother, Bob, came to me and said, "I know the agreement you two originally had was that you would be partners in the single ski. We bought all that equipment, we did the best we could, but we never made any skis, and we never made any money. I'm afraid we can't honor the partnership."

That was a crushing blow for me. I'd developed a new concept in skiing, put years of energy into it, only to have the entire project collapse. It was my first really bitter taste of failure, and the most frustrating thing I'd ever had to deal with. I was thirty-four years old; I'd lost my work, my direction, and my hope for the future. I had no idea what to do next.

The only bright spot in my life was Diane. She was still back in Sun Valley, but something about being apart rekindled our fires. We started writing letters back and forth to each other. I finally called her and asked her if she would come to California.

Diane said she would come if I wanted her to.

It was the first time Diane and I had spent time alone together. It was also the first time she'd seen me on my own territory. I rented a house on Neptune Avenue, on the bluff overlooking the ocean. We went swimming in the ocean and for long walks on the beach. San Diego was all new to her, and I had fun showing it to her.

Later that summer, Diane came right out and said what we'd both been thinking: "Why don't we get married?"

I'd already been married once, and wasn't eager to do it again. But I knew I might never get another chance with a woman like Diane. I told her, "You arrange the wedding. I'll be there."

So we became engaged, and later that summer we were married in Encinitas.

For our honeymoon, Diane and I drove to Cabo in the Ford Falcon her father had bought as governor of Oregon. On the way down, we stopped in El Rosario and had lobster tacos at Espinosa's. I'd stopped there many times over the years on my surfing expeditions to Baja, and I'd gotten to know Señora Espinosa, the owner, fairly well. The government had recently finished paving the road all the way from Tijuana to Cabo San Lucas, so I asked Señora Espinosa if the improved road had been good for her business. She sighed, shook her head, and said, "The bad road brought the good people, and now the good road brings the bad people."

In Cabo we camped at Alfonso's. We went surfing every day, speared fish for our dinner, and drank rum and Cokes. Diane loved it. She ran on the beach and went snorkeling—she'd never seen tropical fish before and couldn't believe their brilliant colors.

Diane loved the simplicity and the freedom of Cabo as much as I did, and we both knew that if our life together could be like this, we would be happy.

I used the money I had left from my place in Oregon to buy a house in Hailey, Idaho, just down the road from Sun Valley. Diane and I planned to live there, but first we had to go to Washington to pick up her furniture, which she'd stored with her mother. So right after the honeymoon, we headed north for Seattle in the Falcon.

I suppose this should have been a happy time for me. But it wasn't. As we drove up I-5, it was raining hard and the sky looked very dreary. I felt like I was going back to the cold mountains where, after being in Cabo, I didn't want to be. In many ways, I felt frustrated and confused. I didn't know what to do about my single ski, and I was worried about how I would support my new wife. Even though Diane did her best to understand my worries, I felt the panic of being married again. I felt like I was driving into the heart of that dark cloud I could see ahead of me on I-5.

We stopped in Oregon so Diane could show me to the governor's mansion in Salem, the place where she'd been raised. The mansion was on top of a hill and had big, white stately columns in front. Her father was no longer governor (in fact, he had passed away), but the security guards still allowed us to walk around the grounds.

I could see that Diane had been raised as a little princess. I should have felt proud to have her for my wife, but instead I only felt inadequate, as if I didn't really deserve this woman.

In Seattle we rented a moving van, but even loading the furniture was depressing. Not only was Washington cold and gray, but with each piece of furniture I loaded into the van, I felt like I was adding a few more pounds to the weight I already felt.

None of this was Diane's fault. She was wonderful to me. It was just that I felt like a failure, and no matter how bright our prospects together might have been, I felt miserable.

After we settled into our house in Hailey, Diane went to work teaching modern dance at the creative arts center there, doing what she loved most. Every morning she would go to work full of joy and enthusiasm. I kept busy remodeling our little house, but I knew that work would end someday, and I dreaded thinking about what would happen next.

The thing that saved me that season was one last chance to push my single ski. A surf and ski photographer, and old friend of mine, Dick Barrymore, was there. One day he said to me, "Hey, I'm gonna go helicopter skiing up in the Cariboos, up in British Columbia. If you'd like to bring your single ski and come along, I'd like to take you. We'll make a movie featuring the single ski."

I'd never been helicopter skiing before, but I'd heard a lot about it—virgin powder and long, open runs. I was excited about having a new adventure, but most of all, I hoped the movie would attract a new sponsor to help me build my single ski.

Barrymore, Corky Fowler (the top hot-dogger on skis at that time), and I flew to Edmonton and then drove to the Starlight Hotel. The guide service at the hotel arranged for us to have a small helicopter, a Hughes 500, meet us at the hotel every morning. The helicopter, which normally cost something like $600 per hour, was free to Barrymore because of the publicity his movie would bring.

Every day we skied mountains that were fantastically beautiful—mile-long runs of perfect, deep powder. In some ways it was a lot like working with Bud Browne on a surf movie, and we had a lot of fun planning out the shots. We had one run that was about three miles long, and just for the fun of it, Corky Fowler and I made figure-eight patterns all the way down the mountain. Watching the film later I counted 187 figure-eights.

That ski trip went a long ways toward nudging me out of the dark mood I'd been in. Later, Dick Barrymore and I traveled around to college campuses showing that film, which he called *Mountain High*. We mentioned in the film, more as a joke than anything else, that we'd set the world figure-eight record. Something about that captured people's imaginations, and skiers from all over began trying to break our figure-eight record.

About this time, 1976, a ski product came out of Utah called the Winter Stick. It was the first snowboard, and looked more like a surfboard than my single ski. The bindings were perpendicular, so you couldn't use it with ski poles, but the body mechanics for the Winter Stick were much more like surfing or skateboarding. It created some excitement in the Rockies, but not much. With a few design improvements, though, the snowboard went on to become hugely successful—and is still growing—mostly, I believe, because of the popularity of skateboarding. There were millions of skateboarders all over the world who had never surfed or skied before, but with the help of the snowboard and just a few hours of practice, they could do as well on ski slopes as expert skiers.

For me, though, the release of the Winter Stick and the snowboards that followed meant the end of my single ski. Snowboards took the design innovations I had made one step further. They leapfrogged my efforts, and the single ski no longer had any marketability.

I ran into Mike Zuetell in Sun Valley one day. I'd known Mike since back in the days when he and his buddies in the 22nd Street Gang had made my life so miserable. Mike and I had become friends over the years. He had been married and divorced, and was now working in Sun Valley as a sales rep for a ski company. Every now and then we would ski together and talk about old times. We always laughed about that scar he had on his forehead from the time Don Hansen threw a ceramic bowl at him in Santa Cruz.

Another old friend, Kemp Aaberg, came to stay with Diane and me for a while. He'd been in Spain studying classical guitar for several years. He was all white and pasty-looking, and hadn't surfed in years. His plans were to move back to California and try to make a living playing the guitar.

Now that the single ski had no future, I had no idea what to do next. I felt demoralized and confused. I wasn't earning any money and had nothing productive to do with my time. I knew all the wealthy people in Sun Valley, but except for my house in Hailey, I didn't have anything. I felt like a high-rolling low-life.

Though I enjoyed skiing and living in the mountains, I knew I belonged near the ocean. The ocean had always been my source of inspiration and strength. In Idaho I was like a fish out of water.

Meanwhile, Diane and I were growing farther apart. (For the sake of privacy, the reasons will go unrecorded here.) When we started having serious problems with our marriage, a friend suggested that we go to an EST workshop—Erhard Seminars Training—in assertiveness and self-improvement, which was becoming a big fad at the time. I didn't want to go, but this guy kept telling us what a big change it would make in our lives, so when the traveling seminar came to Sun Valley, I agreed to go.

That EST workshop was what finally ended our marriage. The focus of the seminar was that you should get on with your life, that you should be doing what you want to do. I didn't like the way the seminar was run; I didn't like the way they cracked people's heads open with an ax, tried to make people spill their guts and go through all their emotional traumas in public. But I couldn't argue with their major premise: People should be happy.

After the seminar, I finally admitted to myself that I had no business being in the mountains. I might have been able to get Diane to go back to California with me if I'd approached her right, but I think we both knew that would only prolong our unhappiness together.

I loaded up my few belongings in the Ford Falcon, gave Diane the keys to the house, and said good-bye.

I was thirty-five years old, had less than $100 in my pocket, no wife, no job, and no notable prospects for the future. Once again I was back to nothing. But after months of watching my marriage fall apart and waiting helplessly for the inevitable, I was relieved it was finally over. I saw a chance to put two failures—my marriage and my single ski—behind me now and get on with my life.

As I started driving across the open range in southern Idaho, with the sun going down and country-western music playing on the radio, I felt more optimistic about the future than I had in a long time.

Gringo Hill

*M*y mother and stepfather had retired to the town of Fall-brook, in north San Diego County about an hour's drive from the coast. They owned about four acres with a small house. Their land had a small creek and was covered with beautiful live oaks. I couldn't see myself moving in with my mother and Walt, and I didn't have enough money to get a place of my own, so I picked out my favorite oak tree and went to work building myself a tree house.

It took only a few days to build my new home, which was about ten-by-fifteen, had a metal roof, and a nice view of the creek. The whole thing didn't cost fifty dollars.

Once I was all moved in, I went to work plotting my future. In spite of my doubts and uncertainty, I felt comfortable being back in Southern California, where I had a lot of friends and could make things happen. I wanted to get involved in some sort of creative project that would, hopefully, earn me some money and fill the hole left by the failure of my single ski.

What I came up with was a formulation for a suntan oil. I knew about oils and scents from the days when we made surfboard wax. I experimented with different combinations until I found one I liked: a mixture of apricot and wheatgerm oil. Then I went to work on the marketing end of it: I found an old whiskey flask, the kind of bottle that might wash up on the beach with a secret message in it, and I designed a label for it. The label looked like a Gauguin painting, with two Polynesian girls holding a bowl of fruit. I named it Endless Summer Suntan Oil, borrowing the name from Bruce Brown's movie.

I installed a phone in my tree house and started calling old friends who might be potential partners in my project. One who liked my idea was Brooks Gifford, an attorney for Ocean Pacific, the giant beachwear manufacturer. Gifford's only concern was that Bruce Brown wouldn't approve of us using the title of his movie. So we decided to go see Bruce and ask for his permission.

I'll never forget how cool Bruce was. When we walked into his house in Dana Point, Gifford had all the paperwork ready to sign. Gifford said, "We're making a suntan oil, Bruce, and we'd love to use the name Endless Summer. Now if you'll just sign here, giving us those rights—"

Bruce just waved the papers aside, then said, "I'll tell you what, guys. You go ahead and make your oil. You don't need anything from me. I'm telling you personally that you can use the title. But I'm not signing anything. Maybe your product will turn out to be as successful as Hawaiian Tropics. I hope so. But if it does become really big, let me know. Then I might want something back for the use of my title."

Gifford sighed and looked perplexed, but I was pleased. After all his success, Bruce Brown still believed that business came down to trusting another person's word.

We made our suntan oil and marketed it up and down the coast, selling it mostly through health food stores and surf shops, directing it toward people looking for a pure, high-quality product and who were willing to pay a little higher price. It was an instant success.

I now had some income, but with four partners taking a cut, my share wasn't enough to live on. To increase the sales of the suntan oil, the next step would have been to spend millions of dollars on advertising. I was broke and had nothing to contribute to that. Besides, running a business never had interested me. The fun part had been creating the product. What I wanted now was some operating capital so I could go on to my next project. So I sold my share to the other partners, and I moved on.

When Rusty Miller moved to Australia (by way of the hippie colony on Kauai), he was eventually joined by my other partner at Surf Research, Garth Murphy. Later, after skiing several winters with me, Bill Engler joined them, too. But now Bill had moved back to North County, and I was really happy to see him again. Bill had always been a good influence on me. He was strong and healthy, mentally focused, a determined worker, and he didn't get side-tracked with wine and women as much as I did. Bill told me, "I feel the call to work with my hands. I feel like I want to build something." I told Bill I felt the same way, so we started talking about a project we could work on together.

Just a few years earlier, when Bill and I had left north San Diego County, we thought the real estate boom had made the place ridiculously expensive. But now we began to realize that the boom had hardly begun. If a person was willing to get his hands dirty and work, he could make some money. Neither of us had ever worked in construction, but we knew that between the two of us we could figure out what needed to be done.

Bill and I combined our finances, went to an estate auction and bought a small house in Oceanside for $29,000 cash. We went right to work remodeling the place, and in only four months we sold it for $75,000.

Construction work was perfect for Bill and me. We were both strong, and we loved the physical activity. We didn't have to work for somebody else or put up with any corporate bull. The work was interesting and creative, and when we took off our nail bags at the end of the day we could see what we'd accomplished. And the pay turned out to be pretty good, too. After years of watching my single ski die a slow death, it felt good to be working hard on a successful project again.

We took all the profit from that first house and bought a much nicer house in Oceanside. This time we threw our foam pads down on the floor and lived right in the house while we were remodeling. We'd wake up in the morning, have a cup of coffee, and go to work—no commuting, no board meetings, no bosses, and no wives. Just swinging a hammer all day long.

Bill had done some amateur boxing, and he still had a set of boxing gloves. So he set up a boxing ring in the living room, and after working all day we'd put on the gloves, set a timer for three minutes, and bang on each other for a while. I still think that's a great way for partners to work out their differences, and it would probably prevent a lot of ulcers, too.

In just a few more months, we sold our second house for

$120,000. This time we bought a lot in nearby La Costa, which was growing dramatically. We didn't have a contractor's license, but we weren't going to let that stop us. We built two custom homes on that lot and sold them both almost as soon as they were finished.

Tom Morey had gone into full production on his Boogie Board by now and was selling something like 100,000 Boogie Boards a year, making it one of the most successful inventions ever to come off the beach. I think a reporter once wrote that every garage in Orange County has a Boogie Board in it. It's one of those inventions that's so simple, it's hard to believe somebody didn't come up with it sooner. But I think those are exactly the inventions that require a visionary like Tom.

I really believe Tom did something quite fantastic with the Boogie Board—I mean more than just make a lot of money. He turned hundreds of thousands of people on to the joy and thrill of riding a wave—not just athletic young men, but little children, middle-aged mothers, senior citizens—people who might never have touched a surfboard.

Tom's Boogie Board factory was in Carlsbad, just a few minutes away from Encinitas, and I liked to stop by and see him from time to time. Over the years, Tom had become a big influence on my thinking. As an example, not long after the first tri-fin surfboard came out, Tom and I were talking about what made the tri-fin work. He told me, "If you want to think a design feature all the way through, imagine it to an absurd extreme, then back it up to the point where it becomes practical. For example, if you can imagine three fins on a surfboard, why not a hundred fins? What would be its advantages and disadvantages?"

Tom actually built a hundred-fin surfboard just for the fun of it, and it worked terrible. But I've used his simple formula ever since—not just designing surf toys, but in all types of thinking. Tom showed me how to make the absurd practical.

Over the years I'd taught a lot of people how to surf, and I had a pretty good idea of what it took to overcome the difficulties of the beginning surfer. Besides the obvious element of balance, you have to learn wave judgment, paddling, timing—a lot of people give up surfing before they ever enjoy the satisfaction of riding one good wave. So I started thinking that a soft surfboard, made from the material Tom was using for his Boogie Board, would be a great learning tool. It would be soft enough that a beginner wouldn't get hurt, it would have smooth edges that would be forgiving, and it would just look and feel fun.

So I stopped by Tom's factory one day to tell him about my idea. He brought me into his office, then listened patiently while I told him what was on my mind. I explained how you could use a foam core, with a fiberglass stringer for rigidity, but instead of covering the thing with fiberglass, like a standard surfboard, you could cover it with soft foam. I said, "It's never going to be a high-performance board, but not everybody needs that. It would be a tool for helping beginners get started."

After Tom had heard me out, he smiled, then shrugged and said, "Hey, Mike, ideas are like assholes— everybody's got one. The hard part isn't coming up with new ideas, but making the ideas work." He pointed out the door of his office and said, "There's my factory, there's the materials. Use whatever you want."

Tom really taught me something there. I'm certain that if I'd used Tom's advice and taken control of the production of my single ski right from the start, that whole disaster would have turned out differently.

After working on houses all day with Bill Engler, I'd go down to Tom's factory at night and experiment with laminating the first soft surfboard. I tried several different templates, trying to find a shape that was both functional in the water and easy to laminate. Eventually, with the help of Tom's people, I put the skin on the first prototype, which looked and felt like a big blob of foam. I took the thing down to the beach and tested it in the water. Right away I thought, Hey, this thing works. We called it the Morey-Doyle, put it on the market, and sold about 3,000 units that first year.

For our next construction project, Bill and I bought a house in Encinitas with a vacant lot next to it. It was on a hill above the old part of town, a prime area overlooking the coastline. We went to work remodeling the existing house, then started on a big, custom,

Spanish-style home on the vacant lot. By the time Bill and I finished building that house, I liked it so much I bought Bill's share and moved in myself.

Later that year I drove to Cabo, and for $7,000 I bought a lot on the hill above Zippers. Using the local workers, I started building a small house in the Mexican style, with brick and plaster, tile floors, shuttered windows (no glass), and a large patio overlooking the ocean. It was simple but comfortable, the kind of place I could leave and come back to without worrying about. Later I hired a local craftsman to make a beautiful woven *palapa* roof over the patio, I planted a few palm trees, and added a big garage to store my surfboards and a dune buggy.

Back in North County, Bill and I started thinking maybe we needed a better training regimen than beating each other in the face with boxing gloves. We were both doing a lot of hard physical work, and we were starting to feel the effects of middle-age—stiffness, a loss of flexibility. It was hard to admit it to ourselves, but maybe we couldn't stay in great shape any longer by just surfing and drinking beer.

We heard about a new exercise program being held at a junior high school in Carlsbad. It was called Jazzercise and was supposedly the first class of its kind in the country. We understood it was mostly for women, but that sounded okay to us. North County still didn't have a lot of girls in those days, and we figured that instead of hanging out at some beach bar, it would make a lot more sense to go where the healthy ones were.

At our first Jazzercise class, Bill and I found a room full of hard, sweaty women. And we were the only guys there. The woman leading the class was a cute blonde, Judi Sheppard. We'd never seen anything like her before. She had a fully aerobicized body, hard and perfect, plus an enormous amount of energy. She liked to scream at the top of her lungs. The women in the class were extremely friendly and gave us lots of attention. One of them said, "This stuff should be easy for a couple of big strong guys like you." Bill and I hopped and bopped until the sweat was pouring down our faces, trying to show them what we could do.

The next day we were so sore, we couldn't get ou
go to work. We took the day off and lay around groan¡
other, sipping on cold beers to ease the pain.

Bill and I kept hearing about another woman, Terry Cole-Whitakker, who was creating quite a splash down in La Jolla as a
minister in the Church of Religious Science. She was preaching
some kind of new-age philosophy and had already attracted a large
and dedicated following. Bill and I weren't the types to get involved
with some California guru cult, but we were curious. So one Sunday
we drove down to La Jolla to listen to Terry Cole-Whitakker speak.
She was undoubtedly the best public speaker Bill or I had ever
heard—full of energy and humor—and we were impressed.

This was a time when a lot of young people in California were
struggling to find a new direction. The hippie era was over, and
people who had dropped out of the mainstream culture were trying
to re-enter it. Terry's main message was that there's no honor to be
gained by being poor, that you have control over your own destiny,
and that prosperity is your divine right. I didn't know what to make
of Terry's message, but I loved the way she presented it. She did
for religion what Judi Sheppard did for exercise.

While Bill and I were pounding nails all day, we'd joke about
what it would be like if he could pair up with one of them and I
could pair up with the other. We could all move in together, and we
would have our entire physical and spiritual lives taken care of.

After going to a few more of Terry Cole-Whitakker's sermons,
I happened to be introduced to her. She was attracted to me, and I
was attracted to her. Terry was married at the time to a Canadian
football player, a big handsome guy, but the marriage was on shaky
ground, and Terry believed in doing what she wanted to do, when
she wanted to do it. One evening she stopped by my house in
Encinitas. We had a couple of drinks and ended up talking long into
the night. After that she and I spent almost all our free time together.

One weekend Terry and I went to a public speakers' convention in Las Vegas, which she had been invited to address. There
were at least a thousand people there, all public speakers who knew
every trick of the trade. You would think they would be so analytical

about the techniques of public speaking that they would be immune to its effects. But they weren't. Terry gave a speech that was so dynamic, so inspiring, so damned good, the entire convention stood and gave her a standing ovation. Oddly enough, I don't even recall what the subject of her speech was now, but it doesn't really matter. That was her talent. She could open the Bible to any page, pick one line at random, and develop an impromptu speech that would make people rearrange their entire lives.

I figured that if a convention of public speakers thought Terry was hot stuff, the general public would go crazy over her. Driving back from that convention, I suggested to Terry that she sell tapes of her speeches. Terry liked the idea and set up a business, separate from her church, called Terry Cole-Whitakker & Associates. Together we created a spiritual tape, a money-and-you tape, and a tape on personal relationships.

Terry did well with all those tapes—at a typical convention we could sell $10,000 worth of them. But the tape on personal relationships outsold the others ten-to-one. I had learned through my own experience, and so had Terry, that more people are confused about personal relationships than about any other element of their lives. They can run their businesses, they can manage their employees, some of them can take care of their health and fitness, but not very many can handle their personal relationships.

The tape on relationships was my idea, and I outlined the thoughts in it, which I know is ironic. I'm the first to admit I've never figured out relationships myself and have only had success with them on a temporary basis. But then it's possible that nobody ever does any better than that. Maybe I didn't know all the answers about relationships, but I'd certainly been around enough to know all the right questions. At any rate, that tape found an eager audience.

In the meantime, Terry's congregation kept growing larger and larger every Sunday until, eventually, she had to move her sermons to a big movie theater in downtown San Diego. She became a media star, and on a superficial level, everything looked wonderful.

Terry's followers were young and affluent, they had very high energy levels, and they liked to have fun. They weren't boring, and they weren't self-righteous, but they were cheap. They never contributed much in the way of collections, which put Terry in a peculiar position. She was like somebody at the top of a multilevel marketing scheme, trying to show all the salesmen below her how easy it was to get rich. She had to put on a show of great prosperity, even though that wasn't necessarily the reality. So Terry became interested in starting a TV ministry, which is where she thought the big money was. I told her I thought she should get out of the church for her own good and move into public speaking. Terry's real talent was inspiring people to pursue their goals, to have the courage to go after what they really wanted in life. The rest of it was just a waste of energy and, I thought, a waste of her talent.

There was an even deeper conflict in Terry's church, which went right to the center of her character. This was the beginning of the decade of greed. Her followers wanted affluence, but they wanted to keep their spirituality, too. People had a real emotional conflict between the two, and Terry seemed to resolve that for them. (She'd written a book titled *How to Have More in a Have Not World*; its basic theme was that you didn't have to feel guilty about wanting to have money.) But in reality, I think Terry had more of a conflict with that dilemma than any of them. She just knew how to talk around it better than they did. I think that was why a reporter nicknamed her "the high priestess of yuppiedom."

Because she had become such a well-known figure in the new-age movement, Terry was invited to participate in every kind of new-age fad imaginable: fire walking, prosperity blessings, crystal healing. She was interested in the occult and had seances at her house. I thought it was all hocus-pocus, but that's the kind of thing Terry liked, and I have to admit it was kind of amusing, like reading your horoscope in the paper.

One time Terry invited a channeler from Los Angeles to come to her house in La Jolla. Dr. Julian (not his real name) was a round, pink-faced little guy who could be very charming and amusing. We all had a few drinks while Dr. Julian went around the room chatting with each of us. Then we settled down to business.

It took a few minutes for Dr. Julian to work himself into a trance. It was an interesting show: His face turned red, his cheeks puffed up, and his whole body bloated up like a little toad. By then the facial features of Dr. Julian had completely disappeared and were replaced by those of his alter ego, whose name I don't recall.

Dr. Julian went around the room and did a reading for each person, describing his or her talents and abilities, and prescribing the role each person should take in Terry's life and business. When he got to Terry he paused, as if summoning his grandest supernatural powers. (It wasn't common knowledge at this time that Terry and I were having an affair, but Dr. Julian, I think, was observant enough to sense it.) Dr. Julian began warning Terry that she should be very careful about her relationships. "Don't allow those closest to you to become a drain on your energy," he said, "because there are wolves all around ready to pounce on you!"

I expected that any second he would to turn to me and shriek, "There's the one! That's the demon in your presence! I command you to tear him to shreds."

But it didn't happen that way. Before Dr. Julian could get to me, I got up and left.

After that little channeling session, I became more and more uncomfortable with Terry and the kinds of people she surrounded herself with.

There were a few people involved in Terry's church, though, who I came to like very much. One was Jack Perl (not his real name), a middle-aged stockbroker from New York who'd made a fortune on Wall Street before moving to Encinitas. Jack was still active in the stock market, but he did all his trading by computer now, from his home, a huge house on the ocean bluff in Encinitas.

Jack looked like the guy who could be on the cover of the health book *Sugar Blues*. He was milky white and kind of soggy looking—in terrible shape. But you could look in his eyes and see there was something going on in there.

Probably the only thing Jack and I had in common was that we were both up at dawn. I went surfing, and Jack worked the stock market. In his office he had a war room with all kinds of display terminals connected to Wall Street. He could push a button and instantly move a few million dollars. His desk was covered with

off to the coastal wilderness where he hoped he wouldn't see another human being. On his saddle he had a rifle scabbard with an old 30-30. As he disappeared into the jungle, Curren looked back at me with a big grin on his face.

Back in California, I stopped by Tom Morey's factory in Carlsbad now and then to see how things were going. Tom was becoming disgruntled about the burden of running his Boogie Board manufacturing company, which by now was doing millions of dollars a year in sales. Like me, he loved the creativity of inventing new toys, but he just didn't care for the day-to-day drudgery of running a company. Tom was starting to talk about moving his family back to Hawaii. That was where he'd been living when he invented the Boogie Board, and in a way he felt it was the source of his inspiration. He talked about getting back to work on his universal language, and most of all, he wanted to begin designing a new swim fin.

Tom asked me what I thought about his plans, and I told him, "Go invent new toys, Tom. That's what you're good at. Let somebody else run the business."

Tom offered me the job of managing his factory, but I told him that job didn't appeal to me any more than it did to him. I did agree to look after things for a while, though, until Tom could figure out what to do with the place.

Eventually, Tom got an offer from the Kransco Corporation to buy the Boogie Board and the soft surfboard, and he decided to take it. He and I flew up to San Francisco to sign the papers.

I got a call one day from my old friend Dave Rochlen, who I hadn't heard from in quite a while. I knew, though, that his clothing company, Surf Line Hawaii, was doing very well. Anyway, Rochlen came right to the point. He said, "Hey, Doyle, you still got those jams I gave you in Hawaii?"

"You mean the ones with the flower print? I wore them for years, but that was a long time ago. Maybe my mom kept them, I don't know."

"Well, if you can find them, let me know. That was the first pair I ever made, and I want to put them in a glass case in my office. I'll give you five thousand dollars for them."

My mom and I tore up her house looking for those jams, but we never did find them.

One day in 1982, I was flying to Utah to go skiing at Snowbird, when I met a Japanese-American fellow, Noren Honda, who lived in Leucadia. Noren was about the most energetic and outgoing person I'd ever met. He was smart, funny, and very charming. Noren liked to surf and was an excellent tennis player. He'd graduated from San Diego State and had been through law school. Noren had a tremendous amount of drive, and I noticed he was in great demand by the women. Before the plane landed, he and I had struck up a friendship.

While we were at Snowbird, Noren told me he was looking around for a business project and asked me if I might be interested in opening a clothing store with him. I thought about it for a few days, then said yes.

So Noren and I opened a store in Encinitas called Doyle Sports, selling mostly simple beachwear items. The store did well right from the start, and before long Noren and I were paying ourselves a decent salary and were having a lot of fun together. Over the next few months, we opened two more stores, one in Laguna Beach and the other in La Jolla.

Noren and I did the buying together, and we both spent a lot of time in the stores, talking with customers and looking after the endless details of a business like that. But we still had a lot free time. I was surfing more than I had in years and swimming a mile or so almost every morning. I bought a seventeen-foot dory, which I took down to the beach a couple of times a week, and went rowing for several hours at a time, just like the old days when I'd been a lifeguard.

After a year or so, the Doyle Sports stores were doing better than ever, and Noren and I got the notion that we could manufacture our own clothing. We figured that with our own retail outlets, we could find out which items sold the best before manufacturing them in large quantities. And by selling our own line of clothes, in our own stores, our profits would be greater all the way around. I wanted to start out simple, with just shorts and T-shirts, but Noren was determined to start out with a full fashion line. I knew from my days at Catalina what that involved: a factory, machinery, material, employees, and a million other details that could go wrong at any time. I knew that route was full of hazards, and besides, it just didn't sound like much fun to me.

From then on things started to sour. The more I rebelled against Noren's plan, the more he resented me. He and I practically lived together night and day, and we started to get on each others nerves, like a married couple. The work became frustrating, and the stress was high. He could be very generous at times, but when he was under stress he felt compelled to make me an employee, rather than a partner, and I couldn't accept that.

Meanwhile, North County was becoming more and more crowded. The people who had just arrived there thought the place was wonderful, because they had just come from someplace worse. But to anybody who had been there for twenty years, the traffic jams and the crowded beaches were intolerable. The place was filling up with dull, upper-middle-class drones—the only people who could afford to buy homes there. The place had lost it's relaxed, beach atmosphere and was fast becoming just another Southern California suburb where everybody drives a BMW with a car phone.

Worst of all, the ocean pollution was horrible. The uncontrolled growth had outpaced the sewer systems, and sewage spills were common. Surfers who were in the water every day were getting all sorts of mysterious rashes on their skin, and during most of the winter (when the surf is best) the beaches were posted with notices saying the water was unsafe. I found myself using the ocean less and less, and I felt deprived, cut off from my source of inspiration and joy.

And yet another thing that bothered me about North County was the excessive use of drugs and alcohol. I have no right to be judgmental about this, because there were times when I was as far off-track as anybody. My personality, by nature, is excessive. Put me in the water, and I'll surf all day. Put a bottle of tequila in front of me, and I'll drink till it's empty. But I've never been the type who could drink day after day. To do that, I would have to give up surfing and so many other things I love. For somebody trying to control their excessive tendencies, though, North County was the wrong place to be. I saw so many people destroy their bodies and make a mess of their lives over drugs and alcohol, I started thinking that living in North County was hazardous to my health.

Bill Engler, in the meantime, had gone in a whole new direction. He took his share of the profits from our construction projects and, along with his uncle, bought some desert land in Imperial County, near the Salton Sea. The land had a hot spring, and they used that warm water to develop a fish farm, growing mostly catfish and tilapia, which they sold to the Asian fish markets in L.A. and San Diego. Bill loved the desert and was totally absorbed in his new project; he spent all his time experimenting with breeding the fish, perfecting his ponds, and studying all he could on aquaculture. Every couple of months or so, I'd drive out to the desert to see him. He was living in a mobile home, surrounded by acres and acres of muddy ponds, which in turn were surrounded by hundreds of square miles of alkali and sand. The place depressed me, but I was happy for Bill. His fish farm was starting to turn a profit, and he was as excited as I'd ever seen him.

My old friend Mike Zuetell, who I hadn't seen since I left Sun Valley, stopped by my house one day. He looked terrible. He'd lost a lot of weight, his teeth were falling out, he had purple splotches on his skin, and he complained about not having any energy. He'd quit his job in Sun Valley and said he hadn't been able to work for some time and was living in his camper. "I'm having some tests done at the veterans hospital in San Diego," he said. "It's all free, but I need a place to stay—just for a few days."

I had a spare bedroom in the back of my house, so I offered it to Zuetell, and he moved in.

Over the next few weeks and months, Zuetell's health deteriorated even more. There were days when he couldn't even get out of bed. I did my best to take care of him. I put him in my car and took him with me when I had errands to run. If I was going out to dinner with friends, I'd take him along.

Every now and then Zuetell would say, in an embarrassed way, that the doctors still didn't know what the problem was, but he was sure he'd be back on his feet in a few more days. He was terrified of not having a place to go, but I assured him he would have a place in my house as long as he needed it.

At a sports trade show up in Long Beach one day, I ran into Dave Rochlen. Rochlen came to all the trade shows. Even though he was the owner and president of Surf Line Hawaii, a successful beachwear company, he would always be right there himself, talking to people, and seeing firsthand what was going on in the industry. And he was still making those wild floral prints that had become his trademark.

Noren and I had a booth at the trade show, trying to move our new line of clothing but not having much luck with it. I never liked the trade shows. I enjoyed meeting people and seeing old friends, but to sit there in that booth was like being in a goldfish bowl.

Anyway, when I saw Rochlen he said, "Hey, Mike, you guys have three shops. Why don't you ever buy my stuff?"

At the time, our own clothing line was more into drab, neutral colors—gray, black, and white. We'd moved away from beachwear, and I thought we'd become too sophisticated for Dave's flower prints. I said, "You know, Dave, I just don't like them."

I knew it wasn't true the moment I said it. But I was tired and frustrated—over so many things. I wasn't happy with the way my partnership with Noren was working out, and I was under too much stress. Rochlen took a long hard look at me, then said, "What the hell has happened to you, Doyle? You've lost something."

I didn't like that at all. It wasn't just the words, but the way he looked into my soul when he said it. I laughed nervously, but I had a bad feeling inside. This was somebody I'd been close to at one time and still had a lot of respect for. I was so shaken, I had to leave our booth for a while. I went to the restroom, glanced at myself in the mirror, then took the same long hard look Rochlen had. And I wasn't very happy about what I saw. I was still healthy, I was still in shape, but that was just a surface illusion. I didn't feel well physically, and I didn't feel good about myself.

What bothered me the most, though, was that I'd lost my direction. It may sound silly, but I knew I wasn't the person who could live on the beach at Malibu like Tubesteak, buy a big bag of brown rice, and collect Coke bottles for a living. I'd become somebody other than the kind of person I'd set out to be.

Rochlen was right. I *had* lost something. I'd lost the sense of freedom that had always been the inspiration in my life. I'd lost the sense of fun and camaraderie with my friends. I was getting sucked down in that Southern California obsession with money, fast women, and manic parties. I give Rochlen a lot of credit for helping me see that. But what could I do to get out of it?

I came home after that trade show to find Mike Zuetell loading his things into his camper truck. He looked frightened and exhausted. All he said was, "It's time for me to go back to Idaho." He'd been at my house for seven months now, and his health hadn't improved. He thanked me warmly for letting him stay there during that time. Then he climbed in his truck and drove away.

A few days later I got word that Mike Zuetell had arrived safely in Sun Valley but had died a short time later.

By this time Noren and I had so many disagreements over our business, we finally decided to resolve them all by ending our partnership. Noren offered to buy my share in the stores, and I quickly accepted. Once that was done and there was no longer the business friction between us, our friendship was rekindled, and Noren and I have remained friends ever since.

It was 1989. I was forty-eight years old and not quite sure what to do with myself now that I had some money in my pocket and a lot of time on my hands.

To some people—even to my friends—I'm sure my life must have looked like chaos. But the fact was, I hadn't felt so optimistic in a long time. I was starting to recognize the patterns of my life, now. Things didn't just fall apart, I tore them down on purpose to get what I really wanted, which was freedom and the sense of adventure that comes from starting all over again. Perhaps other people would see my character differently and say that I couldn't handle commitment, success, or responsibility. The only difference is the point of view. I knew I needed change to be happy.

Surfing affects your lifestyle like no other sport I know of. It's not like bowling, where you can go any night of the week. The surf is only good at certain times—maybe three or four days a month. If you're a serious surfer, you have to design your life around it. You have to make the time to be there when the surf is good.

I've lived my whole life around the patterns of the ocean, and I've taken a lot of criticism for that. I've made a few women unhappy, I've made some employers unhappy, and at times I've made myself unhappy. But I can't help it, I've always known what my priorities are.

There used to be a construction company in La Jolla called "Not When the Surf's Up Construction Company." When the surf was good, they hung up their nail bags and did what they had to do. Those guys were serious surfers.

When I see a car full of surfers going down the highway with a rack of surfboards, my heart still leaps out and goes with them. Probably no man alive has gone on more surf adventures than I have, yet I still haven't had enough. If the conditions are right, I'll walk away from any job or any woman to spend a day in the water with my friends.

I think too many people feel guilty about enjoying themselves. I think the world would be a lot happier place if everybody spent a little time every day doing something they really loved. If there's one thing I've learned, one thing I can tell people that might be useful for them, it's this: It's okay to have fun. That's what I've been doing my whole life, and so far I haven't sailed off the edge of the earth.

That spring I made another trip to Hawaii. I still enjoyed going to Hawaii from time to time, mostly because I saw so many old friends there: Ricky Grigg, Felipe Pomar, Nat Young. When I was young, I thought of a lifetime as being very long, and I thought people would come and go like the other circumstances of my life. But as I approached fifty, I came to realize that a lifetime is really pretty short and the people who were my friends in my youth would be my friends all my life. As I've grown older, my friends have become even more precious to me.

One thing I learned by seeing my old friends was that age didn't have to be the horror some of us had imagined it to be in our youth. The people who had stayed close to the ocean, those who were still physically active—and most of all, those who still had a childlike sense of play—were in remarkably good shape. The people who still enjoyed using their bodies, still had their bodies. In the end, that might be the most beautiful and rewarding thing surfing can give us: a lifelong sense of joy and enthusiasm that helps keep us young.

One day when I was visiting with friends in Honolulu, I walked down to Kahala Beach, where there were usually a lot of windsurfers. Ever since the days when Hoyle Sweitzer had brought his first version of the sailboard by Hansen's shop, more than twenty years earlier, I'd been mostly indifferent to windsurfing. Oh, I'd fooled around with it a bit, but never seriously and never enthusiastically. But windsurfing equipment had improved rapidly in the Seventies and Eighties. The boards and sails were much lighter and maneuverable, making the sport more like surfing than sailing. At the same time, the trend in surfboard design had been toward smaller and smaller boards, until surfing had reached an almost absurd extreme. In the process, it seemed to me that surfing had lost much of its grace and beauty. The aggressive style of slashing and hacking at a wave, as if it were your enemy, seemed ugly and offensive to me. It gave me a headache just watching it. I longed to see the smooth and delicate, ballet-like acrobatics again.

And I found them that day at Kahala Beach. I was thrilled to watch the windsurfers cutting long graceful lines in the water and traveling very quickly over huge areas. Instead of being stuck in one place on a wave, as you are with an undersized surfboard, they would fly off in any direction they wanted to go; then they would pull the sail back like a wing, fly ten or fifteen feet into the air, and float back down.

That same day I borrowed a board and started teaching myself how to windsurf. I couldn't get enough of it. In a very short period of time—I mean in just a few days—I became a windsurfing fanatic, experimenting with different boards, different sails, going out in all kinds of conditions, and learning what size sails to use in what type winds. I couldn't get enough of it. Until then I hadn't even known it was possible for a man approaching fifty to get that stoked again.

When I came back to Encinitas after that trip to Hawaii, I decided it was time I made a major change in my life. The lifestyle I wanted was no longer possible in California. The only place I felt truly comfortable anymore was at my house in Mexico. I'd always worried that the realities of earning a living would make it impossible for me to live there, but I didn't care anymore. It didn't matter if living in Mexico made no sense. I had to follow my instincts. That might lead to misery, or it might lead to happiness, but at least I wouldn't be stuck in the middle anymore. So, in a leap of faith, I sold my house in Encinitas as quickly as I could and headed straight for my place in Cabo.

It's important for me to live in a place where I feel comfortable with the ocean, because when I'm in the ocean I feel in touch with nature. I'm able to understand the interconnectedness of all the living things, the plant life, the fish, even the water. When I'm in the ocean I realize how insignificant my life is. And that gives me the desire to live in harmony with other creatures. I think a lot of the destructiveness in this world is a result of people losing touch with nature.

Cabo is on a peninsula, which to me is like an island you can drive to. There's still room to move here, still a lot of open space. You can pull over to the side of the road and take a pee anytime you want without getting arrested. The latitude here, just below the Tropic of Cancer, feels right to me. The sky is clear, and the colors of the sky and land are beautiful. No matter where you go in the world, the lifestyle at this latitude is more relaxed, which seems to annoy a lot of people from the northern latitudes but suits my temperament perfectly.

The thing I love most about Cabo, though, is being close to the water. Here my childhood dream of waking up, looking out my window and seeing the ocean, has come true. I can get wet any time I want, here. The ocean is always warm, and it's still unpolluted. I love the colors of the water here, and the species of fish. Cabo is home to me. Cabo is my salvation.

I didn't have a lot of money, but that didn't matter. My house was paid for, and I could always afford a bag of brown rice and some vegetables, which was what my worn-out body needed. And I could catch fish anytime I wanted. I wasn't worried about putting a business together, about inventing something, about living up to my reputation as a famous surfer. In Cabo, all that was gone.

I swept out my house, knocked the dust off the furniture, and gave the palm trees a good watering. I had lots of time to think, lots of time to adjust to my new life. I was a bit lonely at first, but I was lonely by choice.

I started working out regularly again. Every morning I hiked to the top of the hill behind my house, and every afternoon I swam a mile or so in the ocean. If the waves were good, I surfed at Zippers, or, when the wind conditions were right, I went windsurfing at Punta Gorda. If neither the wind nor waves were any good, I rowed my dory out to sea. Before long I was back in top physical condition again.

At first I had a lot of free time on my hands, and I filled it by teaching myself how to draw. To me art is a form of happiness. A room without art is sterile, but a room with art makes you feel good. I've always loved art and have always known that I had a talent for it. But in my younger days I never had the patience to sit down and begin. In Cabo, though, I became intrigued with learning the techniques of drawing. I bought paper and pencils, and began doing sketches of people's bodies, of faces, and trees. I took my sketchbook with me everywhere.

After a while I decided I wanted to start working in color, but I didn't know where to begin. It was a big step because it takes an artist to work with color. Who was I to say I was an artist? It took me a while to realize that learning to paint was a lot like learning to surf. You have begin from total ignorance. So I asked my mother to ship me some canvas, some brushes, and a bunch of acrylic paint. When they came in the mail, I just sat down and started painting.

My first attempts were awful. I threw them away in disgust and told myself I would never be a painter. But the next day I fished them out of the trash can and started over. It wasn't as if I had a choice. One good thing about reaching middle age is that you realize you can't keep putting off the things you've always wanted to do. I knew if I didn't keep painting until something good happened, I would regret it the rest of my life.

Finally, one day after weeks of trying, I made a very simple one-line drawing of a cat. It looked like something a kid would draw. But I drew it with my right hand (I'm left-handed) and I drew it upside-down. I painted the background yellow, the cat pink, and then, without even stopping to think about it, I painted a bunch of red chili peppers flying through the air around the cat. That was my first complete painting, and I sold it to a tourist a few weeks later for $500. He said, "It's crude, it's childish. I gotta have it."

I painted every day, and I finished at least one painting a week. I liked to work in quick one-hour spurts, go do something else, then come back later, open the door, and see if what I did was any good. I wasn't critical of what I painted, as long as it was original. If I copied something from somebody else, then I hated it.

I looked on painting as a series of linked recoveries, with an unknown plan. I think that's what creativity is, a series of spontaneous decisions. I'd throw some paint on the canvas, back up and look at it. If it was wrong, if I screwed it up, then I started thinking how I could make it right.

I filled my house with paintings, and I sold the older ones to make room for the newer ones. I had a show of my work at the Hotel Palmilla, a beautiful, old Spanish-style hotel just a short ways from my house. Several other hotels and restaurants in Cabo bought my paintings, as well as a few art collectors. Now my paintings sell for $400 to $2000 apiece, and I sell at least one a month.

I hadn't lived in Cabo very long when some of my old friends from California started showing up. First they just came for short visits to check the place out. Then they came for longer stays and started complaining about how they didn't want to go back. Eventually some of them bought land or houses on the hill where I lived, which by now the Mexicans had named Gringo Hill. Garth Murphy already owned a place here. Howard Benedict, my dentist and friend who holds some unofficial world records for wahoo spearfishing, built a vacation house here and flew down often. Bill Engler visited quite a bit; he didn't buy a place, but he always had a bed at my house or Garth's. Jeff King, a talented surfer who had set a world speed record on a sailboard I'd shaped for him, moved down with his wife. Several more friends moved here, too.

Together we started pioneering new surf spots on both sides of the peninsula. That's all over in California and Hawaii, but on the Baja peninsula, particularly on the Pacific side, there were still places where nobody has ever surfed. My friends and I also started doing a lot of open-water sailboarding, six or seven miles from shore, where you couldn't even see the land. Sometimes we would race alongside each other, going so fast we just couldn't hold it together any longer, and we'd fly over the bars and skip across the surface of the water like a stone. There are a lot of sharks in these waters—we knocked our skegs off on hammerheads a few times—but just knowing there was something out there big enough to eat us only added to the thrill. There's also something here they call a "needlefish," which they call a garfish in Florida. They have long alligator beaks with lots of sharp teeth. The sailboard cutting through the water startles them and they jump into the air. I've had needlefish cut right through my sail several times and once I got a needlefish beak stuck in my ass; I had to go to the hospital to get it cut out.

Tom Morey had moved his family up to Bainbridge, Washington, but he and I stayed in touch by sending faxes back and forth to each other. One day he sent me a fax asking what I thought of an idea a friend of his had come up with. The idea was to make little nine-inch surfboards, take them down to the edge of a lake or even a bathtub, and when the waves come lapping in, you shove your little board into the waves and watch it surf. They called it "finger surfing."

I really missed Tom. Over the years we'd never had a business argument and we'd never signed a contract—we never felt we needed to. I'd always appreciated his honesty, even though it stung at times. But I hated the idea of finger surfing. I called him back and said, "Morey, I think that idea stinks. I think it's for people who let themselves get too old and too fat to really surf. They can sit back in their armchairs, stick their little boards in their blubber rolls and pretend they're surfing."

Maybe I was a bit harsh, but Tom didn't get offended. "Doyle," he said, "What you're talking about is the difference between me and you. I'm a maker, you're a doer. You don't want to talk about things, you don't want to fantasize about things, you want to do things. . . . But me, I like ideas, and I like tools, and I like to think about how to get them both to do what I want. I'm a maker. Aside from that, though, my top priority for a lot of years has been to be a good father. I've always tried to be here when my kids need me, and when I look at them now, I think I've done a good job."

Tom was right in his own way. He had a fine family, and he was a very good father. He was living life the way he needed to. "That's all fine, Morey," I said. "But I wish you'd move back to a place with warm water so you can be a father, a maker, and a surfer, too."

I've always felt ambivalent about starting a family, myself. I think most people decide to have a family because they're afraid of being lonely. But I haven't known much loneliness in my life. I've been fortunate to have a lot of friends, and in some ways they've become my family. Yet I realize that friends aren't really the same as a family. I know there are a lot of married men who envy my lifestyle and my freedom, but they should know that I also envy the love they share with their wives and children.

Women have often told me how good I am with kids and what a great father I'd make. One very angry woman who finally realized I wasn't going to marry her and start a family told me, "The reason you get along so well with kids is that you're nothing but a kid yourself!" It was meant to be an insult, but I considered it a great compliment.

I do love children, and I'm not ready yet to scratch a family off my list of possibilities. Who knows, maybe I'll want to start a family when I'm sixty. Other men have.

My stepfather, Walt, had been in poor health for quite a while. I flew back and forth from Cabo to San Diego several times to be with him and my mother. After his health worsened, Walt went on kidney dialysis three times a week, so my mother, after forty years of not driving, got her driver's license so she could take him to the hospital.

In September 1990, when Walt was in the hospital going through one critical situation after another, I flew up to Fallbrook. During that visit, I ran into Garth Murphy, who said, "Let's go down to San Diego and see Mike Miller. He's got an eighty-foot catamaran in the harbor there, and he's sailing soon to Tahiti."

Mike Miller was a friend of ours who'd made a fortune by investing in Quiksilver, an Australian surfwear company that had become enormously successful. His boat was gorgeous. He'd spent five years designing and building it. He had a water desalinization machine, fax, weather satellite, five queen-size beds—everything you could imagine. The boat's name was a real tongue-twister: *Humu-humu-nuku-nuku-a-pua-a*. It's the longest word in the Hawaiian language, and it means trigger fish. Miller called his boat the *Humu-humu* for short.

Jack McCoy, a surf photographer I knew from Hawaii, was on the boat, too, along with Jack's girlfriend, and Mike's girlfriend. Their plan was to make a movie of their round-the-world surf odyssey.

While they were showing me the boat, Jack said, "Hey, Mike, we need another hand on the boat. We're leaving in a few days. Why don't you come with us?"

I looked at Miller, who was in his early forties, six-foot-five, big and gangly. He said, "You got any sailing experience?"

"Some, not much."

"Well, no problem. You can learn on the way."

I thought, I'm nearly fifty years old. I can't just pick up and go sail to Tahiti on an impulse. I thanked them both for their offer, wished them luck on their voyage, then left with Garth.

But for the rest of the day I kept thinking, Why can't I go? Everybody dreams about sailing to Tahiti. I might never get a chance like this again. So the next day I called Mike Miller. "Do I still have a chance to go?"

"Yeah, but we're leaving day after tomorrow."

I gathered up my surfboard and my diving gear—all my water toys—and I was ready to go.

At the last minute Mike Miller's girlfriend decided she didn't want to go, which left the captain in a troubled state of mind. But he was a tough-minded fellow, and he said, "I've been planning this for five years. I'm going, no matter who goes with me."

So as we departed, it was Jack McCoy, his girlfriend Kelly, Mike Miller, and me.

Instead of sailing to Tahiti by way of Hawaii, which is the way sailing vessels leaving from the mainland usually go, our plan was to sail south along Baja, then turn west toward the Marquesas. It was the longest voyage you could take without seeing land and was completely out of the shipping and flying lanes. The boat was new and relatively unproven. (It had been on two trial runs; there had been some problems with the way the sails were chaffing on the shrouds, but they were supposedly fixed now.) To further complicate matters, this was the *chubasco*, or stormy season, in Baja and not a good time to be sailing.

I'd been around the ocean almost all my life, but I wasn't a sailor, I was a waterman—somebody who spends his time within sight of land. My earlier sailing experiences (like the time I sailed to Maui with Joey Cabell) hadn't been all that enjoyable. As we passed the Coronado Islands, just out of the San Diego harbor, and were putting up full sail, I thought to myself, What have you done?

Captain Miller was proud of his boat and eager to prove what she could do. He liked to put up as much sail and run as hard as he could. We didn't just crawl along like a mono-hull; we flew across the water at fifteen knots.

The boat had autopilot, but even with "Otto" on, one of us still had to keep watch at all times. My favorite watch was midnight to four a.m., after everybody else had gone to sleep. The warm tropical waters were rich in plankton, and sometimes the sea was luminescent. All I could see was the glow of the compass, and then the silvery flash of porpoises breaking the surface of the water. For hours at a time I would listen to the high-pitched sound of the porpoises through the fiberglass hull.

After five or six days at sea, I began to shed my attachment to the land and started feeling attached to the boat. There was no more land. The boat was my home.

Because he'd had to leave without his girlfriend, Captain Miller was under stress. He was a strict captain anyway and expected a lot from himself and his crew. We all understood that discipline was necessary for everybody's safety, but we thought he sometimes carried it a bit too far. When you flushed the head, he would have his ear to the door. "That's too much water you're using!" The boat had facilities for making all the fresh water we wanted, but he was used to the old days when you had to really conserve water. After you brushed your teeth, he'd inspect the head and say, "You didn't wipe the counter off after you finished."

At night there was only one safe place to pee off the back of boat. But Miller told us, "I don't want anybody peeing off the back of the boat. I want you to walk out on the end of the hull." The hull was about six inches off the water, and we considered that a dangerous place to pee. One night at two in the morning, on my watch, we were in tremendous seas. I ignored the captain's orders and peed off the back of the boat. He immediately burst out of the cabin where he'd been sleeping and shouted, "I told you to pee off the hull!"

We loved our captain; he was an expert seaman, but we wished he would lighten up a bit. To ease the tension, we started calling him Captain Bligh, and that usually brought a smile to his face.

I found that sailing across the ocean wasn't just blue skies and calm waters. There was usually not enough wind, or else too much wind, lightning, or thunder. But we had a quick crossing—it only took us fourteen days to reach the Marquesas.

I got off the boat long enough to visit the grave of Paul Gauguin, who died on the Marquesas in 1903. Then Jack and Kelly announced, "We've had enough. We're getting off." They took Jack's 1,000 pounds of camera gear and boarded a filthy, oily, tramp

steamer bound for Papeete with pigs and othe⌐
deck. (But the next time I heard from Jack an⌐
married, so maybe the tramp steamer was mo⌐
looked.)

That was a miserable day for me, to see my
the weather was just as bad—stormy and ugly. but ⌐
go on.

Now it was just me and Captain Bligh. We were thirty miles
out of the Marquesas, flying for the Tuamotus, when we hooked
into two huge tuna. "Back the sail down!" the captain ordered. But
when I didn't do it fast enough for him, he hollered, "Not by hand!
Use the power winch!" As I fumbled with the electric winch, I
accidentally hit the high-speed button, the handle spun forward and
broke my thumb. I managed to tape the broken thumb to my hand,
and we landed a seventy-pound tuna.

When we finally reached Tahiti, there were no bare-breasted
girls swimming out to our boat and no natives in dugout canoes
offering us their daughters. There were a lot of transvestites: big fat
guys dressed up in lava-lavas and lipstick.

But on the outer islands we found some really good surf. We
left the boat in the bay, then took a small rubber boat out to the reefs
and surfed every day.

In Samoa, Mike's brother Paul and another friend, J.P., joined
us. Paul buffered his brother some, and conditions on the boat were
much better. We sailed to Tonga, where we found some unbelievable surf, including two spots that had never been surfed before,
and the four of us had a fantastic time surfing, diving, and fishing.

I could have continued on with them, but I was worried about
my stepfather, who was still in the hospital. (I called my mother as
often as possible to see how he was doing.) So I left the boat and
flew home.

All the time I'd been gone, which was just a few weeks, really,
Walt had hung in there. But as soon as I got back to Fallbrook, Walt
went into a tailspin. We put him in the emergency ward, but he never
recovered. I think he chose that time to go because he realized I was
there with my mother.

After Walt passed away, I was worried about my mother. I knew she was strong enough to deal with anything, but I was afraid she wouldn't *think* she was strong enough. And I was living a thousand miles away. But my mother pulled her life together remarkably well. She took up oil painting, something that she, like her son, had always wanted to do. Her yard and garden, which were always works of art, became even more beautiful. A creative side that my mother had kept hidden all her life began to blossom. My mother was a white-haired little lady now, but I could still see a girl inside that tiny body. She wasn't supposed to eat sweets, but every now and then I'd see her sneak a piece of candy anyway. I loved that about her.

All my life my mother has supported me in everything I've done. She kept every newspaper and magazine clipping on my surfing career. She dragged all my aunts and uncles and cousins off to every surf contest I was in, and encouraged them to hoot and holler during my heat to influence the judges. My mother and I have always been very close, but as we grew older we became even closer. We were able to be more honest with each other about who we really were, and able to forgive each other's weaknesses.

In Cabo I got a call one day from Garth. He said Bill Engler had been in a terrible accident. Bill had been working on his fish ponds in the desert, standing on a twenty-five-foot tower, reaching into one of the ponds with a long aluminum pole. Somehow the pole had gotten too close to a high-voltage power line; electricity arced across the gap and down the pole, blowing out the power for that entire area. Bill was knocked unconscious, but as he fell backward his leg got caught in a ladder. When he finally regained consciousness, he was upside down and his leg was twisted 180 degrees at the knee.

Bill was in the hospital in La Jolla, so I called him right away. He was too groggy, I think, to even know it was me. But I kept calling. I stayed in touch with him every few days for weeks, until they finally let him out of the hospital. Garth took him to his house in Encinitas, where Bill convalesced.

It was miraculous that they'd been able to save Bill's leg, he'd

been burned so badly and lost so much flesh. He walk<
for a while and had a limp. But Bill's attitude was re
never lost his optimism and enthusiasm. He began de]
of the duties on his fish farm to his workers, and we :
more of him in Cabo.

Bill, who always had a tremendous amount of self-discipline
and perseverance, was determined to surf again. The first few times
he tried though, it looked hopeless. He could paddle well enough—
his shoulders and arms were powerful—but he had trouble coming
to his feet. Still, every time he came to visit me in Cabo, he practiced
over and over.

Then one day we were all surfing at Zippers. I was sitting on
the beach, and I looked up to see one of the surfers on a longboard
in full control of a four-foot wave. It took me a moment to realize
it was Bill. After days of trying, he'd finally taught himself how to
come to his feet and land with most of his weight on his strong leg.
Once he got that right, he was surfing like his old self. God, it was
beautiful.

In the summer of 1992, Oxbow, a European sportswear company, hired Nat Young (the great Australian surfer who had changed
the direction of surfing at the world championship in San Diego in
1966) to sponsor a longboard surf contest in Biarritz, France. The
idea was to invite a bunch of the surfers from the Sixties—guys
who had been involved with surfing when it had really started to
grow all around the world. These nostalgia events were becoming
quite popular, and I had been to several of them in recent years.

Nat called me up, invited me to the contest, and sent me a check
to cover my expenses. Along with the check came a personal letter
and invitation signed by the mayor of Biarritz.

Joey Cabell was at the Oxbow event. He and I surfed together
every morning, and went to dinner together at night. Nat Young had
invited Mickey Dora to the contest, too, and to everyone's surprise
Dora showed.

The last twenty years or so had been rough on Dora. Back in
1973 he'd tried to buy a bunch of ski equipment using bad checks.
He was arrested, he pleaded guilty, and was put on probation. Under

the terms of the probation, Dora was supposed to get a job, a permanent residence, and give up using credit cards. But in 1975 Dora skipped out on his probation officer and disappeared. There were rumors he was in South America, New Zealand, and France, but for a long time nobody really knew where Dora was.

After a few years, in 1981, Dora was arrested by French authorities in, of all places, Biarritz. Dora spent a few months in French jails before being flown back to California, where FBI agents met him at the airport and took him to prison. He served his time, was set free, and moved to South Africa.

I saw Dora every day at the contest in Biarritz. I tried several times to have a conversation with him, but it was impossible. Dora talked in riddles, and, for me at least, none of it made any sense.

As part of our agreement with Nat and the other contest organizers, we all met the mayor of Biarritz. The meeting was held in the middle of town at nine o'clock one morning. Nearly everyone in town had gathered in front of a grandstand decorated with flags. There was a big float, and TV stations from all over Europe were there. We all showed up on time—except, of course, Dora. He was an hour late, as if he'd had a more important engagement that morning. When the time came for the mayor to introduce each of us to the crowd, we stood and waved. When he came to Dora, Mickey was wearing a clear plastic pull-on mask that distorted his features—so he could be there, but at the same time not really be there. After all these years, Dora hadn't changed one bit.

On my way back from France, I stopped in San Diego to see my mother. I was in her back yard one day, working on a wooden bridge over the creek, when I happened to notice my old tree house. It had been there all these years—ever since I'd left Idaho and come back to California—but the live-oak branches had grown around it, the roof had rusted an earthy color, and moss had started growing on the outer walls. It was nearly invisible now.

My old ladder, still nailed to the trunk of the tree, had mostly rotted away. I found a stepladder behind the garage, and with a feeling of uneasiness, I climbed into the tiny home I'd built for myself years before.

I knocked back the spider webs and looked around. The wind and rain had tattered the curtains, and squirrels had filled the corners with two feet of acorn shells. An old pair of blue jeans and one cowboy boot were the only possessions I'd left behind. Other than that, the place was empty—except for one wall, where a crude shelf made of wooden crates was filled with dozens of old surfing trophies.

I couldn't stand up for all the cobwebs so, crouched on one knee, I took down the largest trophy, which weighed nearly ten pounds. It was so covered with dust and grime, I couldn't read the lettering on it. I wiped the brass plate with the back of my sleeve and saw that it read: "Puntas Rocas, 1969, Campéon Olas Grandes."

I put it back on the shelf and took down another: "Duke Kahanamoku Hawaiian Classic, 1969, First Place."

And another: "International Surfing Championships at Makaha, 1963, First Place Tandem."

There were a dozen more, but I didn't need to see them.

There was one more thing I had to do before leaving San Diego. While I'd been in France, the ski museum at Chamonix had expressed an interest in buying my first prototype of the single ski. I wasn't sure where it was, but I thought Bill Bahne might still have it at his factory in Cardiff, so I stopped by there one morning.

Bill wasn't at the factory, but his brother, Bob, was there. He called Bill and asked where the ski was, and in a while Bill arrived with the ski in hand. It was battered and dusty, but just looking at it reminded me of a young man with a lot of dreams.

Bahne looked embarrassed to see me, so I just took the ski, thanked him, and left.

My friends and I went surfing over on the Gulf side of the peninsula at a spot we'd discovered and named Y-Mesa, sort of a Mexican Waimea. A storm had kicked up fifteen-foot waves, and as we paddled out it was still raining so hard that as each raindrop hit the water, a droplet bounced back up about four inches, then collapsed down into a bubble. The whole surface of the ocean was covered with bubbles. There was no breeze. You could barely distinguish the wave from the sky because the color of everything was a greenish gray. As we dropped in down the faces of those waves, everything was silent until the lip of the wave cracked over the top of us. Only by the white water could we tell where we were. It was such a thrill, we were all hooting and hollering like a bunch of kids.

Later that afternoon, the wind started picking up. As I was paddling into a twelve-foot wave, the spray was blowing into my eyes so hard I could barely see. By the time I realized I'd caught the wave, it was already pitching over the top of me. I jumped to my feet as quickly as I could and was immediately in a vertical drop. I thought I was going to pearl when I hit the bottom, because the wave was just too steep. But my board had huge nose rocker and tail kick, and when I hit the trough, the board took the transition as smooth as silk. I lay the board on its right rail, drove hard off the bottom, back to the top of a big pitching curl, lay it on the left rail, stuck there on top for a second, then dropped in again.

I've never felt more in control on any wave I've ever rode. As soon as it was over I felt a surge of satisfaction—the feeling you can get when you put aside fear, and trust your mind and body.

All the rest of that day I had an overwhelming feeling of exhilaration.

*I*t was only a week or so after that wonderful day at Y-Mesa that I found myself in the dory several miles off the coast of Cabo San Lucas, about to be swept into oblivion.

After canoe paddling for three hours—from about nine o'clock till noon—the wind was still howling all around me. The muscles in my arms and shoulders were fluttering with fatigue, and I was worried they might cramp up altogether. Both my knees were so bloody and sore, I could barely kneel on them. Every few minutes or so I allowed myself a peek at the coastline. I could make out the larger hotels now, and I figured I must be three or four miles closer to shore. But that still left me eleven miles from land. Even worse, I'd drifted down the coast another four miles toward Cabo San Lucas, leaving me only eight miles from the tip of the peninsula and the open ocean beyond. I could actually see the tip of Cabo—land's end— and it seemed to be drawing closer to me at a faster rate than the shore. My situation was really more desperate than ever.

But at least I had a few points sliding in my favor: I was strong and healthy. I had friends I loved, and who loved me. I had never been more happy or felt more enthusiastic about my future. I had lots to look forward to. I wasn't ready to check out yet.

Maybe that's really the whole point of adventure. It reminds us we're made of flesh and blood. We can check out at any time, but in the end the choice is our own.

I figured I still had two or three hours before I drifted past the cape. I had the will, the strength, and the stamina to go on fighting, *but I had to come up with a better plan than canoe paddling, and I had to come up with it very quickly.*

Over the last half-hour or so, I'd noticed that the wind had shifted slightly and was now blowing more sideshore than offshore. That meant, on the one hand, that I no longer had to make headway directly into the wind; on the other hand, it meant that I was being swept even faster toward the cape. If I'd had something to use as a makeshift sail, I might have been able to take advantage of the shift in wind. But all I had was my T-shirt.

Then it occurred to me that the side of the dory itself was a kind of sail. That was working to my disadvantage, driving me hard to the cape. Still, it occurred to me there might be a way. . . .

I placed my one oar in the port oarlock and rowed a few hard strokes with both arms, driving the dory in a long arc until the bow had turned into the wind. Then I let the wind blow the bow back again in an even longer, slower arc. To my surprise, I was able to gain a considerable distance this way.

So I went to work with a passion, now. Three hard strokes and wait . . . three strokes and wait . . . three strokes and wait. It was slower than rowing with two oars, and my course zigzagged all over the water, but I was making real progress, not just thrashing around. I knew I had a real chance.

At three o'clock that afternoon, seven hours after I'd slipped my dory into the water at Zippers, I reached shore a couple of miles west of the Twin Dolphins Hotel. The wind and the current had swept me twelve miles down the coast and less than three miles from the tip of the peninsula.

I dragged my dory onto the beach and walked up to the highway with my fishing gear under my arm. Before long a taxi coming back from Cabo came by, and I waved it down.

As I climbed into the taxi, the driver smiled and said, "Been fishing?"

Where Are They Now?

Kemp Aaberg has become a master of the flamenco guitar. He's married and lives in Santa Barbara, where he works as a parcel deliveryman. He's in terrific shape and competes in triathlons. I understand he's one of the best distance runners in his age group in the country.

Joey Cabell spends his summers running his restaurant in Hawaii, sailing and surfing; but every winter he goes back to Aspen, where he's become a snowboarding enthusiast. He and Gail divorced, but Joey has remarried now and has a child by his new wife.

Corky Carroll is the head tennis pro at a club in Orange County. He recently remarried, has a young child, and lives in Huntington Beach. He surfs regularly at Trestles and Cottons. Every now and then, he likes to sneak down to Puerto Escondido, in Mexico.

Lance Carson is living close to his favorite surfing spot, Malibu. He's in great physical shape and surfing better than ever. He makes a Lance Carson-model surfboard and markets his own line of beachwear.

Pat Curren prefers a nomadic way of life but was last seen somewhere between Cabo and Costa Rica. He loves Jack Russell terriers more than humans. He still surfs—not long ago he gave in to peer pressure and made himself a lightweight tri-fin. He's actually been seen doing S-turns on it.

Ricky Grigg is a professor of oceanography at the University of Hawaii and has a home at Sunset Beach. He still surfs fearlessly and still has a childlike twinkle in his eye.

Don Hansen still owns the largest surf shop in north San Diego County. He doesn't surf anymore but has become a ski enthusiast. He owns a ranch in Montana, had the South Dakota stain removed from his teeth, and looks great.

Fred Hemmings became a state senator in Hawaii and at this writing is running for Lt. Governor. I understand he's a staunch political conservative and had a radio talk show once described as "the Hawaiian version of Rush Limbaugh." Fred's friends say he's mellowed with age and has learned to take out his aggression by running marathons.

Rusty Miller lives near Byron Bay, Australia and publishes a tourist guide for that area. He and his wife have a couple of kids and a farm with an organic garden and chickens. He still competes in longboard contests and does extremely well.

Tom Morey has moved his family back to Southern California—this time to Capistrano Beach. He has abandoned finger surfing for the real thing. He spends his time working on new inventions: swim fins; a finless surfboard; and his pet project, Storm Drive, a back-up power source for autos, boats, and spacecraft.

Dale Velzy builds redwood and balsa showpiece surfboards for collectors. Last time I saw him, at San Onofre, he was charming as ever, driving a cherry-red hot rod, and had a beautiful woman on his arm.

Nat Young has become a national hero in Australia. He has a family, a ranch, a beach house, and several surf shops. He promotes a French clothing line, surfs and skis all over the world, and recently appeared in a Rolex ad.

On a calm winter morning, former surfing champion Mike Doyle rows his dory off the tip of Baja California for a day of deep-water fishing. A violent shift in weather and a disastrous mistake leave him helplessly adrift, fifteen miles from shore, in a howling wind. During those lonely hours of truth, as he fights to save himself, Doyle looks back on his extraordinary life and the fascinating people who have filled it.

Morning Glass is the autobiography of one of the greatest watermen in history, a man who witnessed the birth of the surfing phenomenon and became a folk hero to millions. Above all, this is the story of a man with a creative passion and a fierce craving for adventure, struggling to find his own place in the world.

To order *Morning Glass* by mail

Please send $16.00, check or money order, to:

Manzanita Press
PO Box 720
Three Rivers, CA 93271

The price includes tax, postage, and handling.